Congressional Preemption

Congressional Preemption

Regulatory Federalism

Joseph F. Zimmerman

State University of New York Press

Published by
State University of New York Press, Albany

For information, address State University of New York Press,
194 Washington Avenue, Suite 305, Albany, NY 12210-2365

Production by Marilyn P. Semerad
Marketing by Michael Campochiaro

Library of Congress Cataloging-in-Publication Data

Zimmerman, Joseph Francis, 1928–
    Congressional preemption : regulatory federalism / Joseph F.
    Zimmerman.
        p. cm.
    Includes bibliographical references and index.
    ISBN 0–7914–6563–2 (hardcover : alk. paper)
    1. Federal government—United States. 2. Central-local government
    relations—United States. I. Title.

JK325.Z558 2005
320.473′049—dc22

                                                                    2004027748

                        10 9 8 7 6 5 4 3 2 1

For Peggy

In appreciation of her continuing support

Contents

Preface

A federal system automatically creates national-state state relations which may be cooperative and/or conflictive in nature. The United States Constitution grants Congress authority to provide only one service—the postal service—within states with the exceptions of services provided on federal properties such as military bases. In consequence, there are few opportunities for conflict and more opportunities for national-subnational cooperation in service provision.

Constitutional amendments and congressional preemption statutes removing regulatory powers from subnational governments have produced a major restructuring of the United States federal system, demonstrating the framers of the United States Constitution did not intend to establish a federal system with rigid national-state jurisdictional boundaries. The first two preemption statutes were enacted in 1790. Subsequently, the number enacted, if any, in a given year was small until the mid-1960s, when the number increased sharply and made the federal system increasingly fluid and complex in nature. These statutes, simple and complicated ones, surprisingly have attracted the attention of relatively few political scientists. This volume, building upon an earlier one, seeks to encourage research on the ramifications of the preemption revolution that removes powers completely or partially in various regulatory fields from state and local governments.[1]

In exercising its preemption powers, Congress often acts *de novo* without consideration of the effectiveness of similar types of preemption statutes enacted earlier or their potential unforeseen adverse impact upon subnational governments. The United States Supreme Court, for example, interpreted the Airline Deregulation Act of 1978 as a field preemption statute that deprived state attorneys general of authority individually and collectively to enforce state deceptive practices laws against airlines. Investigations by the New York attorney general in 2001 and 2002 revealed the ineffectiveness of the United States Security and Exchange Commission, empowered by nine congressional statutes, to police the investment banking industry adequately. To date, Congress has not conducted an in-depth study of the various restructuring provisions incorporated into these statutes, but periodically has responded to state and local government officers' complaints about a particular statute by enacting an amendment offering a degree of relief.

The impact of individual preemption statutes on the federal system in general and individual states varies considerably. A number of complete preemption statutes had no immediate impact because state and local governments had not legislated in the concerned areas. Others, particularly economic deregulation ones, have had a major impact. Not all preemption statutes are state unfriendly and it is noteworthy that state government officers on rare occasions have requested Congress to enact a supersession statute because of their inability to solve a national problem within their state.

Evidence presented in this volume reveals several major preemption statutes have failed to achieve their declared goals and the national government is dependent upon states for assistance in ensuring the effectiveness of certain other complete and partial preemption statutes. Congress recognized the need for subnational governmental assistance by including limited regulatory authority turn-back provisions in certain complete preemption statutes which authorize the head of the concerned national department or agency to sign an agreement with individual states allowing them to enforce the statutes or to conduct inspections using federal standards.

The most important type of preemption statute establishes and/or authorizes national government officers to promulgate minimum national regulatory standards subject to supersession by state standards provided they are as strict or stricter and are enforced. This preemption type, by forging a national-state partnership, has had the greatest impact upon the federal system as regulatory responsibility rests in most cases with states and the role of national departments and agencies is limited to monitoring. Paradoxically, this preemption type has encouraged states to exercise dormant regulatory powers or exercise more fully their regulatory powers.

The pace of congressional enactment of supersession statutes declined slightly since 1995 when the Republican Party assumed control of both houses of Congress, yet the importance of several subsequent statutes, such as the *Telecommunications Act of 1996* and the *Gramm-Leach-Bliley Financial Modernization Act of 1999*, should not be underestimated. The former act encourages a continuing revolution in the provision of telecommunication services and the latter removed the remaining legal barriers between the banking industry and the insurance industry. Technological developments and lobbying by civil rights, economic, environmental, and other interest groups ensure Congress will continue to preempt completely or partially regulatory powers of subnational governments in the foreseeable future.

Brief Cases Studies in this volume are employed to test the safeguards of federalism theory, which posits states may participate in the congressional law-making process to seek the prevention of enactment of unwanted preemption bills into law, and the Blackmun thesis, which holds states should seek relief from preemption statutes in the political branch of the national government, Congress, rather than in the judicial branch.

The preemption revolution has several implications for democratic theory. The principle of subsidiary, incorporated in the draft constitution of the European Union, posits responsibility for a function should be lodged in the government(s) closest to the people capable of exercising the responsibility effectively. The shifting of the public policy decision-making locus from individual local governments and state governments to the national political arena in Washington, D.C., reduces the ability of voters to hold legislators accountable and responsible for their decisions. The voluminous preemption statutes (the Clean Air Act Amendments of 1990 has 314 pages) and implementing rules and regulations make it extremely difficult for the citizenry to determine which plane of government is responsible for each governmental regulatory function. In addition, government officers often do not understand fully the statutes and implementing rules and regulations.

Two theories of United States federalism have been developed. The simple dual theory posits the national government and state governments each possesses autonomous powers and engages in little or no interaction. The more complex cooperative theory, on the other hand, holds the two planes of government are involved in cooperative activities on a daily basis. Minimum standards preemption statutes are based upon the theory of cooperative federalism. While each theory retains a degree of explanatory value, both fail to explain congressional coercive use of delegated powers to mandate subnational governments to initiate specified actions or to forbid these units to initiate specified actions. This volume presents a more general theory of federalism containing dual, cooperative, and coercive postulates, and emphasizing the ever-changing facilitator, inhibitor, and initiator intergovernmental roles played by Congress.

This volume also describes several innovative congressional statutes which encourage state legislatures to enact harmonious regulatory statutes under the threat of preemption if they fail to enact them or to encourage states to enter into interstate regulatory compacts. The concluding chapter seeks to promote a reinvigoration of the federal system by offering advice to Congress when exercising preemption powers to ensure achievement of national goals without unnecessarily depriving subnational governments of important regulatory powers and recommendations to states to cooperatively initiate harmonious regulatory actions to discourage enactment of congressional preemption statutes.

Acknowledgments

A scholarly book on a complex subject is never the work of a single individual as the author draws heavily upon available literature in preparing a research design and incorporates pertinent literature in the text with the assistance of research associates.

Identifying and collecting pertinent literature would have been a time-consuming process for the author without the assistance of others. I am pleased to acknowledge a special debt of gratitude to my research associates—Eric R. Amidon, Winston R. Brownlow, and Dai Li—who were most proficient in searching the political science and public law literature and locating books, government documents, articles, and unpublished works pertaining to the subject of congressional preemption. A debt of appreciation also is owed to Addie Napolitano for her expert preparation of the manuscript for publication, to freelance professional copyeditor, Lisa Metzger, and to Marilyn Semerad for expediting production of the manuscript. Any errors of fact or misinterpretations naturally are my sole responsibility.

Chapter 1

CONGRESSIONAL PREEMPTION

The extent to which political power should be confided to the national government has been a controversial issue since the drafting of the U.S. Constitution in 1787 with no consensus reached at any time on the optimal degree of power centralization. The Constitution's drafters decided a static division of regulatory powers between the national government and the states would be undesirable and hence formulated a lithe document generally enabling Congress to employ its delegated powers, including the necessary and proper clause, to respond effectively to new regulatory challenges—brought about by domestic, foreign, and technological developments—without the need for a constitutional amendment. In particular, incorporation in the fundamental document of provisions for formal constitutional amendments, delegation of expressed powers to Congress in broad terms, and inclusion of the necessary and proper clause and the supremacy of the laws clause ensures there will be continuing changes in the distribution of regulatory powers between the two planes of government. The latter clause is of great importance as it authorizes Congress to enact statutes invalidating regulatory statutes and regulations of subnational governments that conflict with congressional statutes. Hence, Congress can employ its constitutional powers to remove completely or partially concurrent and reserved regulatory powers of the states. A total of 522 preemption statutes were enacted in the period 1790–2004.

Authors commonly cite the interstate commerce clause and the supremacy of the laws clause as sources of authority for Congress to enact preemption statutes. The former clause is not the only delegated power employable to remove authority from states. Congress also is authorized to enact preemption statutes relating to bankruptcy, naturalization, copyrights, patents, and taxation. It is important to note the supremacy of the laws clause does not delegate a power to Congress and is limited to "conflict preemption," that is, a court may invalidate a state constitutional or statutory provision if it conflicts with a congressional statute based upon a delegated power. Does invalidation of a specific state statute on the ground of a conflict deprive this state and sister states of all concurrent powers to regulate in the given field? The answer is no, but state law enactments in the field subsequent to a court's conflict decision, of course, may be subject to court challenges if they conflict with a congressional statute. The reader should note it is the courts, not Congress, that determine whether there is a direct conflict between a federal law and a state law of a magnitude triggering activation of the supremacy of the laws clause (see chapter 6).

"Conflict preemption" is not the only source of statutory preemption. Congress prospectively can preempt completely or to a limited extent state regulatory authority in the absence of any conflicting state constitutional and statutory provisions by exercising its delegated powers; the necessary and proper clause also allows enactment of preemption and other laws not based upon a specifically delegated power. In 1819, Chief Justice John Marshall of the U.S. Supreme Court in *McCulloch v. Maryland* opined "let the end be legitimate, let it be within the scope of the Constitution, and all means which are appropriate, which are plainly adapted to that end are constitutional."[1] In consequence, the national legislature may enact a "field preemption" statute completely depriving state legislatures of authority to enact regulatory statutes and state administrators to promulgate rules and regulations in a specified field for the first time. This type of preemption has a major impact on the nature of the federal system (see chapter 4).

Can Congress be required to exercise any of its delegated powers? The answer is no and for decades commentators referred to the "silence of Congress." Furthermore, there is no constitutional provision forbidding Congress to devolve one or more of its delegated powers upon the states with the exception of coinage. The initial Congress in 1789 decided to devolve to states authority to regulate marine port pilots.[2] The current Shipping Statute, last revised in 1983, contains a provision nearly identical to one contained in the 1789 devolution act and stipulates "pilots in the bays, rivers, harbors, and ports of the United States shall be regulated only in conformity with the laws of the States."[3]

Of greater importance is the *McCarran-Ferguson Act of 1945*, which specifically reversed the 1944 decision of the U.S. Supreme Court holding insurance was interstate commerce by devolving authority to states to regulate the insurance industry.[4] In 1999, Congress, as described in chapter 5, enacted a statute preempting thirteen specified areas of state insurance regulation and threatening to establish a national system of licensing insurance agents if twenty-six state legislatures failed to establish a uniform licensing system by November 12, 2002.[5]

A third example of congressional devolution of powers is a minor one and dates to 1978 when Congress authorized states to preempt to a limited extent the congressional prohibition of interstate off-track wagering.[6] The statute allows interstate simulcasts of horse races provided the concerned state regulatory agency and the concerned horsemen's association do not object to the simulcast. The U.S. District Court for the Eastern District of Kentucky in 1993 agreed with a plaintiff's contentions that the act violated the First Amendment's guarantee of freedom of speech and is unconstitutionally vague.[7] The decision was appealed and the U.S. Court of Appeals for the 6th Circuit in 1994 reversed the lower court decision by finding that the act does not regulate commercial speech in view of the fact off-track betting can take place in the absence of simulcasting, the act regulates a very narrow subject and consequently a "less strict vagueness test" is applicable to the act, and it "does not delegate legislative power to private parties."[8]

This book focuses upon the continuous readjustment of the respective competences of Congress and the states resulting from the accretion of congressional powers by means of conditional grants-in-aid, crossover sanctions attached to conditional grants-in-aid, tax credits, tax sanctions, congressional preemption of state regulatory authority, and occasional congressional devolution of powers to states. Preemption statutes may be placed in three broad classes: complete, partial, and contingent. The latter refers to preemption statutes applicable to a state or local government only if a specified condition or conditions exist within the unit or states failed to enact harmonious regulatory policies in a field by a stipulated date.

Particular attention is placed upon (1) criteria utilized by the U.S. Supreme Court to determine whether a congressional statute lacking an explicit preemption clause is preemptive, (2) national goal achievement, (3) fiscal implications of congressional mandates and restraints placed on subnational governments, (4) accountability for action or inaction where responsibility for the performance of governmental functions is shared by two or three planes of government, and (5) modification of the dual and cooperative theories of U.S. federalism.

Centralization of Political Power

The newly drafted United States Constitution was not a universally revered fundamental law in 1787–1788. Opponents, termed anti-federalists, raised numerous objections against the proposed document and were particularly disturbed by a provision in Article VII: "The ratification of the conventions of nine states shall be sufficient for the establishment of this constitution between the States so ratifying the same." They specifically maintained the document was illegitimate and violated Article XIII of the Articles of Confederation and Perpetual Union, which required that any amendment to the articles be subject to the approval of the unicameral Congress and each state legislature.

An even greater fear was generated by the constitutional delegation to Congress of preemption powers whose employment could result in the conversion, without a constitutional amendment, of the federal system into a unitary system governed by the English common law ultra vires doctrine. The states in effect would be subject to the complete domination of Congress as local governments were subject to the complete control of state legislatures at the time. In a letter, Elbridge Gerry, a Massachusetts delegate to the 1787 Philadelphia constitutional convention, reflected the views of many citizens:

> My principal objections to the plan, are, that there is no adequate provision for a representation of the people—that they have no security for the right of election—that some of the powers of the Legislature are ambiguous, and others indefinite and dangerous—that the Executive is blended with and will have an undue influence over the Legislature—that the judicial department will be oppressive—that treaties of the highest importance may be formed by the President with the advice of two thirds of a quorum of the Senate—and that the system is without the security of a bill of rights.[9]

Chapter 2 explains Alexander Hamilton, John Jay, and James Madison wrote eighty-five letters to editors of New York City newspapers (subsequently published as *The Federalist Papers*) to allay anti-federalist fears of over-centralization of political powers, and the Bill of Rights was proposed and ratified as amendments to the U.S. Constitution in response to these fears.

Concern continued in the late eighteenth and early nineteenth centuries that a federal leviathan would devour the states. A change in attitudes was in part a product of Roger B. Taney replacing John Marshall as chief justice of the U.S. Supreme Court in 1835. Under Marshall, the Court tended to give an expansive reading to the delegated powers of Congress. The Taney Court, on the other hand, issued a series of rulings commonly described as dual federalism ones enhancing the powers of the states. In general, the court was protective of "states rights" until 1937, as explained in chapter 6.

Congress and state legislatures to a large extent exercised their respective powers independently of each other during the early decades of the federal system, although Congress enacted two complete preemption statutes in 1790 establishing a uniform copyright system and a uniform patent system.[10] The federal system during this period could be described accurately as largely "symbiotic" in terms of national-state relations: the two planes of government coexisted in close proximity, yet had relatively little contact with each other and one plane generally did not encroach seriously upon the preserve of the other. Although it was not recognized at the time, ratification of the Fourteenth, Fifteenth, and Sixteenth Amendments, which delegated additional powers to Congress, in the period 1868 to 1913, enhanced greatly the prospects the federal system in the future would undergo significant structural changes. Furthermore, ratification of the seventeenth amendment, providing for popular election of U.S. senators, reduced the influence of state legislatures over congressional enactment since the legislatures no longer elected the senators.

Inventions and technological developments have spurred enactment of many preemption statutes. Congressional response to inventions, however, is not always rapid. An Act to Regulate Commerce, creating the Interstate Commerce Commission (ICC) to regulate railroad fares and tariffs, was not enacted until 1887.[11] Congress responded to several subsequent technological developments by extending the jurisdiction of ICC to cover interstate telephone and telegraph companies, transoceanic cable companies, bus and trucking firms, and electric power transmission lines. In 1996, Congress abolished the commission as deregulation statutes removed many of its functions (see chapter 4).[12]

Preemption powers for more than a century were exercised on a limited basis with only twenty-nine such statutes enacted by 1900; several subsequently were repealed.[13] The primary foci of these statutes were commerce, health, and safety. It should be noted Congress enacted seven civil and voting rights preemption statutes, based on the Fourteenth and Fifteenth Amendments, in the period 1866 to 1875. The U.S. Supreme Court in the latter year, in *State v. Reese*, invalidated most provisions of the 1870 and 1871 Voting Rights Acts on the ground they also protected the voting rights of white citizens while the Fifteenth

Amendment protects only the voting rights of blacks.[14] Congress in 1890 repealed the remaining provisions of these acts and no voting rights act was enacted again until 1965.

The Great Depression of the 1930s revealed inadequate state government responses to immense economic and social problems and led to predictions that the states and the federal system would vanish. Luther Gulick, director of the Institute of Public Administration in 1933, concluded "the American State is finished" and added:

> The revolution has already taken place. The States have failed; the Federal Government has assumed responsibility for the work. The Constitution and the law must be made to conform to avoid needless complications, judicial squirmings, and great waste of time and money. Without clean-cut constitutional revisions, the States will continue to maintain their futile duplicating organizations at great expense
>
> All essential powers affecting economic planning and control must be taken from the States and given to the Nation....
>
> What would the States then become? They would become organs of local government. They would abandon their wasteful and bungling endeavors and pretense of competency in the field of national economics and settle down to perform honestly and successfully their allotted tasks in creating and maintaining the organs of local government and service.[15]

Harold J. Laski, a British Fabian socialist and academic who examined the federal system, unconditionally declared in 1939 federalism was obsolete and in 1948 concluded "the States are provinces of which the sovereignty has never since 1789 been real."[16]

Felix Morley in 1959 reported Alexander Hamilton's forecast in *The Federalist Papers* was correct: Political power would shift to the national government if the states failed to "administer their affairs with uprightness and prudence."[17] Morley added: "State governments, with a few honorable exceptions, are both ill-designed and ill-equipped to cope with the problems which a dynamic society can not, or will not solve for itself. State constitutions are in many cases unduly restrictive. Their legislatures meet too briefly and have the most meager technical assistance....Governors generally have inadequate executive control over a pattern of local government unnecessarily complex and confusing."[18]

Dennis W. Brogan, an English academic and commentator, in 1960 also concluded states possessed relatively few important powers, and explained:

> There is, of course, an irreducible minimum of federalism. The States can never be reduced to being mere counties, but in practice, they may be little more than mere counties. The Union may neglect to exercise powers that

it has and so leave them to the States (subject to varying Supreme Court doctrines as to whether the States can legislate freely in the mere absence of federal legislation, on matters affecting interstate commerce for instance). But in a great many fields of modern legislation, States' rights are a fiction, because the economic and social integration of the United States has gone too far for them to remain a reality. They are, in fact, usually argued for, not by zealots believing that the States can do better than the Union in certain fields, but by prudent calculators who know that the States can do little or nothing, which is what the defenders of States' rights want them to do.[19]

The reader should note the above conclusions were drawn prior to the preemption revolution, explained below, which commenced in 1965. Congress subsequently removed partially or completely a large number of regulatory powers from the states, but today no federalism scholar would agree the federal system is obsolete or states are mere counties.

Congress in the twentieth century increasingly relied upon conditional grants-in-aid (see chapter 3) to persuade states to implement national policies while continuing to enact a limited number of preemption statutes. Only sixteen preemption statues were enacted during the 1940s and twenty-four during the 1950s, with most relating to commerce and health. The federal system underwent significant changes by 1950 as the result of congressional enactment of numerous conditional grant-in-aid statutes, which influenced the delivery of many services by subnational governments, and a number of preemption statutes that totally or partially removed regulatory authority from the states.[20] As a result, the federal system could be described accurately as a mutuality model reflecting the general interdependence of the governmental planes—national, state, and local—and the reliance of one plane upon the others for performance of a number of functions and/or functional components, standard setting, or financial assistance.

A federalism revolution commenced in 1965 as Congress enacted preemption statutes with greater frequency in a wide range of regulatory fields.[21] Thirty-six preemption statutes, many relating to civil rights and environmental protection, were enacted in the period 1965 through 1969. A total of 102 such statutes were enacted during the 1970s, 93 during the 1980s, 83 during the 1990s, and 41 between 2000 and 2004. The bulk of these statutes involve commerce, finance, and health, but banking has emerged as an important preemption area. The reasons for the sharply increased use of congressional preemption powers were the growing awareness of the interstate nature of many public problems, general failure of states to enact harmonious regulatory statutes and form effective cooperative programs to solve problems, activism by certain members of Congress seeking to establish a leadership record in solving major problems as part of their strategy of winning the presidency in a future election, and success of public and private interest groups lobbying Congress to enact preemption statutes. It should be noted a number of the post-1965 preemption statutes amend earlier preemption statutes as illustrated by the *Bankruptcy Reform Act of 1994, Federal Trademark Dilution Act of 1995, Riegle-Neal Amendments Act of 1997,* and *Internet Tax Nondiscrimination Act of 2001.*[22]

Mandates and restraints increasingly were included in the new preemption statutes. A mandate requires subnational governments to initiate a specific course of action, such as removal of listed pollutants from public drinking water supplies. A restraint prevents these governmental units from initiating an action; dumping sewage sludge in the ocean is an example.[23]

The pace of enactment of preemption statutes slowed somewhat after the Republican Party assumed control of Congress in 1995. Seventy-five such laws, including several important ones, were enacted in the period 1995-2004. They reflected in part the Republican-controlled Congress's responses to pressure from business interest groups for the establishment of harmonious regulatory policies. The 104th Congress was sensitive to criticisms of unfunded federal mandates by subnational governmental officers and enacted the *Unfunded Mandates Reform Act of 1995* establishing new mandatory congressional procedures for the enactment of mandates.[24] The following year, Congress enacted the *Safe Drinking Water Act Amendments of 1996,* providing relief from expensive directives contained in the *Safe Drinking Water Act Amendments of 1986.* These directives had left numerous small local governments with the choice of either bankruptcy or abandonment of their drinking water supply systems and also placed major financial burdens on larger local governments.[25]

The *Telecommunications Act of 1996* preempts all state and local government legal barriers to firms providing any interstate or intrastate telecommunications service, but authorizes states to manage their public rights-of-way and to require providers to pay reasonable fees for the use of rights-of-way on a nondiscriminatory basis.[26] The act also stipulates local governments cannot require or prohibit the provision of telecommunications services by a cable operator.[27] And the *Internet Tax Nondiscrimination Act of 2001* forbids subnational governments to tax sales made via the Internet.[28]

The reader should be aware that state government officers are not always opposed to preemption statutes. The *Commercial Motor Vehicle*

Safety Act of 1986, for example, was enacted by Congress at the request of several states. These states were unable to solve cooperatively the problem created by commercial vehicle drivers who, holding operator licenses issued by a number of states, continue to drive with a license issued by one state after the suspension or revocation by another state of their respective license for a serious violation of that state's motor vehicle law or regulation.[29]

No one can deny that state legislatures are weaker today in terms of their unrestrained freedom to exercise all powers originally reserved to them at the time of the ratification of the U.S. Constitution. State legislatures today, however, are exercising powers they generally did not exercise prior to 1965. In other words, the universe of their exercised powers has been expanded tremendously by congressional minimum standards preemption statutes. This has resulted in state legislatures exercising what had been latent powers simultaneously with the loss of their freedom to exercise other specified regulatory powers because of congressional enactment of preemption statutes that remove all or specified regulatory powers in a given field from states. As explained in subsequent chapters, Congress increasingly relies upon the states to conduct regulatory programs meeting or exceeding minimum national standards, and the states typically possess considerable discretionary authority in administering these programs.

Changing Roles

Congress has drawn upon its latent delegated powers to expand its influence over the provision of services by subnational governments by means of conditional grants-in-aid, crossover sanctions, and tax credits (see chapter 3), and similarly to expand its regulatory policy sphere by enactment of preemption statutes. The latter have resulted in significant role changes for Congress, the president, federal bureaucrats, national and state courts, state governors, state legislatures, state bureaucrats, local government chief executives and governing bodies, local government bureaucrats, interest groups, and citizens.

Congress no longer confines its attention almost exclusively to foreign affairs, national defense, and major public works projects such as the Boulder Dam; it has become involved deeply in designing programs to solve rural, urban, metropolitan, and interstate problems that traditionally were the responsibilities of state and local governments. The enlargement of congressional responsibilities is attributable in part to lobbying by special interest groups and activism by certain members of Congress who have sought to establish a leadership record. Congressional activism in one regulatory field has generated interest group pressures in other fields.

As chief executive, the president is responsible for preparing and transmitting an annual executive budget to Congress and directing myriad federal departments and agencies. The president increasingly has been subject to intense pressure by interest groups and citizens as partial congressional preemption statutes have become more common.

The role of many federal bureaucrats, whose numbers have remained nearly constant since 1946, has been enhanced dramatically as a product of congressional enactment of "skeleton" preemption statutes outlining new programs or policies and authorizing departments and agencies to draft and promulgate implementing rules and regulations. As explained in subsequent chapters, their responsibilities include reviewing and accepting or rejecting state and local government applications for federal grants-in-aid and analyzing state regulatory standards for conformance with national minimum standards statutes and regulations prior to delegating regulatory primacy in a given field to applicant states.

The national judicial system continues to play its customary referee role, but also has become deeply involved in policymaking in areas such as public schools and the environment, even to the point of establishing a judicial receivership of several public school systems, as described in chapter 6. State courts have been deprived of jurisdiction over specified types of lawsuits by preemption statutes.

The traditional balance of power between a governor and the state legislature has been altered by partial congressional preemption statutes and their implementing rules and regulations which grant to governors powers not delegated by his/her state constitution and/or statutes. The new roles of governors are examined in chapter 5.

Minimum standard preemption acts have forced state legislatures to amend their statutes to bring them into conformity with national standards or lose responsibility for the preempted functions and possibly national grants-in-aid.

The importance of state bureaucrats who administer programs covered by minimum national standards has increased because they draft and promulgate implementing regulations. In drafting regulations, bureaucrats typically work closely with their federal counterparts who are required by law to review state rules and regulations for conformity with national minimum standards. Development of acceptable state rules and regulations often necessitates extensive negotiations between bureaucrats on the two planes of government.

Chief executives of general purpose local governments are not responsible for administering federal minimum standards preemption acts, but are subject to their provisions and implementing rules and regulations. They may have to seek clarification or waivers of the standards or extensions of time for their governments to meet newly established standards.

Minimum standards preemption statutes can also impact local government bodies. If their facilities fail to meet minimum air, water, and drinking water national standards, these governing bodies will have to appropriate funds for necessary improvements to existing facilities and/or construction of new facilities. Federal mandates imposed on state and local governments are examined in chapter 7, which also addresses the question whether subnational governments should be reimbursed in full or in part for the costs incurred in complying with the mandates.

A positive correlation exists between the expansion of national governmental programs and the growing influence of private and public interest groups, which naturally transferred part of their attention from state capitols to the national capitol as Congress became more deeply involved in traditional state and local governmental functions. Groups unable to achieve fully or partially their goals by lobbying state legislatures and governors redirected resources to influence Congress, the president, and the national bureaucrats with varying degrees of success.

Do business firms prefer national or state regulation? Congressional preemption has changed the political landscape in terms of interest group politics and the extent of state regulatory authority. Many economic interest groups historically lobbied against national government regulation in the belief they would be more successful in influencing state legislatures not to enact stringent regulatory statutes and state administrators whose promulgated regulations might not be as strict or vigorously enforced compared with national regulations and their enforcement. The motor vehicle industry in the mid-1960s was a major exception as it lobbied for complete congressional preemption of motor vehicle safety standards and regulation of new motor vehicles emissions. Motor vehicle companies were fearful that absent such preemption they might have to manufacture vehicles with specific safety features and emission control systems for sale in each state with non-harmonious standards. The trucking industry and the teamsters union similarly lobbied Congress to remove state authority to establish maximum truck sizes and weights (see chapter 4).

Preemption Criteria

When and under what conditions should Congress preempt the regulatory authority of states and their political subdivisions? The importance of this question increased with the acceleration in the pace of congressional enactment of preemption statutes. President Dwight D. Eisenhower, reflecting the concern of many citizens that the national government had become too powerful, appointed in 1953 the Commission on Intergovernmental Relations. The commission was charged with conducting an in-depth study of power distribution in the federal system.

The commission addressed the controversy over congressional removal of state regulatory authority and identified the following conditions as justifying Congress exercising its preemption powers:

(a) When the National Government is the only agency that can summon the resources needed for an activity. For this reason, the Constitution entrusts defense to the National Government. Similarly, primary responsibility for governmental action in maintaining economic stability is given to the National Government because it alone can command the main resources for the task.

(b) When the activity cannot be handled within the geographic and jurisdictional limits of smaller units, including those that could be created by compact. Regulation of radio and television is an extreme example.

(c) When the activity requires a nationwide uniformity of policy that cannot be achieved by interstate action. Sometimes there must be an undeviating standard and hence an exclusively national policy, as in immigration and naturalization, the currency, and foreign relations.

(d) When a State through action or inaction does injury to the people of other States. One of the main purposes of the commerce clause was to eliminate State practices that hindered the flow of goods across State lines. On this ground also, national action is justified to prevent unrestrained exploitation of an essential nature resource.

(e) When States fail to respect or protect basic political and civil rights that apply throughout the United States.[30]

The above criteria may be viewed as common sense ones restating the powers delegated to Congress by Section 8 of Article I of the U.S. Constitution and Section 5 of the Fourteenth amendment.

The commission also formulated the following principles to guide congressional regulation to ensure states retain essential reserved powers:

First, the fact the National Government has not legislated on a given matter in a field of concurrent power should not bar State action.

Second, national laws should be framed that they will not be construed to preempt any field against State action unless this intent is stated.

Third, exercise of national power on any subject should not bar State action on the same subject unless there is a positive inconsistency.

Fourth, when a national minimum standard is imposed in a field where uniformity is not imperative, the right of States to set more rigorous standards should be carefully preserved.

Fifth, statutes should provide flexible scope for administrative cession of jurisdiction where the objectives of the laws at the two levels are substantially in accord. States legislation need not be identical with the national legislation.[31]

The first principle is simply recognition of the well-established principle of constitutional law that either or both planes of government may exercise concurrent powers. The second principle is easy to state but difficult to implement, and questions may be raised whether the principle is workable in all situations. The third principle is nothing more than a restatement of the supremacy of the law clause of the U.S. Constitution. The fourth principle underlies the type of minimum standards preemption employed by Congress since 1965, which is examined in chapter 5. The fifth principle was implemented by the *Atomic Energy Act of 1959*, which authorizes the Nuclear Regulatory Commission to turn over certain regulatory powers to states signing an agreement with the commission provided the state statutes and administrative regulations are consistent with the federal statutes and administrative regulations, a subject explored in chapter 4.[32]

The commission in effect urged Congress to be more careful in the future when enacting statutes not to preempt the regulatory powers of the states unnecessarily, but it did not attack U.S. courts for their decisions.

The U.S. Advisory Commission on Intergovernmental Relations, established by Congress in 1959, issued a report in 1984 recommending that Congress enact a preemption bill into law only to achieve one of the following goals:

1) to protect basic political and civil rights guaranteed to all American citizens under the Constitution;
2) to ensure national defense and proper conduct of foreign relations;
3) to establish certain uniform and minimum standards in areas affecting the flow of interstate commerce;
4) to prevent state and local actions which substantially and adversely affect another State or its citizens; or
5) to assure essential fiscal and programmatic integrity in the use of federal grants and contracts into which state and local governments freely enter.[33]

These principles do not differ significantly from the conditions identified by the Commission on Intergovernmental Relations nearly two decades earlier.

A much different answer to when and under what conditions Congress should preempt the regulatory authority of the states was provided by President Ronald Reagan, who in 1987 listed the following as "Fundamental Federalism Principles":

(a) Federalism is rooted in the knowledge that our political liberties are best assured by limiting the size and scope of the national government.

(b) The people of the States created the national government when they delegated to it those enumerated governmental powers relating to matters beyond the competence of the individual States. All other sovereign powers, save those expressly prohibited the States by the Constitution, are reserved to the States or to the people.

(c) The constitutional relationship among sovereign governments, State and national, is formalized in and protected by the Tenth Amendment to the Constitution.

(d) The people of the States are free, subject only to the restrictions in the Constitution itself or in constitutionally authorized Acts of Congress, to define the moral, political, and legal character of their lives.

(e) In most areas of governmental concern, the States uniquely possess the constitutional authority, the resources, and the competence to discern the sentiments of the people and to govern accordingly. In Thomas Jefferson's words, the States are "the most competent administrations for our domestic concerns and the surest bulwarks against anti-republican tendencies."

(f) The nature of our constitutional system encourages a healthy diversity in the public policies by the people of the several States according to their own conditions, needs, and desires. In the search for enlightened public policy, individual States and communities are free to experiment with a variety of approaches to public issues.

(g) Acts of the national government—whether legislative, executive, or judicial in nature—that exceed the enumerated powers of that government under the Constitution violate the principle of federalism established by the Framers.

(h) Policies of the national government should recognize the responsibility of—and should encourage opportunities for—individuals, families, neighborhoods, local governments, and private associations to achieve their personal, social, and economic objectives through cooperative effort.

(i) In the absence of clear constitutional or statutory authority, the presumption to sovereignty should rest with the individual States. Uncertainties regarding the legitimate authority of the national government should be resolved against regulation at the national level.[34]

Reagan's principles essentially reflected the position of individuals and organizations favoring states' rights, emphasized the vital role played by individual states as laboratories of democracy, and advised Congress to exercise restraint in exercising its delegated powers. Richard S. Williamson, President Reagan's first assistant for intergovernmental relations, explained in 1982 the president was seeking "to change the presumptions which have been directing Americans and led them in recent years to turn first to the federal government for answers. He is seeking a 'quiet revolution,' a new federalism which is a meaningful American partnership."[35] Nevertheless, President Reagan signed more preemption bills into law than any other president to date.[36]

The Changing Nature of National-State Relations

The U.S. Constitution to a large extent assigns responsibility for the restructuring of the federal system to Congress by delegating to it sweeping powers in broad terms without guidelines or restrictions governing their use. When pressures build for action to solve a major problem Congress generally responds by developing a solution *de novo*. No comprehensive study has been conducted by Congress or any other organization to identify and assess (1) the effectiveness of the various structural approaches employed by Congress to remove regulatory powers completely or partially from subnational governments or (2) the impact of preemption statutes on the viability and fiscal capacity of these governments.

A federal system is described aptly as an *imperium in imperio*, an empire within an empire, with legislative bodies on the national and state planes of government exercising relatively autonomous political power in their respective area of competence as well as concurrent powers (see chapter 5). The U.S. Constitution delegates specific powers to Congress and reserves all other powers unless prohibited to the states and the people. Congress, however, is authorized to employ its delegated powers, including the necessary and proper clause reinforced by the supremacy of the law's clause (art. VI), to preempt certain concurrent powers exercised by state legislatures. In other words, certain concurrent powers are coordinate ones and other powers are subordinate ones subject to complete or partial preemption by Congress. A power fundamental to semi-sovereign states, such as the power to levy taxes, is not subject to preemption unless its exercise places an undue burden on interstate commerce or denies a citizen equal protection of the laws.

Although Congress has possessed the power to preempt completely certain concurrent powers since 1789, the power was not employed between 1790, when the *Copyright Act* and the *Patent Act* were enacted, and 1946 when the *Atomic Energy Act* was enacted.[37]

Several of the original complete preemption statutes—atomic energy, grain standards, and railroad safety are examples—have been amended by Congress in recognition of the significant roles states can play in the administration of these statutes. These amendments authorize

the responsible federal administrator to make limited regulatory authority turn-backs to states meeting stipulated conditions. Congress also has
authorized the governor of one state to petition the secretary of transportation for removal of a decision made by a complete preemption
statute and the governor or state legislature to veto a federal administrative decision based upon a complete preemption statute—*Nuclear Waste
Policy Act of 1982*—subject to a subsequent veto override by Congress
(see chapter 4).

Congress incorporated contingent preemption provisions in the
Voting Rights Act of 1965, described in chapter 4, by stipulating the
act will apply to a state only if two conditions prevail within the
state.[38] In 1999, Congress enacted the *Gramm-Leach-Bliley Financial
Modernization Act*, which contains a contingent preemption provision
providing a federal insurance agent licensing system would be implemented if twenty-six states failed to adopt a uniform licensing system
for agents by November 12, 2002.[39] This provision was effective:
thirty-five states on September 10, 2002, were certified as having a
uniform licensing system.[40]

Congressional mandates requiring state and local governments to
initiate a particular course of action currently are the major irritants in
national-state relations. Subnational governments described as galling
the 1985 decision of the U.S. Supreme Court that validated congressional extension of the provisions of the *Fair Labor Standards Act* to
their employees.[41]

A revolution, albeit a relatively silent one, in intergovernmental relations has been worked since 1965 by limited congressional preemption
of traditional state and local responsibilities. Chapter 5 examines the various types of limited preemption statutes enacted by Congress, including
ones creating an *imperium in imperio*, adopting a state standard, authorizing additional uses of a federally regulated product as determined by a
state standard, combining partial preemption and *imperium in imperio*,
and providing for voluntary state transfer of regulatory responsibility to
the national government.

In effect, a regulatory *imperium in imperio* under partial preemption
exists at the sufferance of Congress, which in its wisdom at any time
may assume complete responsibility for a regulatory function. The principal distinction between a genuine *imperium in imperio* and one created
by minimum standards partial preemption statutes is that the latter's
establishment is dependent upon a state voluntarily submitting a plan,
containing state standards at least as stringent as national ones and an
enforcement program, to the appropriate federal department or agency
and accepting the regulatory primacy delegated to it by the department

or agency if the plan is approved. Under regulatory primacy, only the state exercises regulatory authority and the role of the concerned national body is to monitor state exercise of the authority.

The Accountability-Responsibility Problem

Congress in enacting limited preemption statutes has produced a complex national-state intertwining of powers that makes it difficult for government officers, and particularly for citizens, to determine which plane is responsibility for solving major governmental problems. A genuine system of "dual" federalism with no shared powers would facilitate citizen determination of the plane of government responsible for a function or a functional component. The reluctance of Congress to enact limited preemption acts on a regular basis until 1965 preserved in general a governance system in which accountability and responsibility could be fixed with relative ease. It, of course, must be recognized that federal conditional grants-in-aid allow subnational government officers to blame Congress for certain unpopular actions by maintaining they were "mandated" to take the actions. In fact, the so-called mandates could have been avoided by failing to apply for or accept grants-in-aid from the national government.

Although limited congressional preemption statutes subject states to national controls, the extent and variety of these controls vary considerably from one statute to another, as outlined in chapter 5. While the argument can be advanced that the system may function more effectively if preemption statutes are tailored to address each problem in the most effective manner, one product of this approach is citizen confusion.

Citizen control of governments is reduced by complete and limited preemption as the decision-making forum is shifted from subnational legislative bodies to the more remote Congress. This disadvantage may be offset in the eyes of many citizens by advantages that can flow from congressional preemption statutes. Recommendations are presented in chapter 7 to clarify the responsibility of the national and state planes of government under partial preemption statutes.

Congressional Preemption and Goal Achievement

Congressional exercise of its preemption powers is justified primarily on the ground that it is the most effective and efficient manner in which to solve major nationwide problems. Unfortunately, as noted earlier, there have been few studies of the effectiveness and efficiency of the various types of complete and limited preemption statutes enacted by Congress.

Studies of a complete preemption program with a provision for the turn-back of limited regulatory authority—the agreement states program in the nuclear area—reached the positive conclusion the program is effective and popular with the states. Citizens generally are aware that the air quality and water quality partial preemption statutes have failed to achieve their goals because Congress has been forced to grant extensions of time for achievement of mandated standards by the states and their political subdivisions.

A 2002 U.S. General Accounting Office limited study focused on federal and state responsibilities for standard setting and implementation in regulatory programs and noted: "...[there are a] rich variety of ways in which the federal government and the states can work toward achieving shared regulatory objectives. Each variation reflects circumstances and sensitive issues specific to the program concerned, and each program is unique in some way. But comparative analysis reveals both underlying features of program design and trade-offs between the various options available. Explicitly considering these features and trade-offs could help guide decisions about how to structure future federal-state regulatory programs."[42] This study is examined in more detail in chapter 7, which also examines the question whether Congress, in mandating the achievement of statutory goals by specific dates, was realistic in view of the fact no consideration was given to the technical feasibility of achieving certain statutory goals or the financial and political capacity of subnational governments to comply with the standards by the dates specified.

Field preemption by Congress may have undesirable consequences as illustrated by a 1992 decision of the U.S. Supreme Court opining the *Airline Deregulation Act of 1978* strips states of all regulatory authority in the field, thereby making it impossible for state attorneys general individually or cooperatively to enforce state deceptive practices suits against airlines.[43]

Experience also reveals a federal preemption statute is not always successful in achieving its proclaimed goals. Congress has preempted to a substantial degree the authority of states to regulate the financial securities industry. New York State Attorney General Eliot Spitzer in 2002 demonstrated the regulatory inadequacy of the U.S. Securities and Exchange Commission's supervision of financial markets by his investigation of Merrill Lynch & Company. His findings revealed some of its analysts pretended to be providing impartial recommendations to clients to purchase shares of dot-com companies whose business the company's investment bankers were seeking while aware the stocks were not sound investments.[44] The company negotiated a settlement with the attorney general involving the payment of $100 million in fines and issuance of an apology to investors.

Congressional Responsiveness

The unamended U.S. Constitution contained a built-in safeguard ensuring Congress would not intrude upon the reserved powers of the states by enacting unwanted preemption statutes. The constitutional provision (art. I, §3) authorizing the election of senators by state legislatures was an effective mechanism to allow them indirectly to veto preemption bills approved by the popularly elected House of Representatives. The Constitution of the Federal Republic of Germany currently contains a similar provision providing members of the *Bundesrat* are members of the *Kabinett* (cabinet) of each *Land* (state). The *Bundesrat* may disallow bills enacted by the *Bundestag* (parliament) if they encroach upon the powers of the *Länder* (states).

Allowing the drafters of the Constitution to speak for him, Jackson Pemberton in 1976 attributed the fundamental changes in federal-state relations to the adoption of the Seventeenth Amendment:

> We noted with concern that the universal nature of legislatures is to legislate too much, and that unless some opposing force were supplied, the United States Congress would eventually infringe every State prerogative until the rights of the people vested in the States were consumed. We talked much of the need for Senators to preserve the sovereignty of their States because they were the best defenders of the rights of the people had already lost to their States' governments. Hence, Senators were elected by the State legislature, were to answer to the State, and were to represent the interests of the State in the Congress. Amendment XVII destroyed that balance and the Senate became another house.[45]

Ratification of this amendment in 1913 removed a safeguard against congressional encroachment on state regulatory powers, yet Congress did not enact preemption statutes on a regular basis until the 1960s. Chapters 4 and 5 explain the reasons for the sharp increase in such statutes.

One focal point of this book is the extent to which Congress gives credence to the preemption concerns of state and local governments. In 1824, Chief Justice John Marshall of the U.S. Supreme Court referred to Congress's interstate commerce power by noting, "the wisdom and the discretion of Congress, their identity with the people, and the influence which their constituents possess at elections, are...the sole restraints on which they have relied to secure them from its abuse."[46] One hundred and twenty-nine years later, Herbert Wechsler expanded Marshall's conclusion by developing the political safeguards theory of federalism, explaining states can utilize the political process to fend off bills in Congress designed to preempt one or more of their reserved powers.[47]

Justice Harry A. Blackmun of the U.S. Supreme Court drew upon this theory in 1985 to uphold the constitutionality of a congressional preemption statute by opining, "the principal and basic limits on the federal commerce power is inherent in all state participation in federal government action."[48] The statute extended national minimum wage and overtime pay requirements to non-supervisory employees of state and local governments, thereby subjecting many of these governments to a new major fiscal burden.

States in the early 1960s also objected to many conditions attached by Congress to grant-in-aid programs and maintained they were burdensome and amounted to an indirect form of preemption. President Lyndon B. Johnson initiated several administrative actions in response to these criticisms and President Richard M. Nixon proclaimed his "New Federalism" policy was designed to shift political power to state and local governments (see chapter 3). President James E. Carter, a former Georgia governor, was sensitive to the criticisms of federal rules and regulations and an economic deregulation movement commenced during his administration.

President Ronald Reagan, who assumed office in 1981, has been the most successful president in terms of persuading Congress to reduce the number of conditions attached to grants-in-aid by replacing numerous categorical grants-in-aid with block grants and directing federal departments and agencies to expedite delegation of regulator primacy to states under minimum standards preemption statutes.

Fiscal Implications of Congressional Mandates

General purpose local governments complained for decades about state legislative mandates requiring the undertaking of specified activities and/or provision of services meeting minimum state standards on the ground these mandates impose substantial unreimbursed costs on local governments. Lobbying by local governments led to amendment of fifteen state constitutions and enactment of statutes in sixteen states providing mandate relief.[49] The various amendments and statutes either make it more difficult for state legislatures to impose mandates or require the state government to reimburse local governments in full or in part for costs incurred in implementing the mandates.

Congress uses its preemption powers to impose costly mandates and restraints on subnational governments. The restraints forbid them to initiate specific actions and the units may have to employ more expensive alternatives. These governments lobbied Congress to reimburse them for mandated costs for three decades without success. In 1995, the Republican Party assumed control of Congress, which enacted the *Unfunded Mandates Reform Act of 1995*.[50] Chapter 7 contains a typology of congressional mandates and explores the impact of the *Unfunded Mandates Reform Act of 1995* in terms of achieving its stated goals.

Federalism Theory

Scholarly writings on the U.S. political system contain numerous references to theories of U.S. federalism, but the references tend to be little more than general phrases, most commonly "dual federalism" and "cooperative federalism." Dissatisfaction with the explanatory values of these descriptors, commencing in the 1960s, led to a myriad of new descriptors. William H. Stewart in 1984 identified 497 such figurative descriptions.[51]

The dual federalism theory is a simple one positing a complete separation of state and national powers. Similarly, the theory of cooperative federalism typically is defined as a governance system in which activities of the three planes of governments are carried out on a cooperative basis. Neither theory adequately explains the federal system more than two hundred ten years after its inauguration.

Chapter 2 explains in some detail congressional possession of certain exclusive powers which states are forbidden to exercise. Furthermore, state legislatures possess exclusive reserved powers—such as provision of services and control of local governments subject to state constitutional limitations—which generally are not subject to congressional control. These facts accord with the theory of dual federalism.

Cooperation between the national, state, and local planes of government in exercising powers is extensive. Examples of national government cooperation with subnational governments include the Internal Revenue Service and state tax departments exchanging computer tapes containing income tax returns, the Federal Bureau of Investigation operating a fingerprint service for state and local police forces, and Congress authorizing grants-in-aid to assist subnational units.

Neither theory, however, takes account of the sharply increased use of preemption powers by Congress since 1965. In effect, the national legislature has produced a quiet revolution in the U.S. federal system in the absence of constitutional amendments by employing its powers of complete and partial preemption to structure new regulatory relationships between the planes of government.

Daniel J. Elazar, who made important contributions to federalism theory, explained in 1987 "the center-periphery model of statehood is challenged by the champions of a new model, which views the polity as a matrix of overlapping, interlocking units, powers, and relationships. The efforts to come to grips intellectually with all of these phenomena have been slower than the movement in the real world. The accepted intellectual models have tended to lag behind actual developments."[52]

Elazar's comments are most pertinent. It is apparent a full appreciation of the complexities and dynamics associated with the ever-changing division and sharing of governmental powers cannot be gained from current federalism theories, which focus upon the paradigms of centralization and noncentralization of political power. This linear view of political powers is useful in positing the extremes, but is not helpful in promoting a full understanding of the nuances of a complex federal system composed of centralization, noncentralization, and decentralization elements.

Federalism is an abstract organizational principle; it does not determine precisely the boundary lines between national and state powers. A federal constitution can provide for a sharp and static distribution of powers between the two governmental planes or a dynamic changing distribution of powers. An examination of the U.S. Constitution reveals three broad spheres of power: a national controlling sphere, a state controlling sphere, and a shared national-state sphere. In practice, the shared sphere also includes general purpose local governments. The drafters of the Constitution sought to establish "a more perfect Union" and this goal has been achieved in the sense the planes of government have become more united through inter-linkages. The goal of "a more perfect Union" is depicted on the reverse side of the Great Seal of the United States: the shield with a horizontal bar represents Congress, linking the thirteen vertical bars (states) together, thereby suggesting Congress had been assigned the major responsibility for integrating states into the national polity.

The review of congressional complete and circumscribed preemption statutes in this volume reveals a new synthesis of elements to be incorporated into a more general theory of federalism which has greater explanatory value than the two current major theories. It will become apparent that more than a separation of all political powers between two planes of government and cooperative interplane relations must be embodied in a dynamic theory of federalism. The intertwining of regulatory programs, produced by fiscal incentives and prescriptions, and constantly changing relationships between the planes are key characteristics of a functioning federal system in the twenty-first century.

A comprehensive nonequilibrium theory of dynamic federalism must encompass elements of *imperium in imperio*, cooperative interplane interactions, informal congressional preemption, total congressional preemption, and partial congressional preemption, a subject examined in chapter 7.

An Overview

An in-depth analysis of metamorphic federalism commences with chapter 2, which examines the strengths and weaknesses of the confederacy established in 1781 by the Articles of Confederation and Perpetual Union, the growing dissatisfaction with the articles, and the conversion of the confederacy into a federal system by the U.S. Constitution effective in 1789. This chapter explores the intent of the constitution's drafters and the expansion of the powers of the national government by statutory elaboration, judicial interpretation of constitutional grants of powers to Congress, and constitutional amendments.

Chapter 3 reviews congressional use of incentives—conditional grants-in-aid and tax credits—to persuade states and local governments to adopt and implement national policies. This chapter makes a clear distinction between incentives and genuine congressional mandates.

The subject of chapter 4 is complete congressional preemption of the regulatory authority of states in specified fields. Experience with several complete preemption statutes reveals states, if authorized, could play a role in implementation of the statutes, and Congress amended a number of these statutes by authorizing a limited turn-back of regulatory authority to the states.

Chapter 5 explores the nature of the *imperium in imperio* system established by the U.S. Constitution and congressional use of its delegated powers to remove regulatory powers partially from states.

Congressional preemption statutes have been challenged on numerous occasions on the ground they violate the Tenth Amendment to the constitution. Furthermore, Congress does not always include a provision in a statute stipulating whether the regulatory powers of states are preempted totally or partially. Chapter 6 focuses on major U.S. Supreme Court decisions relative to whether Congress exceeded its delegated powers in enacting a preemption statute or intended to preempt the powers of states without so stipulating.

Chapter 7 reviews the findings presented in the preceding chapters, draws conclusions with respect to the desirability and effectiveness of various types of complete and partial preemption statutes, and offers a more dynamic and general theory explaining the nature of the U.S. federal system in the first decade of the twenty-first century.

Chapter 2

ESTABLISHMENT OF A FEDERATION

Three major governance changes occurred within the original thirteen states in the period 1776 to 1789. The Declaration of Independence in 1776 instituted the first change and made clear that thirteen new nation-states had been created. These states formed a loose coalition, superintended by the Second Continental Congress, for the purpose of prosecuting the Revolutionary War against the United Kingdom. The second major governance change was the 1781 ratification of the Articles of Confederation and Perpetual Union by the thirteen states establishing the third confederacy in the world. The demonstrated inadequacies of the articles led to the third governmental transformation with the 1788 ratification of the U.S. Constitution and its effectuation in 1789. The newly established first federal system has been undergoing continuous changes as the result of ratification by states of congressionally proposed constitutional amendments, judicial decisions interpreting the scope of the delegated powers, and Congress' use of statutory elaboration to make concrete the powers delegated to it in general terms.

The initial adoption of a confederation and the subsequent adoption of the innovative federal system are attributable to the fear of a strong national government that might be a threat to individual liberties. The debate between advocates of a strong national government and advocates of states' rights has been a continuing one. It has been accentuated since the mid-1960s by the explosion in the number of preemption statutes removing completely or partially regulatory powers in specified fields from states.

The dramatic expansion in the use of latent powers by Congress during the Great Depression of the 1930s struck fear in the hearts of the more conservative elements in the nation and was responsible for numerous proposals in the immediate post-World War II period to shift powers from Congress to the states. Relatively few successful initiatives to strengthen the position of states were implemented until President Richard M. Nixon was able to persuade Congress in the early 1970s to enact several of his "New Federalism" proposals into law. His resignation as president in 1974 terminated major efforts to alter significantly the nature of the federal system until the inauguration of Ronald Reagan as president in 1981. Initially, Reagan experienced considerable success in implementing several of his recommendations, a subject examined in chapter 3.

However, centralization trends continued throughout the Nixon and Reagan presidencies and are traceable in origin to the *Water Quality Act of 1965*, the first partial preemption statute to establish minimum national standards and provide for federal assumption of responsibility for water pollution abatement if a state failed to adopt and implement a pollution abatement plan meeting minimum national standards.[1] Congressional preemption of state regulatory authority subsequently attracted relatively little academic study for more than two decades, yet preemption has had a major impact upon the nature of the federation (see chapter 5).

This chapter examines the development of the Articles of Confederation and Perpetual Union, their weaknesses, the intent of the drafters of the U.S. Constitution relative to the powers delegated to Congress and the powers reserved to states, and expansion of congressional powers.

The Articles of Confederation and Perpetual Union

Member states of a confederation retain all powers not denied to them by their respective constitution, and the national government possesses only powers expressly delegated to it by the states. The nature of a confederation would lead one to assume the thirteen newly independent states would have few objections to forming a confederacy since they would retain ultimate control of the system. Nevertheless, there was strong opposition by states to giving up any of their powers to a national body, no matter how weak its powers might be. Leading political statesmen, including Samuel and John Adams of Massachusetts and Thomas

Jefferson and Patrick Henry of Virginia, strongly opposed any movement to restrain the freedom of state legislatures to enact statutes.[2]

The Second Continental Congress, a unicameral body with equal representation from each of the thirteen states, coordinated efforts to expel the British during the Revolutionary War. This body understood the need for a fundamental law to unite the states and in 1777 drafted and submitted the Articles of Confederation and Perpetual Union to the states for ratification. Eight states ratified the document the following year and four additional states ratified the articles in 1779. Maryland, however, refused to ratify the document until 1781 because of Virginia's claims to the "western lands." Virginia in that year acceded to Maryland's position by ceding the lands to the proposed union. Maryland thereupon ratified the articles, and they became effective immediately.

Major Provisions

Article II is the most important one and stipulates "each State retains its sovereignty, freedom and independence, and every power, jurisdiction and right, which is not by this confederation expressly delegated to the united States in Congress assembled." Notice the use of "united" to signify a national government was not being established and the confederation was composed of states united for express purposes. Article III describes the mutual relations of the states as "a firm league of friendship with each other." The articles did not establish an executive branch or judicial branch.

Each state legislature was authorized to appoint and send two to seven delegates to the Congress and to recall a delegate at any time. No delegate could serve for more than three years during any six-year term of Congress. Each state had one vote in the Congress regardless of the number of members appointed to represent the state.

The articles delegated relatively few powers to Congress. It was empowered to borrow and coin money, declare war, establish a postal system and standards of weights and measures, negotiate treaties with other nations, and regulate relations with Indian tribes. Congress also could establish quotas for each state to furnish men and money for the army. Predestining the demise of confederacy was the failure of the articles to authorize Congress to levy taxes and to regulate interstate commerce.

Major Defects

The articles' defects were revealed relatively quickly by experience. Specifically, the defects were the failure to grant adequate powers to

Congress which was (1) dependent upon voluntary contributions of funds by states; (2) powerless to regulate interstate commerce; (3) lacked authority to enforce its enacted statutes which individual states were free to ignore; (4) hampered in obtaining foreign credit; and (5) unable to suppress domestic disorders.

The paper money printed by Congress soon became worthless because of its inability to raise funds by taxation and several states commenced to issue paper currency. Perhaps of greater importance in terms of leading to the abandonment of the articles were state-erected interstate trade barriers which gradually strangled commerce among sister states. Firewood from Connecticut and cabbage from New Jersey are examples of commodities taxed by New York during this time period.[3] Furthermore, the moneyed and property classes were disturbed greatly by Shays's rebellion in western Massachusetts in 1786, which resulted in Captain Shays and his followers occupying most of Massachusetts west of Worcester until the rebellion was suppressed by an army led by General Benjamin Lincoln and financed by wealthy Boston citizens.[4] Shays's demands included lower taxes, cheap money, and suspension of mortgage foreclosures. New Hampshire in the same year was forced to call out its militia to disperse a mob seeking to coerce members of the General Court (state legislature) to authorize the printing of paper money.[5]

With the defects of the articles becoming more apparent with the passage of each year, the boundary commissioners of Maryland and Virginia recommended in 1785 that each state send delegates to a meeting in Annapolis the following year to consider remedies. This conference, attended by delegates from only five states, memorialized Congress to convene a convention in Philadelphia in 1787 for the purpose of drafting curative amendments to the Articles of Confederation and Perpetual Union. Congress, with reluctance, called the convention.

The Constitution of the United States

All states, except Rhode Island and Providence Plantations, sent delegates to the convention held in Philadelphia from May to September 1787. Delegates generally were dissatisfied with the articles but opposed to establishment of a unitary or centralized national governance system. They took an innovative step and drafted a constitution establishing an *imperium in imperio* by dividing powers between the thirteen states and Congress (see figure 2.1). In effect, they merged a unitary system with a confederate system by delegating specified powers to the national Congress, which could enact uniform national laws, while reserving to

Figure 2.1
Power Division in the United States

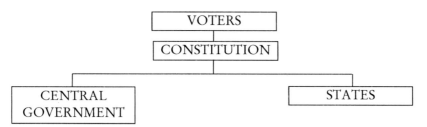

the states all other powers not prohibited. State legislatures were thereby allowed considerable freedom to enact statutes significantly different from statutes enacted by sister state legislatures. No constitutional attempt, however, was made to maintain a balance of powers between the national government and the states.

The proposed constitution reflected the sharp divisions between the thirteen states at the time. Incorporated into the document were compromises between states with large populations and states with small populations, northern and southern states, and eastern seaboard and inland states. New Jersey delegates at the convention proposed continuation of the system of voting in the confederacy's unicameral Congress, with each state having one vote. Virginia delegates, on the other hand, maintained votes accorded to each state should be in proportion to its percentage of the national population, thereby favoring states with large populations. The famous Connecticut compromise provided for a bicameral Congress, with the senate composed of two members from each state elected by its state legislature for a six-year term and a directly elected house of representatives with seats apportioned among the states on the basis of their respective population with the proviso each state would have at least one member.

Distribution of Powers

The decision to establish a federal system presented the drafters of the fundamental law with three options relative to the distribution of functional responsibilities between the national and state planes of government. First, specific responsibilities could be assigned to each plane. Second, specific functions could be confided to the national government with all other powers, except prohibited ones, reserved to the states. Third, the states could be granted specific powers and all other powers, excepted prohibited ones, could be reserved to the national government.

The convention decided the constitution should delegate enumerated or expressed powers to Congress including exclusive ones—foreign affairs, coinage of money, and declaration of war. Included in the list of delegated powers is a clause, commonly termed the necessary and proper clause, authorizing Congress "[t]o make all laws which shall be necessary and proper for carrying into execution the foregoing powers, and all other powers vested by this Constitution in the Government of the United States, or in any department or officer thereof" (art. I, §8). The delegates acted upon the assumption that all other powers not specifically forbidden would be reserved to the states. The Tenth Amendment to the Constitution made explicit this assumption.

Congress and the states are forbidden by the Constitution (art. I, §§9–10) to exercise certain powers: enactment of bills of attainder and ex post facto laws, and granting titles of nobility. Congress specifically was forbidden (art. I, §9) to lay duties on exports from any state, grant preference to the ports of one state over ports of other states, require vessels bound to or from a state to pay duties in another state, draw funds from the Treasury without an appropriation, or prohibit the importation of slaves into any state prior to 1808.

The Constitution (art. I, §10) contains preemption provisions removing powers from states: "No State shall enter into any treaty, alliance or confederation; grant letters of marque and reprisal; coin money, emit bills of credit; make any thing but gold and silver coin a tender in payment of debts; pass any bill of attainder, *ex post* facto law, or law impairing the obligation of contracts; or grant any title of nobility."

Two types of concurrent powers are authorized by the Constitution. The first type includes the power of states to levy taxes immune from formal congressional preemption or court invalidation unless they impose a burden on interstate commerce or violate the privileges and immunities or equal protection of the laws clauses of the constitution. The second type encompasses powers expressly delegated to Congress and not prohibited to states, as illustrated by regulation of interstate commerce. The existence of concurrent powers can result in clashes between a congressional statute and a state statute. The Constitution's drafters were aware such conflicts would occur and incorporated the supremacy of the law's clause in Article VI providing for the prevalence of the congressional statute in the event of a conflict. In other words, the exercise of this type of concurrent power by a state legislature is subject to complete or partial preemption by a congressional statute.

The Constitution (art. I, §10) also allows state legislatures to exercise certain otherwise prohibited powers with the consent of Congress—

levying of import and tonnage duties, keeping troops in time of peace, and entering into compacts with sister states. The U.S. Supreme Court, however, has not always ruled these powers can be exercised only with congressional approval. In *Virginia v. Tennessee*, the Court in 1893 opined such approval is required only if two or more states desire to enter into "political compacts" affecting the balance of power between the states and the Union.[6] In 1975, the Court held the prohibition of levying "imposts or duties on imports" without congressional consent does not prevent imposition of an ad valorem property tax on imported tires.[7] The Court in 1986 issued a similar ruling holding it was constitutional for a county in North Carolina, a major tobacco producing state, to levy an ad valorem property tax on imported tobacco stored in customs-bonded storehouses for future incorporation in domestic manufacturing on the grounds the tax did not violate the import-export clause of the constitution and was not preempted by a congressional statute.[8]

It is important to note citizens within states receive all their public services, except the postal service, from state and/or local governments. The mix of state and local services provided varies considerably between the states. Congress, of course, is free to authorize the provision of services on federal properties, such as education for children on military bases located within states.

Ratification Campaign

Opposition to the proposed constitution was strong in all states and especially in New York and Virginia. The drafters were aware it would be impossible to persuade all thirteen states to ratify the proposal and decided it would become effective upon ratification by conventions of voters in nine states.[9] It should be recalled that Article XIII of the Articles of Confederation and Perpetual Union stipulated they could be amended only by the affirmative vote of Congress confirmed by each of the thirteen state legislatures.

The visible strength of the opposition to the proposed fundamental law induced Alexander Hamilton, John Jay, and James Madison to write a series of eighty-five letters to editors of New York City newspapers, signed *Publius*. These letters explained the document with emphasis on the incorporated prohibitions protecting the liberties of individuals and the sections ensuring states would retain important powers.[10] These letters remain the best exposition on the design of the proposed constitution.

Hamilton contended, in "The Federalist Number 17" "it will always be far more easy for State governments to encroach upon the national authorities than for the national government to encroach upon the State authorities. The proof of this proposition turns upon the greater degree of influence which the state governments, if they administer their affairs with uprightness and prudence, will generally possess over the people."[11] He described in "The Federalist Number 33" the necessary and proper clause as "the sweeping clause," and sought to ensure readers it could not be used to expand without limit the delegated powers of Congress.[12] Referring to the delegated taxation power, Hamilton asked: "What are the proper means of executing such a power but *necessary* and *proper laws?*"[13]

James Madison, in "The Federalist Number 44," also justified the clause by explaining employment by the drafters of the first alternative—assignment of specific powers to each plane—would have resulted in a "complete digest of laws on every subject to which the Constitution relates" and the second alternative would involve the enumeration of "the particular powers or means not necessary or proper for carrying the general powers into execution" and "the task would have been no less chimerical.... "[14] Constitutional silence on the subject would have been a third alternative, but Madison concluded "all the particular powers requisite as means of executing the general powers would have resulted to the government by unavoidable implication."[15]

Citizens fearful of the creation of a national leviathan were reassured by Madison in "The Federalist Number 45": "[t]he powers delegated by the proposed constitution to the federal government are few and defined" and in "The Federalist Number 46" he predicted "a local spirit will infallibly prevail much more in the members of Congress than a national spirit will prevail in the legislatures of the particular States."[16] Experience under the Constitution reveals these prognostications generally were accurate until 1965 when Congress commenced to exercise its preemption powers with greater frequency to remove important regulatory powers completely or partially from state and local governments, and to impose mandates upon them, a subject examined in chapters 4 and 5.

Members of the Pennsylvania convention considering the proposed national constitution were divided, with minority members maintaining "the powers vested in Congress...must necessarily annihilate and absorb the legislative, executive, and judicial powers of the several States, and produce from their ruin one consolidated government, which from the nature of things will be an iron handed despotism, as nothing short of the supremacy of despotic sway could connect and govern these United States under one government."[17]

These members directed their criticism in particular at the "complete and unlimited" power of Congress "over the purse and the sword," and prophesied:

As there is no one article of taxation reserved to the state governments, the Congress may monopolize every source of revenue, and thus indirectly demolish the state governments, for without funds they could not exist; the taxes, duties, and excises imposed by Congress may be so high as to render it impracticable to levy further sums on the same articles, but whether this should be the case or not, if the state government should presume to impose taxes, duties, or excises on the same articles with Congress, the latter may abrogate and repeal the laws whereby they are imposed, upon the allegation that they interfere with the due collection of their taxes, duties, or excises, by virtue of the following clause, part of section 8th, article 1st, *viz.* "To make all laws which shall be necessary and proper for carrying into execution the foregoing powers, and all other powers vested by this Constitution in the government or the United States, or in any department or officer thereof."[18]

The above fear was realized partially in 1942 when Congress raised income tax surtaxes sharply, with the highest rate set at ninety-one percent.

The Federalist Papers did not allay the Anti-Federalists' fear of a strong national government. To persuade the larger states to ratify the proposed constitution, the proponents agreed the first item of business of the new Congress under the constitution would be the proposal of a bill of rights. Thomas Jefferson wrote to James Madison and implied the Virginia convention should not ratify the proposed fundamental law unless a bill of rights was incorporated into the document.[19] The Massachusetts, New York, and Virginia conventions ratified the proposal with the condition that a bill of rights be added as soon as the constitution became effective. New Hampshire, in June 1787, became the ninth state to ratify the constitution and also recommended the adoption of a bill of rights. Elections for presidential and vice presidential electors and members of the U.S. House of Representatives were held in 1788, state legislatures each appointed two senators, and the new national government became effective in 1789.

The Tenth Amendment is known as the states' rights amendment and attempts to make it crystal clear Congress possesses only enumerated powers by stipulating "the powers not delegated to the United States by the constitution, nor prohibited by it to the States, are reserved to the States respectively, or to the people." This division of powers approach to establishing a governmental system—an *imperium in imperio*—often is labeled dual or layer cake federalism and underlies the theory of dual federalism. In practice, there is a sharing by the national and state governments of many powers—a marble or "rainbow" cake—by the three planes of government (federal, state, and local) rather than

the complete separation of national and state powers suggested by the
theory of dual federalism.

Expansion of National Powers

The possibility one plane of government would encroach upon the preserve of the other plane concerned Thomas Jefferson, who wrote in
1814, "I have always thought where the line of demarcation between the
powers of the General and the State governments was doubtfully or
indistinctly drawn, it would be prudent and praiseworthy in both parties, never to approach it but under the most urgent necessity."[20] The
potential for national government encroachment upon the reserved
powers of the states has been increased significantly by accretions of
congressional powers resulting from statutory elaboration of delegated
powers, generally broad judicial interpretation of delegated powers, and
ratification of constitutional amendments delegating additional powers
to Congress and authorizing popular election of U.S. senators. The
enlarged powers of Congress in particular generated a continuing ideological debate over the proper roles of the national government and the
states (see figure 2.2).

Figure 2.2.

Distribution of Powers, U.S. Constitution, 1789 and 2005

1789

Exclusive Federal Powers	Concurrent Powers	Art. 1 §10	Exclusive State Powers

2005

Exclusive Federal Powers	Concurrent Powers	Art. 1 §10	Exclusive State Powers

*Based upon a "zero-sum" model where an increase in the powers of the federal govern-
ment results in a corresponding decrease in the powers of the states.*

Statutory Elaboration

There is no constitutional requirement Congress must exercise a delegated power and Congress failed to exercise a few of its delegated
powers for many decades. To cite two examples, Congress did not use

its authority to regulate interstate commerce in a comprehensive manner until enactment of an *Act to Regulate Commerce of 1887* or its power to supersede most provisions of state bankruptcy laws until 1898.[21]

Congress first employed its preemption powers to remove two concurrent state regulatory powers in 1790 when it enacted the *Patent Act* and the *Copyright Act*, but nevertheless it had enacted only twenty-nine total and partial preemption statutes by the end of the nineteenth century.[22] The pace of enactment of such statutes picked up slowly during the first four decades of the twentieth century. Shortly after the end of World War II Congress enacted two major preemption statutes. The *Atomic Energy Act of 1946* completely preempted responsibility for the regulation of ionizing radiation until a 1959 amendment authorized the Atomic Energy Commission (now Nuclear Regulatory Commission) to enter into agreements with states allowing them voluntarily to assume certain regulatory responsibilities.[23] Thirty-two states have assumed such responsibilities as of 2004, a subject addressed in chapter 4 in terms of its implications for intergovernmental cooperation and conflict. Another example of a complete preemption statute is the *Uniform Time Act* of 1966, preempting responsibility for determining the dates on which standard time is changed to daylight saving time and vice versa.[24]

An explosion in the rate of enactment of preemption statutes commenced in 1965 and involved new types of complete and partial preemption statutes. Many of these statutes relate to environmental protection because Congress concluded major environmental problems could not be solved by relying upon state and local governments to initiate corrective action even with the encouragement of federal grants-in-aid. Two preemption statutes—*Water Quality Act of 1965* and *Air Quality Act of 1967*—marked a new phase in congressional use of its powers of supersession by establishing a new type of partial preemption statute which specifies minimum water quality and air quality standards that states, by statutes and administrative regulations, are allowed to exceed.[25]

The first act requires each state, desiring to retain regulatory authority, to adopt "water quality standards applicable to interstate waters or portions thereof within such State," as well as an implementation and enforcement plan. The administrator of the Environmental Protection Agency (EPA) is authorized to promulgate water quality standards which become effective at the end of six months if a state fails to establish and enforce adequate standards. The federal role has been strengthened by other statutory enactments, particularly the *Federal Water Pollution Control Act Amendments of 1972*, which established July 1, 1977, as the date for achieving "water quality which provides for protection and propagation of fish, shellfish, and wildlife," and required the elimination of the "discharge of pollutants into navigable waters by 1985."[26] The *Air Quality Act of 1967* established a similar procedure with respect to states assuming responsibility for air pollution abatement with the exception of emissions from new motor vehicles. The rate at which preemption statutes were enacted did not significantly slow subsequent to the Republican Party gaining control of Congress effective in 1995, as noted in chapter 1.

Judicial Interpretation

The U.S. Supreme Court, under the chief justiceship of John Marshall, commenced in the second decade of the nineteenth century to issue decisions interpreting broadly certain delegated powers of Congress, as illustrated by the development of the doctrine of implied powers in *McCulloch v. Maryland* in 1819 and the doctrine of the continuous journey in *Gibbons v. Ogden* in 1824 (see chapter 6).[27] Political scientist Woodrow Wilson in 1885 was convinced "Congress must wantonly go very far outside the plain and unquestionable meaning of the Constitution, must bump its head directly against all right and precedent, must kick against the very pricks of all well-established rulings and interpretation, before the Supreme Court will offer its distinct rebuke."[28]

The U.S. Supreme Court always has possessed the authority to invoke the Constitution's supremacy of the law's clause as the ground for invalidating a state statute that conflicts with a congressional statute. In the nineteenth century, the Court developed its dormant interstate commerce doctrine to place restrictions on the use of the states' police power (a broad regulatory power) and taxation powers to ensure the free flow of interstate commerce in the absence of congressional statutes regulating interstate commerce. In 1976, the Court extended the guarantees of the First Amendment to the U.S. Constitution by partially preempting state corrupt practices statutes restricting political campaign contributions and expenditures.

The Court in *Buckley v. Valeo*, which involves the *Federal Election Campaign Act of 1971* and its 1974 amendments, opined the individual contribution limits, disclosure and reporting requirements, and public campaign financing provisions were constitutional, but ruled as violative of the First Amendment the limits placed on the amount of money a candidate can spend from his/her personal funds.[29] The Court specifically held the limitation of personal expenditures by candidates "imposes a substantial restraint on the ability of persons to engage in protected First Amendment expression."[30] The Court added: "The candidate, no less than any other person, has a First Amendment right to engage in the discussion of public issues and vigorously and tirelessly to advocate his own election and the election of other candidates. Indeed, it is of particular importance that candidates have the unfettered opportunity to make their views known so that the electorate may intelligently evaluate the candidates' personal qualities and their positions on vital public issues before choosing among them on election day."[31]

Building upon this decision, the Court in 1978 invalidated a Massachusetts corrupt practices act restricting contributions of a corporation to referendum campaigns involving issues "that materially affect its business, property, or assets" by ruling a corporation has the right guaranteed by the First Amendment to spend its funds to publicize its opposition to a proposed Massachusetts constitutional amendment that would authorize the general court (state legislature) to levy a graduated income tax.[32]

These two decisions, by preempting state statutes limiting personally financed campaign expenditures and corporate referendum campaign expenditures, have had an adverse impact on the nature of political campaigns. The *Buckley* decision has made it extremely difficult for candidates who are not exceptionally wealthy to win a seat in the U.S. Senate, a governorship in a large state, or the office of mayor in a city such as New York. These Court rulings also have resulted in a proliferation of political action committees, which provide a significant portion of the funds expended in political campaigns for elected office and in initiative and referendum campaigns.[33]

Many U.S. Supreme Court decisions since the middle of the twentieth century and enactment of total and partial preemption statutes since 1965 generated a major debate relative to whether the Court and Congress have deviated from the intent of the framers of the U.S. Constitution.

The Intent of the Framers

U.S. Attorney General Edwin Meese III in 1985 initiated a national debate on the intentions of the drafters of the U.S. Constitution when they included various provisions in the fundamental document. He maintained the majority of the justices of the U.S. Supreme Court in their federalism decisions were not adhering to the intent of the Constitution's framers.

> A jurisprudence seriously aimed at the explication of original intention would produce defensible principles of government that would not be tainted by ideological predilection. A Jurisprudence of Original Intention also reflects a deeply rooted commitment to the idea of democracy. The Constitution represents the consent of the governed to the structure and

powers of the government. To allow the court to govern, simply by what it views at the time as fair and decent, is a scheme of government no longer popular; the idea of democracy has suffered. The permanence of the Constitution is weakened. A Constitution that is viewed as only what the judges say it is, is no longer a constitution in the true sense.[34]

Meese's view drew an almost immediate response from Justice William J. Brennan, Jr., of the U.S. Supreme Court:

> There are those who find legitimacy in fidelity to what they call "the intentions of the Framers." In its most doctrinaire incarnation, this view demands that Justices discern exactly what the Framers thought about the question under consideration and simply follow that intention in resolving the case before them.... It is arrogant to pretend that from our vantage we can gauge accurately the intent of the Framers on applications of principle to specific, contemporary questions.... Typically, all that can be gleaned is that the Framers themselves did not agree about the applications or meaning of particular constitutional provisions, and hid their differences in cloaks of generality.[35]

Judge Robert H. Bork of the U.S. Court of Appeals for the District of Columbia Circuit in the same year delivered a rejoinder to Justice Brennan's views:

> In short, all an intentionalist requires is that the text, structure, and history of the Constitution provide him not with a conclusion but with a premise. That premise states a core value that the framers intended to protect. The intentionalist judge must then supply the minor premise in order to protect the constitutional freedom in circumstances the framers could not foresee.... Thus, we are usually able to understand the liberties that were intended to be protected. We are able to apply the First Amendment's free press clause to the electronic media and to the changing impact of libel litigation upon the media; we are able to apply the Fourth Amendment's prohibition on unreasonable searches and seizures to electronic surveillance; we apply the commerce clause to state regulation of interstate trucking.... At the very least, judges will confine themselves to the principles the framers put into the Constitution. Entire ranges of problems will be placed off-limits to judges, thus preserving democracy in those areas where the framers intended democratic government. That is better than any non-intentionalist theory can do.[36]

Professor H. Jefferson Powell of the University of Iowa Law School examined the cultural factors which influenced legal interpretation when the U.S. Constitution was drafted and ratified, and concluded "the claim or assumption intentionalism was the original presupposition of American constitutional discourse...is historically mistaken."[37]

The Meese initiated constitutional debate is not as heated in the opening decade of the twenty-first century in part because a five-member majority of the U.S. Supreme Court has been more protective of the rights of states since 1990. Nevertheless, it is a healthy sign the U.S. governance system remains a vigorous one with important federalism issues debated continually even if each side of an issue uses pejorative terms to describe the other side.

The judiciary will continue to play important roles as the umpire of the federal system in view of the delegation of powers in broad terms to Congress and the impossibility of divining the precise intentions of the framers when the U.S. Constitution was drafted. Chapter 6 examines in more detail the preemption of state constitutional provisions and statutes by judicial interpretation of the U.S. Constitution.

Summary

This chapter reviews the provisions of the Articles of Confederation and Perpetual Union, describes briefly their defects, examines the distribution of exercisable powers between Congress and the states under the U.S. Constitution, outlines the methods by which the powers of the national government have been expanded and the regulatory powers of states reduced, and reviews the debate over the intentions of the framers of the fundamental law.

The information in this chapter is designed to promote a fuller understanding of the nature of informal, complete, and circumscribed congressional preemption of the reserved powers of subnational governments, topics analyzed in the following three chapters. Informal preemption (see chapter 3) refers to congressional use of conditional grants-in-aid, crossover sanctions, and tax credits to encourage state and local governments to adopt policies desired by Congress.

Chapter 3

SPENDING POWER PREEMPTION

The U.S. Constitution (art. I, §8) grants broad regulatory powers and a broad spending power to Congress in order to "provide for the common defense and general welfare of the United States." As noted in chapter 2, Congress is not authorized to provide services other than the postal service within states except on federal properties. Historically, Congress sought to achieve certain national goals by assisting states through land grants, and it did not enact a statute authorizing a financial grant-in-aid to states until 1887. The early land grants and the 1887 money grant did not limit the discretionary authority of the states. Congress for the first time in 1894 attached conditions to grants. They became relatively common in the 1930s and commenced to influence the service policymaking decisions of state and local governments.

It is difficult for subnational government policymakers to refuse to apply for large conditional grants-in-aid and thereby subject their governmental units to the attached conditions. We refer to such grants as spending power preemption. Such preemption differs in law from formal congressional preemption, which removes completely or partially regulatory powers in given fields from state and local governments which cannot be avoided. In effect, subnational governments by accepting conditional grants initiate a type of voluntary preemption of part of their discretionary authority. Congress also has enacted statutes authorizing conditional tax credits for private individuals and business firms to induce state legislatures to enact parallel laws on the same subjects.

The 1950s and the 1960s witnessed a dramatic increase in the number of grants-in-aid programs and the funds appropriated to state and local governments by Congress. The grant proliferation generated considerable criticism by state and local government officers. The Johnson, Nixon, and Reagan administrations responded by initiating actions that modified the national government's intergovernmental roles.

Conditional grants-in-aid are not the only form of national financial assistance to state and local governments. Congress also provides assistance in the form of commodities (for example, food stamps), exemption of interest paid on municipal (state and local) bonds from the federal income tax thereby enabling borrowing at a lower cost, in-lieu property tax payments, loans, services-in-aid (for example, Federal Bureau of Investigation's fingerprint service), and technical assistance in a wide variety of areas.

This chapter traces the historical development of spending power preemption in the form of conditional grants-in-aid and related crossover sanctions, examines the criticisms of the grant-in-aid system and the national response to the criticisms, and explains the tax credit and tax sanction systems.

Historical Development of Categorical Grants

The Articles of Confederation and Perpetual Union and the U.S. Constitution are silent relative to whether Congress may grant land and/or funds to state and local governments. Nevertheless, the unicameral Congress under the articles enacted the Northwest Ordinance of 1785 reserving one square mile in each township for educational purposes in the area covered by the ordinance.[1] In 1837, the U.S. Treasury experienced a large surplus and Congress distributed the surplus to states as "loans with no expectation of repayment."[2] Congress in 1850 granted swamp lands to the states, but did not make another major land grant until enactment of the *Morrill Act of 1862*, designed to encourage states to establish colleges of agricultural and mechanical arts.[3] In 1887, the *Hatch Act* authorized the sale of federal lands to raise funds for annual grants of $15,000 to promote the establishment of an agricultural experiment station at each such college.[4] The *Morrill Act of 1890* also relied upon the sale of federal lands to fund instructional grants for these colleges.[5] Congress in 1914 decided there was a need for disseminating the results of research at the agricultural experiment stations and enacted the *Smith-Lever Act*, providing funding for a county agent system.[6]

The *Weeks Act of 1911* represented a break with the policy of providing grants to states. V.O. Key, Jr., reported that for several years "this act was not administered as a grant, but the funds were used to pay directly the salaries of 'federal patrolmen,' who held state commissions, and were selected and supervised by the state forester who also was a federal employee with a nominal salary."[7]

In 1916 Congress turned its attention to the development of highways on which to move the United States' mail expeditiously. It authorized grants to states to construct highways.[8] Five years later, Congress declared its goal was the establishment of a national system of highways and authorized expanded grants-in-aid for states.[9] Subsequently, Congress enacted numerous highway grant-in-aid acts, including the *National Defense and Interstate Highways Act of 1956*.[10]

Vocational education was supported for the first time when Congress enacted the *Smith-Hughes Act of 1917*, authorizing grants-in-aid to states for agricultural, home economics, industrial and trade vocational education.[11] Such grants were expanded by the *Vocational Rehabilitation Act of 1920*.[12] Public health grants to states for the prevention of venereal diseases date to 1918; grants promoting hygiene for infants and mothers date to 1921; and grants providing unemployment relief, public employment, and public assistance were authorized in the 1930s to combat the Great Depression.[13] Subsequently, Congress authorized grants to state and local governments for a wide variety of other purposes.

Key conducted the first major national study of federal grants-in-aid and titled a chapter in his 1937 book "The Role of Associations and Conferences."[14] He described the American Association of State Highway Officials, organized in 1914, as "an extremely powerful body but probably less so than the land-grant college body."[15] These associations (1) promoted enactment of favorable bills by Congress; (2) influenced the formulation of federal administrative policies and practices; (3) coordinated interstate activities with the activities of federal departments and agencies; and (4) served as a clearinghouse for the informal exchange of information and opinions.

Key reached several conclusions: (1) Federal grants have influenced new and expanding state government activities; (2) conditions restrict the ability of states "to meet new problems"; (3) grants have been used primarily for service programs and not regulatory programs; (4) "states are welded into national machinery of sorts and the establishment of costly, parallel, direct federal services is made unnecessary"; and (5) the grant-in-aid system has the virtue of administrators who "remain amenable to local control."[16]

A constitutional challenge to conditional congressional grants-in-aid to states was made and the U.S. Supreme Court in 1866 opined "it is not doubted that the grant by the United States to the State upon conditions, and the acceptance of the grant by the State constitute a contract.... The contract was binding upon the State, and could not be violated by its legislation without infringement of the Constitution."[17] Whether Congress could use grants-in-aid to require states accepting grants to exercise their reserved powers to implement provisions of a maternity act was the subject of a 1923 U.S. Supreme Court decision in *Massachusetts v. Mellon*; the Court ruled the provisions of the act were constitutional.[18]

Attached Conditions

The first conditional grant-in-aid act was an 1808 statute appropriating $200,000 to the states for arming and equipping their respective militias.[19] Continuing grants-in-aid to subnational governmental units are traceable in origin to the *Hatch Act of 1887*, which authorized grants to states to promote the establishment of agricultural experiment stations at state colleges of agriculture.[20] Authorization for a federal administrator to withhold funds from states failing to comply with grant conditions dates to the *Morrill Act of 1890*.[21] The *Weeks Act of 1911* authorized grants for state forestry programs and for the first time required state matching grants and made the programs subject to federal inspection.[22] Modern conditional grants-in-aid generally require the recipient state or local government to provide matching funds, often on a two-thirds federal, one-third state or local government basis. The matching funds in some instances can be in the form of contributions of land for a nationally aided project.

The *Carey Act of 1894* was the first one to contain a mandatory application condition. In order to be eligible for the receipt of a grant, a state had to prepare a comprehensive irrigation plan for arid land.[23] A state accepting a grant was subject to a type of de facto partial preemption by being required to implement the plan. Subsequent grant-in-aid acts often contain a requirement that the state seeking a grant must prepare a comprehensive plan to ensure grant funds will not be wasted.

The *Federal Road Aid Act of 1916* inaugurated the next major innovation in the use of the grant-in-aid device by including the first "single state agency" requirement; that is, the state highway department must administer a federally aided highway program.[24] A 1921 amendment to this act extended the influence of the national government by stipulating state highway departments receiving federal moneys were subject to an evaluation of their competence by the secretary of agriculture.[25] This condition-of-aid did not cause a controversy, but the requirement that a single state agency must administer the grant program in the *Social Security Act of 1935* generated rifts in federal-state relations.[26]

The sharp increase in federal grants-in-aid to states for highway construction induced certain states to divert revenues from their highway user taxes to other purposes. The *Hayden-Cartwright Act of 1934* was designed to prevent this diversion by a maintenance-of-effort requirement section containing a penalty—one-third of the federal highway aid—to a state diverting highway user tax revenues.[27] A similar requirement is contained in most grant-in-aid statutes today.

Congress became concerned with the competence and political neutrality of state and local governmental employees administering programs funded in part with national moneys because many were selected and promoted on a political patronage basis in state and local governments lacking a constitutional or statutory civil service merit system. In consequence, Congress inserted a provision in the *Social Security Act of 1935* mandating state and local government employees administering grant programs authorized by the act must be selected and promoted in accordance with the merit principle.[28] Growing concern about the possible waste of federal grants by politically appointed subnational government employees led to insertion of a crossover sanction in the *Hatch Acts of 1939* and *1940* forbidding any subnational government employee receiving part or all of his or her salary from federal funds from engaging in partisan political action.[29]

For decades Congress generally viewed local governments as creatures of their respective state government and all federal grants-in-aid were made only to state governments. The *United States Housing Act of 1937* initiated a new trend by authorizing federal grants to be made to general purpose local governments.[30]

Growth of Federal Grants-in-Aid

Federal financial assistance for state and local governments today is essential for their continued fiscal health. The current subnational governmental dependence upon federal funds is a dramatic change from the period prior to 1915, when such aid to states totaled less than $5 million annually.[31] The *Federal Road Aid Act of 1916* produced a sharp increase in federal aid to states. The aid amounted to approximately $100 million annually in the period 1918 to 1930, with highway aid accounting for 80 percent of the total. Congress responded to the Great Depression by authorizing new grants and increasing funding for existing grants to stimulate the economy, yet such aid amounted to less than 10 percent of federal appropriations annually during the 1930s.

Twenty-nine programmatic categories of federal aid were authorized in the period 1946 to 1960.[32] An explosion in federal grants-in-aid
to state and local governments occurred in the period 1961 to 1966,
when thirty-nine of ninety-five program categories of grants were
authorized. Grants subsequently increased by approximately 15 percent
annually, from $7 billion to over $91 billion in 1980.[33]

The proportion of federal fiscal assistance devoted to different
functions has varied over the decades. The early grants related primarily
to agriculture, including the *Federal Road Aid Act of 1916* designed to
facilitate the transport of farm crops to markets. Enactment of the *Social
Security Act of 1935* changed the proportion of aid devoted to agriculture and highways by establishing a new social services program.
Approximately 60 to 65 percent of federal grants were devoted to
health, labor, and welfare in the period 1950 to 1955, with welfare
grants accounting for approximately 50 percent of the funds.[34]
Enactment of the *National Defense and Interstate Highways Act of 1956*
resulted in the bulk of the grant funds being devoted to highways.[35] The
"Great Society" programs, enacted by Congress during the Johnson
administration in the 1960s, emphasized once again health, labor, and
social service programs.

Categorical grants-in-aid assume one of two forms—formula or
project. The former provides for distribution of federal funds to subnational governments on the basis of a formula composed of several factors, including population and per capita income. Project grants are
capital ones, illustrated by sewerage treatment plants and light rail systems. Assistant Director Carl W. Stenberg of the U.S. Advisory
Commission on Intergovernmental Relations in 1980 attributed "the
presence of so many separate or functionally related programs administered by various agencies" to "differences in individual missions and
clienteles."[36] The sharp reduction in the number of education, health and
human services, and labor categorical grants in the post-1981 period is
attributable to the enactment of block grants-in-aid, a topic examined in
a subsequent section.

Figure 3.1 presents data on federal grants-in-aid to state and local
governments by major granting departments in fiscal year 2000. The
total of all grants was $323.9 billion, with grants awarded by the
Department of Health and Human Services accounting for 54.6 percent
of the total and far outstripping Department of Transportation grants
totaling only $37.1 (11.1 percent). Figure 3.2 contains similar data classi-
fied by major programs for fiscal year 2000. Healthcare accounted for
$133.0 billion (40.9 percent) compared to only $13.0 billion (4.5 percent)
for elementary and secondary education.

Figure 3.1 Federal Aid to State and Local Governments, Amounts and Percentages by Major Agency: Fiscal Year 2000

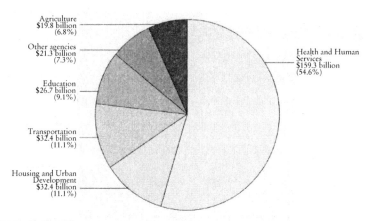

Figure 3.2 Federal Aid to State and Local Governments, Amounts and Percentages by Major Program: Fiscal Year 2000

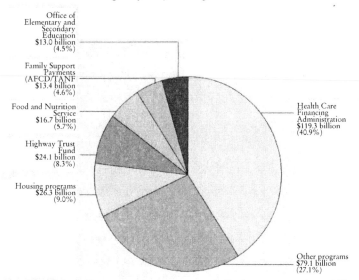

Note: Total federal aid to state and local governments in fiscal year 2000 was $291.9 billion

Federal Aid to States for Fiscal Year 2000

U.S. Census Bureau

Source: www.census.gov/govs/faads/o22sumus.htm

Table 3.1 Direct Federal Aid to Illinois State Agencies

(Ranked per 2002 actual amounts. Dollars are in thousands.)

Function	FY 2001	%	Estimate FY 2001	%	% Change 2001-2002
Block Grants for Community Mental Health Services	16,249	4.6%	16,245	4.5%	0.0%
Family Planning—Services	8,327	2.4%	6,700	1.9%	-19.5%
Immunization Grants	4,254	1.2%	6,127	1.7%	44.0%
All Other Programs	37,175	10.6%	39,486	11.0%	6.2%
Labor & Employment	**317,128**	**3.0%**	**349,601**	**3.3%**	**10.2%**
Workforce Investment Act (WIA)	118,181	37.3%	154,946	44.3%	31.1%
Unemployment Insurance State Administration	119,990	37.8%	118,428	33.9%	-1.3%
Employment Services	35,439	11.2%	35,771	10.2%	0.9%
Employment & Training Administration Pilots—Demonstration & Research Projects	14,979	4.7%	11,346	3.2%	-24.3%
All Other Programs	28,539	9.0%	29,110	8.3%	2.0%
Defense	**265,513**	**2.5%**	**257,247**	**2.4%**	**-3.1%**
Army & Air National Guard	231,598	87.2%	226,961	88.2%	-2.0%
Civil Defense (Emergency Services)	33,915	12.8%	30,286	11.8%	-10.7%
Housing	**214,413**	**2.0%**	**225,958**	**2.1%**	**5.4%**
Low Income Housing (Sect 8)	140,849	65.7%	151,987	67.3%	7.9%
Community Development Block Grants—State's Program	39,361	18.4%	39,361	17.4%	0.0%
HOME—Investment Partnerships Program	26,024	12.1%	26,500	11.7%	1.8%
Interest Reduction Payments—Rental & Cooperative Housing for Lower-Income Families	4,994	2.3%	5,149	2.3%	3.1%
All Other Programs	3,185	1.5%	2,961	1.3%	-7.0%
Environmental Protections	**126,415**	**1.2%**	**139,093**	**1.3%**	**10.0%**
Water Pollution Control	99,487	78.7%	111,082	79.9%	11.7%
Performance Partnership Grants	16,824	13.3%	17,876	12.9%	6.3%
Superfund State Site—Specific Cooperative Agreements	2,486	2.0%	3,850	2.8%	54.9%
All Other Programs	7,618	6.0%	6,285	4.5%	-17.5%
Law Enforcement	**103,836**	**1.0%**	**109,319**	**1.0%**	**5.3%**
Violent Offender Incarceration & Truth-in-Sentencing Incentive	26,055	25.1%	25,559	23.4%	-1.9%
Crime Victim Assistance	24,824	23.9%	22,841	20.9%	-8.0%
Byrne Formula Grant Program	19,688	19.0%	20,434	18.7%	3.8%
Juvenile Accountability Incentive Block Grants (JAIBG)	8,337	8.0%	8,620	7.9%	3.4%
State Criminal Alien Assistance Program(SCAAP)	1,503	1.4%	7,356	6.7%	389.4%
State Medicaid Fraud Control Units	4,819	4.6%	5,403	4.9%	12.1%
Juvenile Programs	4,643	4.5%	4,620	4.2%	-0.5%
Violence Against Women Formula Grants	5,098	4.9%	4,131	3.8%	-19.0%
Community Oriented Policing Grants COPS	2,190	2.1%	2,000	1.8%	-8.7%
All Other Programs	6,679	6.4%	8,355	7.6%	25.1%
Agriculture & Natural Resources	**32,523**	**0.3%**	**39,078**	**0.4%**	**20.2%**
Mine Lands	12,458	38.3%	13,216	33.8%	6.1%
Fish & Wildlife Assistance	9,039	27.8%	10,721	27.4%	18.6%
Intrastate Meat & Poultry Inspection	4,669	14.4%	5,102	13.1%	9.3%
Outdoor Recreation-Acquisition, Dev.& Planning	2,600	8.0%	2,600	6.7%	0.0%
Wildlife Conservation & Restoration	1,630	5.0%	2,600	6.7%	59.5%
All Other Programs	2,127	6.5%	4,839	12.4%	127.5%
Energy Conservation	**11,671**	**0.1%**	**11,142**	**0.1%**	**-4.5%**
Weatherization Assistance for Low-Income Persons	8,210	70.3%	9,324	83.7%	13.6%
State Energy Program	1,417	12.1%	1,570	14.1%	10.8%
All Other Programs	2,044	17.5%	248	2.2%	-87.9%
Miscellaneous	**18,104**	**0.2%**	**16,640**	**0.2%**	**-8.1%**
State Library Program	5,606	31.0%	6,028	36.2%	7.5%
Abraham Lincoln Presidential Library & Museum	9,975	55.1%	8,000	48.1%	-19.8%
All Other Programs	2,523	13.9%	2,612	15.7%	3.5%
Grand Totals	**10,650,824**	**100.0%**	**10,717,685**	**100.0%**	**0.6%**

Source: Intergovernmental Issues 23, Summer/Fall 2002, p. 14. Reprinted with permission of the Illinois Commission on Intergovernmental Cooperation.

The 50 state governments derived $253,691,979 (22 percent) of their revenues from the federal government. Local governments secured a much lower amount—$31,686,906 (3.8 percent)—from the federal government and a much larger amount—$296,327,653 (35.2 percent)—from their state governments.[37] Revenues raised by local governments from their own sources totaled $511,016,885, or 61 percent of their total revenues. Table 3.1 highlights the importance of a wide variety of federal grants-in-aid to Illinois state departments and agencies.

Sanctions

Congress discovered it could achieve additional national policy goals by attaching new conditions to existing grant-in-aid programs and imposing sanctions for violations of the conditions. The sanctions are of two types. The first type is the crosscutting sanction which, as noted, dates to 1921. This type applies to all federal grant-in-aid programs. To restate, the sharp increase in federal grants to state and local governments during the Great Depression raised a concern in Congress whether the subnational government employees administering grant-in-aid programs may have been selected by political considerations rather than merit, with the result federal moneys may have been wasted. This concern induced Congress to enact a crosscutting sanction requiring state and local governments accepting federal grants to employ the merit system in appointing and promoting personnel financed partially or totally with national funds or to lose part of the grant funds.[38]

The second type is a crossover sanction. The oil embargo imposed by Arab nations in 1974 resulted in long lines at gasoline stations and made conservation of petroleum essential. One congressional response to the energy shortage was enactment of a statute in 1974 that threatens to withhold 10 percent of highway grants if a state fails to establish fifty-five miles per hour as the maximum speed limit on its highways.[39] A second congressional response was passage of a 1975 act that provides for withholding of highway grant funds from a state that fails to allow motorists stopped at a red traffic light to make a right turn if no motor vehicle is approaching the intersection from the left.[40]

Driving motor vehicles while intoxicated is a major problem in all states and a high percentage of such operators in the early 1980s were under the age of twenty-one. Congress in 1984 decided to attack this problem by means of a cross-over sanction involving the loss of federal highway grants if a state failed to increase its minimum age for the purchase of alcoholic beverages to twenty-one.[41] South Dakota challenged the constitutionality of the crossover sanction on the ground the

Twenty-first Amendment to the U.S. Constitution grants states exclusive authority to regulate the sale and consumption of alcoholic beverages. The U. S. Supreme Court in 1987 rejected the challenge.[42] All states subsequently complied with the act. Congress in 1998 enacted a statute threatening to reduce highway grants to states if they failed to strengthen penalties against repeat intoxicated drivers or lower their blood alcohol content (BAC) standard to 0.08 percent.[43] The New York state legislature reluctantly lowered its BAC standard to 0.08 percent in December 2002.[44] Six states—Colorado, Delaware, New Jersey, Minnesota, Pennsylvania, and West Virginia—failed as of late 2003 to enact a compliance statute.[45]

In 1986, Congress employed a similar sanction threatening states with the loss of part of their Alcohol, Drug Abuse, and Mental Health Block Grant if they failed, with the assistance of national grants, to develop a state comprehensive mental health services plan.[46]

The *Department of Transportation and Related Agencies Appropriations Act of 1991* employs a crossover sanction directing each state legislature to enact a law that requires the automatic revocation of the operator license of a motor vehicle driver convicted of a drug-related crime or lose 10 percent of its federal highway grant.[47] This statute contains an innovative section that authorizies a state legislature to avoid the directive by enacting an "opt-out" resolution; the governor must then send a letter of concurrence with the resolution to the secretary of transportation. Congress apparently enacted the section on the assumption no state legislature would dare to incur public wrath by opting out of the requirement. Nevertheless, many states did opt out, and Congress included in the *Department of Transportation and Related Agencies Appropriations Act of 1992* a stipulation that the crossover sanction in the 1991 act should "be treated as having not been enacted into law."[48] Congress changed its mind again and reinserted the requirement in the *Transportation Equity Act for the 21st Century of 1998.*[49]

Criticisms of Categorical Grants

The initial federal grant-in-aid programs were subjected to little criticism because of their limited scope and the small amounts of grant funds. The growth in the number and dollar amount of grant programs by 1920 commenced to produce opposition. Charges were levied that unelected federal bureaucrats were dictating "sovereign states" to initiate specific actions. In addition, this early opposition emphasized the power to tax and the power to spend should not be separated; grants in effect are bribes to subnational governments to administer national government programs; and business firms and citizens in wealthy states should not be taxed by Congress to fund the provision of services in the poorer states.[50]

Similar charges were made during the Great Depression and World War II. The post-war period witnessed increased concern about undesirable aspects of such grants and resulted in the Commission on Intergovernmental Relations, appointed by President Dwight D. Eisenhower, in 1955 cautioning, "the National Government must refrain from taking over activities that the States and their subdivisions are performing with reasonable competence, less the vitality of state and local institutions be undermined."[51]

Grant proponents countered the criticisms by stressing such aid fosters cooperative services by the three planes of governments; helps to overcome inflexible state consitutional provisions; assists subnational units to finance services they otherwise could not afford to provide; promotes tax equity by redistributing tax resources nationally; enables these units to preserve their viability; and improves the quality of state and local governmental administration.[52] A governor of a southern state wrote to the author in 1987 that "grants-in-aid generally give the State the option to conform in its own way to federal mandates rather than being instructed by federal legislation on exactly how compliance will be dealt with. This flexibility is certainly much better than a comprehensive federal statute outlining what will be done."

The early pro and con grant arguments tended to be ideological in nature. Commencing in the 1960s, the arguments focused more heavily on the administrative discretion of subnational units, economy and efficiency in service provision, programmatic accountability, and effectiveness in achieving programmatic goals.

Post-1960 Criticisms

The sharp growth in the number of narrow categorical grant-in-aid programs in the late 1950s and 1960s led to considerable controversy over the impact of such programs on the discretionary authority of state and local governments.[53] Opponents of the greater congressional influence over subnational policies acquired through grant conditions were disturbed by attempts to influence traditional state and local governmental policies previously ineligible for federal conditional grants-in-aid.

A 1978 U.S. Advisory Commission on Intergovernmental Relations report highlighted that "at least through the 1950s, federal assistance activities were confined by an effort to restrict aid to fields clearly involving the national interest or an important national purpose."[54] The report added, "the concept of the national interest lost most of its substantive content" subsequent to 1965 with "any action passed by both legislative chambers and signed by the President being accepted as appropriate."[55]

State and local government officers generally welcomed the receipt of national government grants, but were disturbed by the impact of narrow conditional categorical grants-in-aid on their units and cited twenty adverse effects.[56] Specific criticisms are listed below:

1. *Reduced Subnational Governmental Discretionary Authority.* Complaints frequently were made that the attached conditions limited their policymaking discretion unduly and resulted in lower quality services and/or unnecessary administrative costs. Charles L. Schultze in 1976 doubted that important national purposes were served by conditional grants and concluded they "simply reflect the substitution of the judgment of federal legislators and agency officials for that of state and local officials."[57]

2. *Dominance by Federal Bureaucrats.* Federal conditional grants-in-aid statutes contain provisions authorizing federal departments and agencies to promulgate rules and regulations granting federal bureaucrats a veto power over subnational governmental plans, policies, and implementation of federally assisted programs. U.S. Senator James L. Buckley of New York in 1978 evoked fears of national administrative imperialism: "The federal bureaucracy has grown into what is essentially a fourth branch of government that has become virtually immune to political direction or control. It is peopled by men and women who are now possessed of broad discretionary power over many areas of American life—so many, in fact, that one begins to wonder to what extent ours [government] can still be described as a government of laws rather than of men."[58] He was convinced that only by reducing federal government involvement in the governance process, by shifting responsibilities to subnational governments, would it be possible to "expand the amount of time that the President and members of Congress can devote to each of the matters for which they remain responsible."[59]

3. *Impact on Gubernatorial-Legislative Relations.* The position of the typical governor vis-à-vis the legislature has been strengthened by federal conditional grants-in-aid since most grants are applied for and received by executive agencies under the control of the governor. The governor's position also has been strength-

ened by powers delegated under provisions of partial preemption statutes (see chapter 5).

The U.S. Advisory Commission on Intergovernmental Relations surveyed state budget officers and reported in 1978 that federal categorical grants requiring no state matching funds or only in-kind matching "strengthens the discretionary power of the Governor and administrators and weakens the Legislature's control over the budget and administration."[60]

Several state legislatures responded to this development by enacting statutes stipulating federal grant funds cannot be expended in the absence of a legislative appropriation. Courts in Colorado and New Mexico invalidated such statutes on the ground the funds are "custodial funds" controlled executively by the executive branch.[61] On the other hand, the New York Court of Appeals in 1981 opined a statute subjecting federal funds to appropriation by the state legislature was constitutional.[62]

The U.S. Supreme Court issued an important decision in 1973 holding a state's constitutional spending prohibitions were not preempted and whether a grant-in-aid falls within the state prohibition is a matter of state law and not federal law.[63] In 1979, the court affirmed a decision of the Pennsylvania Supreme Court holding a state law requiring all received federal funds be deposited in the general fund of the commonwealth was a valid exercise of legislative power.[64]

4. *Increased Subnational Bureaucratic Independence.* Many state and local government officers and observers were disturbed by subnational governmental agencies applying for and receiving federal funds that enabled them to be more independent of elected officers and thereby evade in part regular budgetary and personnel controls. G. Homer Durham was an early critic and in 1940 wrote, "some of the largest and politically most powerful state agencies, such as highway administration with an almost total absence of merit personnel, are no longer dependent on their operating jurisdictions for funds."[65]

5. *Distorted Expenditure Patterns.* Federal funds are blamed for a reduction in the ability of subnational governments to determine their own priorities and for the resulting distortion of their spending patterns. Most federal grants require recipient units to contribute funds to federally aided programs and projects. The required percentage varies between programs and projects. Not

surprisingly, subnational governments often seek to maximize federal grant contributions. In 1980, the U.S. General Accounting Office concluded local governments experiencing a fiscal crisis or a taxpayer revolt were unable to reduce their own spending for federally supported activities without losing the federal aid and may have to eliminate programs not supported with federal grants or not institute reductions in any supported program.[66]

6. *Encouragement of Increased State-Local Spending.* The requirement of a nonfederal financial contribution to a federally aided program or project increases total government spending above the level of spending that otherwise probably would occur. It must be recognized increased subnational government spending is one of the objectives of federal grant-in-aid programs.

7. *Agency-Client Group Relationships.* The proliferation of federal grant programs in the 1960s is attributable in large measure to interest groups, which subsequently establish what amount to agency-client relationships. These groups have individualistic goals and by promoting categorical grant programs to achieve their goals, they make it more difficult for state and local governments to integrate administratively related programs in the most effective manner.

8. *Ineffective Congressional Review of Proposed Spending.* This criticism dates to the 1930s. Key concluded in 1940, "the strength of these pressure groups, rather than any rational consideration of governmental finance, has been the controlling factor behind federal and state aid."[67]

9. *Conflicting Grant Objectives.* Congress responds to pressures from divergent interest groups and the result is enactment of many grant-in-aid programs with goals conflicting in part with the goals of other grant programs. Outstanding examples involve transportation grants-in-aid. Highway grants encourage citizens to use their motor vehicles rather than public transportation services in urbanized areas and to use their vehicles in lieu of traveling on passenger trains for longer journeys. The diversion of traffic from public transportation facilities has forced their operators to reduce services and to increase fares, which in turn has promoted an additional decline in the number of passengers and revenues.

10. *Duplicative and Overlapping Grant Programs.* The U.S. Advisory Commission on Intergovernmental Relations in 1967 illustrated this criticism by citing "federal grants for water and

sewer projects. No less than four such programs are available, administered by four different agencies."[68]

11. *Voluminous Federal Rules and Regulations.* The sharp increase in the number of federal grant-in-aid programs was accompanied by the promulgation by various federal departments and agencies of voluminous and complex rules and regulations to implement the programs. Critics contended the delivery of services and completion of construction projects by subnational governments were hampered and made more expensive by the rules and regulations.

12. *Lack of Adequate Subnational Governmental Input into the Framing of Rules and Regulations.* State and local government officers often complained they received no advance notification of proposed federal rules and regulations for grant-in aid programs until they read the proposals in the *Federal Register.* They maintained they often were not accorded adequate time to review the proposals and to offer constructive suggestions for their revision.

13. *Complex Application Procedures.* Subnational officers objected to unnecessarily complex procedures in the grant application process, including the requirement for multiple copies of applications, which significantly raised administrative costs.

14. *Insufficient Federal Field Delegation.* Critics were disturbed by the failure of the Washington, D.C., offices of federal departments and agencies to delegate sufficient discretionary authority to federal field officers, thereby resulting in what observers considered to be too many levels of review of grant applications, requests for changes in approved plans, and required reports.

15. *Inflexible Programmatic Requirements.* The elapsed time between preparation of a grant-in-aid application and its approval by a federal department or agency could be as long as eighteen months. This long approval process may necessitate programmatic revisions for the most effective attainment of grant objectives due to changed conditions. Furthermore, obtaining approval for revisions was difficult.

16. *Single-Agency Requirement.* Many federal grant-in-aid programs in the 1960s required that a single state agency be responsible for administration of each program in order to fix responsibility and avoid programmatic duplication. This requirement was highly controversial and several governors

maintained their states lost the ability to reorganize their respective executive branch to achieve goals most effectively and economically. The U.S. Supreme Court in 1979 upheld the
constitutionality of the requirement.[69]

17. *Crosscutting Requirements.* As Congress gained more experience with grants, it began to add crosscutting requirements to
grant programs. These requirements are not related directly to
the goals of the particular programs, but are designed to achieve
other policy goals, such as citizen participation and nondiscrimination. The governor of a western state wrote to the
author in 1987 that the threat of loss of federal highway grants-
in-aid if a state legislature does not raise its minimum legal
alcoholic beverages purchase age to twenty-one "amounts to
little more than federal blackmail." This particular grant-in-aid
crosscutting requirement was upheld as constitutional in 1987
by the U.S. Supreme Court, which opined "even if Congress
might lack the power to impose a national minimum drinking
age directly, we conclude that encouragement to state action
found in §158 is a valid use of the spending power."[70]

18. *The Accountability Problem.* Stenberg in 1980 clearly identified
the accountability problems associated with categorical grants-
in-aid: "[T]he highly fragmented intergovernmental assistance
program provides many buck-passing opportunities. Local officials can always blame the 'feds' for unpopular actions or policy
decisions such as fair share housing programs or community
based corrections projects. Both can criticize the insensitivity,
unwillingness, or inability of some States to provide needed
assistance or authority to their local governments."[71]

19. *State-Local Governmental Coordination Impediments.* A major
change in federal grant-in-aid policy occurred when Congress
enacted the *United States Housing Act of 1937*, providing for
direct federal grants-in-aid to general purpose local governments, thereby completely bypassing state governments.[72] By
1967, there were sixty-eight such grant programs.[73]

Several intergovernmental relations observers attributed
establishment of direct federal-local financial relationships to
the failure of most state governments to assume their urban
responsibilities and play a major partnership role in the federal
system. State government officers criticized "bypassing" and
contended they were in the best position to integrate state pro-

grams with federally aided local programs to achieve maximum results at the lowest costs.

Federal government officers suggested state governments that do not wish to be bypassed should "buy into" federal-local grant programs by providing one-half of the funds local governments are required to provide to obtain a direct grant-in-aid. Stenberg examined the experience of New York State in "buying into" a federal-local grant program. He concluded such "buying into" resulted in "more flexible cost-sharing arrangements, expanded local program scope, and reduced local costs," and encouraged local government participation in such programs, facilitated coordination of state-local governmental planning, reduced grant processing time, expedited funding for local government projects, and state-local governmental cooperation.[74]

20. *Local Government Coordination Impediments.* A second major change in congressional grant policy occurred with the enactment of the *Economic Opportunity Act of 1964*, which authorizes grants to private organizations, thereby bypassing general purpose local governments and state governments and causing coordination problems. Furthermore, the numerous federal grants-in-aid provided directly to local governmental agencies made it exceptionally difficult for a general purpose local government to launch a coordinated program to solve problems due to the restrictive conditions attached to each grant.

Federal Responses to the Criticisms

Congress responded to the growing criticism of its grants-in-aid programs commencing in the mid-1960s by creating new organizations and establishing new procedures. The Department of Housing and Urban Development and the Department of Transportation were established to improve program coordination. President Lyndon B. Johnson in 1965 decided to improve high-level federal-subnational governmental communications by designating the Office of the Vice President as the contact point for local government officers and the Office of Emergency Preparedness in the executive Office of the President as the contact point for governors. President Richard M. Nixon, by executive order, transferred responsibility for federal-state relations to a newly established Office of Intergovernmental Relations under the supervision of the vice president to serve as a federal ombudsman for state and local governments.

A new procedure was established in 1966 under which governors and local government chief executives were consulted by federal departments and agencies prior to the promulgation of new or revised grant regulations. The U.S. Advisory Commission on Intergovernmental Relations acted as an intermediary body, channeling proposed regulation changes to national associations of state and local government officers, and transmitting their comments, questions, and suggestions to the appropriate federal departments and agencies.

The exceptionally large number of narrow federal categorical grant programs confused numerous state and local government officers and the confusion was augmented by the grant-in-aid catalogs published by the federal grant departments and agencies. In 1967, the Office of Economic Opportunity was assigned responsibility for publishing a single catalog of federal grant-in-aid programs, a responsibility subsequently assumed by the Office of Management and Budget. The *Vice President's Handbook for Local Officials*, a companion publication, was published and distributed.

President Johnson in 1967 directed the Bureau of the Budget (now Office of Management and Budget) to study grant consolidation, simplification of grant application procedures and financial accounting, and field office structure and location. The budget bureau issued a circular requiring federal departments and agencies to consult governors prior to designating planning and development districts. If a state already had such districts, new districts established by federal departments and agencies were required to conform to the boundaries of the state districts unless there was strong justification for divergent boundaries.

Three major intergovernmental coordination actions were initiated. First, the heads of various federal departments and agencies signed interagency coordination agreements. Second, President Johnson issued an executive order authorizing the secretary of housing and urban development to convene all federal departments and agencies operating in a city whenever greater coordination of federal programs was needed. Third, a similar convener power was delegated to the secretary of agriculture with respect to federal grant programs impacting agricultural and rural development. These convener powers were never employed.

Congressional enactment of the *Intergovernmental Cooperation Act of 1968* improved federal-state-local governmental coordination by disseminating more federal government information to subnational governments, authorizing federal departments and agencies to waive the single-agency requirement and provide technical services to subnational governmental units on a reimbursable basis, and requiring periodic congressional review of grant programs.[75] The act specifically authorized the head of any federal department or agency, upon the request of the governor or other appropriate state officer, to waive the single-agency requirement and approve a different administrative structure. Presidents subsequently launched initiatives to improve the grant-in-aid system. The *Federal Financial Assistance Management Improvement Act of 1999* directed the U.S. General Accounting Office to evaluate the effectiveness of the 1968 act within six years.[76] In 2003, the office released its report, which noted earlier administrative reforms were useful, but failed to address the problems flowing from the fragmented nature of the grant-in-aid system.[77]

The above actions help to improve the administration of federal grant-in-aid programs, but congressional authorization of block grants and general revenue sharing—subjects examined in a subsequent section—had a more significant impact upon the federal system.

Federal Tax Credits and Sanctions

Congress has employed tax credits since 1926 to encourage state legislatures to enact harmonious laws based upon national statutes, and tax sanctions since 1982 to promote the achievement of national goals. The latter are similar to crossover sanctions attached to conditional grants-in-aid, described above.

Tax Credits

Tax credits, a second type of informal or incentive preemption, have been offered by Congress as a device to encourage state legislatures to enact uniform state laws, thereby facilitating harmonious interstate relations benefiting citizens and business firms. Such a credit is very valuable because it allows a taxpayer to deduct all or part of a credit from his or her federal income tax liability, in contrast to a tax deduction which only reduces a person's gross income for tax purposes.

The federal *Revenue Act of 1926* authorized the first tax credit by allowing eligible taxpayers to take an 80 percent credit against the federal estate tax for estate or inheritance taxes paid to a state.[78] All federal estate tax revenue would flow to the United States Treasury if a state legislature failed to enact a statute levying a tax identical to the federal estate tax, and such failure would lead to eligible taxpayers pressuring the legislature to enact such a statute. This act has been totally successful in achieving its goal of encouraging states to enact a uniform estate tax.

The *Social Security Act of 1935* authorized the second tax credit program, this one designed to establish a national system of state-operated unemployment insurance.[79] Employers who pay state unemployment taxes are allowed a tax credit against their federal unemployment insurance tax obligation equal to 90 percent of the taxes paid to a state if its tax law conforms to the federal tax law provisions. This program also was successful in achieving its goal.

The *Economic Recovery Tax Act of 1981* authorized tax credits for a period of five years to promote rehabilitation of homes in historical districts designated by local governments and to assist public transportation authorities.[80] Relative to the latter, a private corporation was authorized to purchase buses, for example, from a public transportation authority for $10 million by using $2 million of its own funds and $8 million of the authority's funds. The private corporation holds title to the buses, depreciates their total costs, and leases them for a moderate fee to the authority, which is responsible for all maintenance and operating costs. This transaction allows the authority to gain $2 million while the private corporation takes advantage of tax-deductible interest payments and accelerated depreciation over a five-year period. Congress did not extend the tax-credit program because of the sharp increase in the size of the federal government deficit and the loss of tax revenue.

Can a federal tax-credit program be developed to replace one or all categorical grant-in-aid programs? The answer is no, but such a program could replace many categorical grant programs. A tax-credit program is a type of informal congressional preemption and generally is as effective as conditional grants-in-aid in achieving national objectives. A major advantage of such a program is administrative in nature; that is, the Internal Revenue Service can administer the program at a considerably lower cost than conditional grant-in-aid programs administered by federal specialized departments and agencies. Do subnational government officers favor tax-credit programs? There is no definitive answer to this question as the answer depends upon the nature of the programs. Beneficiaries of such programs include private citizens and private corporations authorized to employ tax credits, but subnational governments also can benefit in terms of increased revenues.

Tax Sanctions

The *Tax Equity and Fiscal Responsibility Act of 1982* imposed the first tax sanction on subnational governments by stipulating they may issue only registered, instead of bearer, long-term municipal bonds; otherwise, the interest received by bondholders will be subject to the federal income tax.[81] Should a state or local government issue traditional bearer bonds, the interest rate would have to be higher to attract investors who would be required to pay the federal income tax. The constitutionality of this act was challenged and the U.S. Supreme Court in 1988 upheld the tax sanction.[82]

A second tax sanction is included in the *Tax Reform Act of 1986*. It requires state and local governments issuing long-term bonds whose interest is exempt from the federal income tax to rebate arbitrage profits, if any, to the U.S. Treasury.[83] Arbitrage refers to the profit made by investing funds raised by a bond issue, until needed, in U.S. Treasury or other safe securities paying a higher rate than the interest paid by subnational governments to their bondholders.

Block Grants and General Revenue Sharing

Numerous state and local government officers argued for years that federal government financial assistance would be more effective in achieving national goals at a lower cost if subnational governments were granted greater discretionary authority in administering the aid in the form of block grants-in-aid and general revenue sharing. The former dates to 1966 and the latter to 1972.

Block Grants

The Commission on the Organization of the Executive Branch of the Federal Government (Hoover Commission) issued a report in 1949 recommending that Congress establish a system of grants-in-aid to state and local governments "based upon broad categories...as contrasted with the present system of extreme fragmentation."[84] Congress did not act on this recommendation until 1966, when it enacted an omnibus statute including the *Partnership for Health Act of 1966*.[85]

The U.S. Advisory Commission on Intergovernmental Relations in 1977 published a report noting that one formula public health service "program in 1936 had become nine programs in 1966" and Congress prefers categorical grants-in-aid for the following reasons:

> Proponents argued that categorical disease control programs resulted in the most highly targeted impact of limited federal financial aid. It was feared that adding funds to the general health grant would not achieve a greater impact in a particular program area, given the many competing demands on state and local health departments. Programs directed at specific health problems also demonstrated the responsiveness of the federal government to these problems, and to the constituencies which favored categorical grants, because success with Congress made it unnecessary to cope with the ambiguities of state legislative processes. Lastly, an increasing

and permanent federal participation in the financing of health services naturally led to a desire on the part of Congress and administering officials to more actively shape state and local decisions regarding aided activities.[86]

One major criticism of categorical grants-in-aid programs was the administrative burden placed upon the states and the obstacles impeding development of balanced public health programs. Congress responded by collapsing nine formula-grant programs into a single block grant program allowing state officers greater discretionary authority while ensuring national goals will be achieved. This block grant program quickly received the strong support of state health commissioners.

Two years later, Congress enacted the *Omnibus Crime Control and Safe Streets Act* which Michael D. Reagan and John G. Sanzone described as being "so much subjected to 'creeping categorization' that it can best be described as a closely related set of categorical grants masquerading under a block grant guise by being run through a single federal agency...and by utilizing state planning agency structures as a device for federal-state interactions."[87]

President Richard M. Nixon in 1972 proposed four "special revenue sharing" programs, and the 1974 Congress enacted one: community development.[88] This program typically is referred to as the Community Development Block Grant program (CDBG), but differs from a conventional block grant program in four respects: an eligible general purpose local government is required to submit only a simple application; the U.S. Department of Housing and Community Development (HUD) may not reject the application; the recipient is not subject to HUD administrative audits; and there are no maintenance-of-effort or matching requirements.

Richard S. Williamson in 1981 explained there were five reasons why the Reagan administration promoted block grants:

> First, our governmental system, at present, is not working. The federal government is overloaded, having assumed more responsibilities than it can efficiently or effectively manage....It has crowded out state and local governments, treating them as if they were mere administrative provinces of the federal government....
>
> Second, the block grants will permit government decisions once again to be made by state and local officials who can be held accountable for those decisions. There has been a breakdown in accountability between decisionmaker and voters....
>
> Third, significant administrative savings will result. The program proposed for consolidation in just the health and social services areas alone encompass 437 pages of law and 1,200 pages of regulations. Once the awards for 6,800 separate grants are made, over 7 million man-hours of

state and local government and community efforts are required each year
to fill out federally required reports....

 Fourth, block grants will result in greater innovation and permit the
States to serve as true "laboratories of democracy."...

 Finally, enactment of the block grants will reduce the impact of the
budget cuts by permitting state and local officials to target diminishing
resources to areas and individuals whose needs are the greatest.[89]

The U.S. General Accounting Office released in 1984 reports assess-
ing the Maternal and Child Health Block Grant, Preventive Health and
Health Services Block Grant, and education block grants. The reports
concluded grants achieved their objectives of according state governments increased programmatic administrative flexibility and specifically
noted the education block grant "facilitates improvements in administrative procedures and planning and budgeting."[90] SRI International in 1986
reached a similar conclusion relative to the education block grant program, and explained the program "reduced the local administrative
burden associated with the programs it replaced" and "enhanced local
discretion over these federal funds."[91]

General Revenue Sharing

Congress enacted the *State and Local Fiscal Assistance Act of 1972* to
provide state and general purpose local governments with the greatest
degree of discretionary authority in spending the $30.2 billion appropri-
ated for a five-year period.[92]

 The general revenue-sharing program was an entitlement one and
eligible governments were not required to submit an application to the
U.S. Treasury, provide matching funds, meet a maintenance-of-effort
requirement, or be subject to administrative audits by a federal department or agency. Congress renewed the program in 1976 for five years,
but states were dropped as eligible recipients in 1980 when the program
was renewed. Although the program was a popular one, Congress did
not extend the program for local governments in 1986 because of the
sharp increase in the national government deficit (attributable in large
measure to the rearming of the defense forces in response to a perceived
threat by the Soviet Union.)

 As the reader would anticipate, general revenue sharing was exceptionally popular with elected state and local government officers due to
the few restrictions placed by Congress on spending the federally shared
revenue and the strengthening of the ability of these officers to control
bureaucrats since the funds could not be spent without an appropriation

by the local governing body. Certain grant-in-aid funds, in contrast, could be spent by bureaucrats without an appropriation.

Reagan's New Federalism

The media used the term "new federalism" to describe President Ronald Reagan's program to make significant changes in the intergovernmental system. This term had been employed earlier by President Nixon, who sought to decentralize the governmental system of the United States by encouraging Congress to return certain functional responsibilities to the state and local governments and by increasing the fiscal capacity of these units by means of the general revenue- and special revenue-sharing programs. Nixon also promoted centralization by recommending responsibility for income maintenance and functions with spillover costs, such as air and water pollution and energy, be centered in the national government.[93]

The new federalism program of President Reagan, a former California governor, had three policy goals: continuation and expansion of economic deregulation initiated by Congress during the administration of President James E. Carter; a "swap" of certain functions between the national government and states; and congressional enactment of additional block grant programs. In accepting his nomination for the presidency by the 1980 Republican National Convention, he stated: "Everything that can be run more effectively by state and local government we shall turn over to state and local government, along with the funding sources to pay for it. We are going to put an end to the money merry-go-round where our money becomes Washington's money to be spent by States and cities exactly the way the federal bureaucrats tell us it has to be spent."[94]

Specifically, President Reagan recommended that the national government should assume complete responsibility for the Medicaid program and states should assume complete responsibility for Aid to Families with Dependent Children and the food stamp program. He also urged Congress to enact a statute turning back to the states thirty to forty programs, in addition to the programs to be consolidated into his proposed block grants. According recognition to the need of states for additional revenue to finance the turn-back programs, he suggested revenues from specified federal excise taxes—alcoholic beverages, tobacco products, and motor fuel—be made available to states. The president maintained the overall effect of his proposals was revenue neutral, but state officers commenced to fear states would lose revenue. In consequence, the proposals proved to be highly controversial and Congress did not enact the necessary statutes to implement the proposals.

The Reagan administration continued the economic deregulation program and expanded its scope to include subnational governments. Congress in 1981 consolidated fifty-seven categorical grant-in-aid programs into nine new or revised block grant programs, thereby necessitating revision of existing rules and regulations to conform to the new block grant format. The revised regulations totaled only 31 pages, compared to the previous 905 pages, in the *Code of Federal Regulations*. In addition, the Reagan administration reviewed all other rules and regulations and revised many to reduce the administrative burden placed upon state and local governments.

U.S. Comptroller General Charles A. Bowsher studied the effectiveness of the deregulation and reported in 1986:

> Reduced federal regulatory control has enable States to make gains in containing health care costs. For instance, under Medicaid, States are moving toward prepaid plans and States are using prospective payments for nursing home care.
>
> States have also moved decisively in areas where the federal government has stepped back. One example is the States' role in delivering emergency medical services under the preventive health and health services block grant. States strengthened their regulatory roles, and a number have created trust funds from traffic fines to finance local emergency medical services. Local officials are looking more to the States, not the federal government, to set standards and provide assistance.[95]

Congress became concerned the reduction in federal regulation of state and local governmental activities, financed in part with federal moneys, might result in programmatic inefficiencies and unnecessary expenditures. In consequence, Congress enacted the *Single Audit Act of 1984*, the goal of which is to facilitate the determination of whether each subnational government has an internal control system providing "reasonable assurance" federal financial assistance programs are managed "in compliance with applicable laws and regulations."[96] Each state has primary responsibility for arranging for the required audits, and all subsequent audits by federal departments and agencies must build upon the single state audit.

The Urban Institute reviewed the intergovernmental record of the Reagan administration and concluded in 1984: "[T]he Administration has reversed the trend of growing financial dependence of lower levels of government on the national government, put in place a grant structure that is less restrictive and provides less encouragement to local spending, challenged the assumption that there should be uniform national standards for public services, and more fully engaged the States as partners in the effort to contain domestic program costs." [97]

The president in 1986 reviewed his administration's accomplishments in the areas of deregulation, economic growth, the environment, tax reform, and other matters. He was particularly critical of the tendency of the federal government to bypass the subnational governments during the 1970s and commented:

> Today, we have reversed the trend toward centralization. State and local governments are again assuming their rightful role....
>
> Through block grants, we have been able to cut through federal red tape and allow State and local officials to design and administer programs that make sense to them and their taxpayers. Accordingly, the budget I submitted contains proposals for new block grants, and maintains healthy funding levels for the ones already in place.
>
> We are working with State and local government officials and organizations to compile a roster of major federal regulations for revision or elimination. We will also seek to standardize agency grant management practices that will reduce administrative costs and confusion.[98]

The president's program was subject to criticism by a number of subnational governmental officers and their national associations because of the burdens imposed by federal mandates.

Federal Mandates

By 1986, the fiscal problems of many state and local governments were aggravated as the result of the termination of the general revenue-sharing program and the increasing number of federal mandates requiring these governments to initiate specific actions and to bear totally the resulting costs. A federal mandate differs from a condition attached to a federal grant-in-aid program or a crossover sanction because it is a legal requirement. The affected subnational governments cannot avoid the mandate, as they can avoid a grant condition or a crossover sanction by not applying for or accepting a federal grant-in-aid. (The large sum of federal moneys available under a number of grant programs, of course, makes it difficult for subnational governments not to accept the grant funds.)

A number of congressional statutes prohibit a specified type of subnational governmental action and the prohibition may make it imperative that a concerned subnational government initiate a different and more costly action to achieve a goal. The *Ocean Dumping Ban Act of 1988* is a restraint forbidding the dumping of sewage sludge in oceans.

Municipalities located near an ocean thereby need to utilize an expensive alternative disposal method, such as incineration or a landfill.[99]

As noted, the 104th Congress enacted the *Unfunded Mandates Reform Act of 1995*, authorizing the use of parliamentary rules to make it more difficult for Congress to impose such mandates on state and local governments (see chapter 7).

Summary

This chapter examines the development and use of spending power preemption by means of conditional grants-in-aid and tax credits, criticisms of this informal type of preemption, and administrative and political responses to the criticisms.

State and local government elected officers welcomed the regulatory relief provided by Congress and the president in the form of block grants and removal and reduction of administrative burdens since the mid-1960s. This movement toward administrative decentralization, however, was offset by the sharp increase in the number of preemption statutes enacted by Congress commencing in 1965. Chapter 4 examines the various types of congressional complete preemption statutes and chapter 5 is devoted to a similar examination of preemption statutes removing partially the regulatory authority of the states in specified fields.

Chapter 4

COMPLETE FIELD PREEMPTION

The framers of the U.S. Constitution recognized their inability to foresee all future developments that would affect the newly established economic and political union, and in consequence authorized Congress to utilize delegated powers to enact statutes preempting completely or partially the regulatory authority of states in various fields. Congress also may enact a devolution statute empowering states to exercise regulatory powers in a field assigned to Congress by the Constitution.

Although Congress enacted preemption statutes completely removing regulatory authority from states as early as 1790, these statutes and partial preemption ones had a relatively minor impact on the federal system prior to 1965. Congressional preemption statutes regulating interstate commerce did not forbid state legislatures to exercise the police power—to protect and promote public convenience, health, morals, safety, and welfare—provided an undue burden was not placed on commerce among sister states. The January 1940 issue of *The Annals of the American Academy of Political and Social Science*, titled "Intergovernmental Relations in the United States," contains not a single reference to congressional preemption.[1] A second volume, published in 1974, on the other hand, has three articles referring to congressional preemption.[2] And a third volume of *The Annals*, published in 1990, also includes three articles containing references to congressional preemption.[3]

Do states always oppose complete preemption bills in Congress? The answer is no. State government officers tend to be pragmatic and on occasion recognize states cannot solve particular nationwide regulatory problems. This is reflected in the following National Governors' Association's 1980–1981 policy position:

> The Association is concerned with increasing costs to truckers as well as consumers resulting from the lack of uniformity in allowable vehicle weights and dimensions which still exists among many States....
> The Association urges that Congress immediately enact legislation establishing national standards for weight (80,000 gross; 20,000 per single axle; 34,000 for tandem), and length (60 ft.).[4]

Congress responded by enacting the *Surface Transportation Assistance Act of 1982* and the *Motor Vehicle Width Regulations of 1983*.[5]

National associations of state government officers have also called upon Congress to clarify the authority of a federal department or agency which has been assigned complete responsibility for a preempted function. The National Conference of State Legislatures, for example, expressed its concern relative to the danger to the general public posed by the transportation of high-level nuclear wastes across state borders to a disposal site. It maintained the national government should be responsible "for the protection of the public against damages and personal injury incurred as a consequence of any accident in the transportation or disposal of high-level nuclear wastes," and added, "The Nuclear Waste Policy Act authorizes the U.S. Department of Energy (DOE) to enter into written cooperation and consultation agreements with the States to address the liability concerns of the States. However, the federal government (through its agent the U.S. Department of Energy) asserts that its liability for accidents incurred during the transportation or disposal of high-level nuclear waste is limited by existing federal law which, it claims, circumscribes its authority to protect the States."[6]

This chapter probes the nature of congressional statutes that totally remove from states their regulatory powers in specified fields. A typology will be developed and two brief case studies involving complete assumption by Congress of regulatory authority will be presented.

The Nature of Congressional Preemption

Chapters 1 and 5 describe the sources of and reasons for the increased use of preemption powers by Congress in the period 1965 through 2004, and note certain state and local government laws may be preempted by treaties entered into by the United States with other nations as well as by congressional statutes. The provisions of treaties with respect to conflicting subnational governmental statutes and administrative rules and regulations vary. The *Uruguay Round Agreements Act of 1994* stipulates:

"No State law, or the application of such a State law, may be declared invalid as to any person or circumstance on the ground that the provision or application is inconsistent with any of the Uruguay Round agreements, except in an action brought by the United States for the purpose of declaring such law or application invalid."[7]

Congress at any time may broaden the coverage of a partial preemption statute, as it did in 1991 by amending the *Employee Retirement Income Security Act of 1974* to include within its coverage telephone and electric cooperative welfare plans.[8] In 2000, the act was amended again "to clarify the application to a church plan that is a welfare plan of State insurance laws that require or solely relate to licensing, solvency, insolvency, or the statute of such plan as a single employer plan."[9] The 2000 statute also provides "the church plan shall be subject to State enforcement as if the church plan were an insurer licensed by the State."[10]

In 1991, Congress amended the *Commercial Motor Vehicle Safety Act of 1986* and directed the secretary of transportation to promulgate regulations within one year establishing "a program which requires motor carriers to conduct preemployment, reasonable suspicion, random, and post-accident testing of the operators of commercial motor vehicles for use, in violation of law or federal regulation, of alcohol or a controlled substance."[11] State and local governments are forbidden to adopt any law or rule inconsistent with the regulations issued by the secretary "except that the regulations issued...shall not be construed to preempt provisions of State criminal law which impose sanctions for reckless conduct leading to actual loss of life, injury, or damage to property, whether the provisions apply specifically to commercial motor vehicle employees, or to the general public."[12]

Congress in 1994 expanded the coverage of the *Petroleum Marketing Practices Act* by forbidding a state or a local government to enact a law or promulgate a regulation requiring "a payment for the goodwill of a franchise on the termination of a franchise or nonrenewal of a franchise relationship authorized by this title."[13]

Many congressional regulatory statutes contain an expressed complete preemption provision applicable to an entire regulatory field or a segment of the field. The *Flammable Fabrics Act of 1967* stipulates it is intended to supersede any law of any state or political subdivision inconsistent with the act's provisions.[14] In other words, a state legislature or a local governing body may enact a law regulating flammable fabrics only if it is consistent with the provisions of the federal statute. A somewhat similar provision is contained in the *Telephone Operator Consumer Services Improvement Act of 1990*, which stipulates its requirements do not apply to an aggregator of services in a state with a statute or regulation requiring an aggregator "to take actions that are substantially the same as those required" by the act.[15] *The Radiation Control for Health and Safety Act of 1968* is a more stringent preemption act because it allows a state legislature or local governing body to enact only a regulatory standard "identical to the federal standard."[16]

The *United States Grain Standards Act of 1968* lacks a consistency provision and explicitly forbids a state or a local government to "require the inspection or description in accordance with any standards of kind, class, quality, condition, or other characteristics of grain as a condition of shipment, or sale, of such grain in interstate or foreign commerce, or require any license for, or impose any other restrictions upon, the performance of any official inspection functions under the Act by official inspection personnel."[17]

A limited type of complete preemption is illustrated by the *Gun Control Act of 1968*: "No provision of this chapter shall be construed as indicating an intent on the part of the Congress to occupy the field in which such provision operates to the exclusion of the law of any State on the same subject matter, unless there is a direct and positive conflict between such provision and the law of the State so that the two can not be reconciled or consistently stand together."[18] In other words, the scope of this preemption statute is limited because the removal of state regulatory authority is complete only if a direct and positive conflict exists between the act and a state statute. The *Drug Abuse Control Amendments of 1965* contains an identical provision.[19]

Many congressional statutes lack an explicit preemption clause. Nevertheless, such an act facially may suggest it is a complete preemption one, as evidenced by the wording of the *Children's Bicycle Helmet Safety Act of 1994*.[20] Other statutes lacking an explicit preemption declaration have been held to be preemptive by courts. Chapter 6 examines the criteria employed by the U.S. Supreme Court to determine whether a congressional statute is a preemptive one completely or partially removing regulatory authority from states and their political subdivisions. Congress, of course, is free to overturn a court decision holding a state or local government law is preempted by enacting a remedial statute. The *Civil Rights Act of 1991* reversed the decision of the U.S. Supreme Court in *Wards Cove Packing Company v. Atonio*.[21] The Court had opined the statistical evidence of a higher percentage of positions held by nonwhite cannery employees compared to the few noncannery positions held by nonwhites did not constitute a prima facie violation of Title VII of the *Civil Rights Act of 1964*.[22]

To what extent can states protect their regulatory authority against potential congressional preemption? Chief Justice John Marshall of the

U.S. Supreme Court provided an answer in 1824, relative to congressional employment of the interstate commerce clause, when he opined: "The wisdom and the discretion of Congress, their identity with the people, and the influence which their constituents possess at elections, are, in this, as in many other instances, as that, for example of declaring war, the sole restraints on which they have relied to secure them from its abuse."[23]

This thesis was employed by Herbert Wechsler in 1953 to develop the political safeguards of federalism theory, which holds states can engage in the national political process to help elect members of Congress who will protect the states' reserved regulatory powers.[24] Justice Harry A. Blackmun of the U.S. Supreme Court endorsed this theory in 1985 by writing, "the principal and basic limits on the federal commerce power is inherent in all state participation in federal government action."[25] In particular, he suggested states should seek protection of their regulatory powers not in the courts, but in the political branch of government, that is, Congress.

Many state government elected officers disagree with the justice's position. One of our research goals is to examine the political safeguards theory in terms of Congress's responsiveness to their calls for relief from congressional preemption statutes causing problems for subnational governments or imposing substantial costs upon them (commonly termed "unfunded mandates") and the Blackmun thesis relative to preemptive decisions of courts (see chapter 7).

The next two sections contain a typology of complete preemption statutes and two brief case studies illustrating the degree of congressional responsiveness to the concerns of subnational government elected officers with respect to two such statutes.

A Typology of Complete Congressional Preemption

Seventeen types of congressional statutes removing all regulatory authority from states and their political subdivisions are identified in this section. This typology will be of assistance in determining the type(s) of congressional preemption most effective in mobilizing needed resources at the lowest possible cost to achieve the goals of each statute without seriously impeding the functioning of subnational governments or imposing costly burdens upon them.

Unaided Complete Preemption

The U.S. Constitution (art. I, §8) delegates to Congress the power "to promote the progress of science and useful arts, by securing for limited times to authors and inventors the exclusive right to their respective writings and discoveries...." Acting under this grant of power, Congress enacted the first copyright and the first patent act in 1790.[26] Subsequently, Congress enacted copyright extension acts in 1831, 1909, 1976, and the *Sonny Bono Copyright Term Extension Act* and the *Digital Millennium Copyright Act* in 1998.[27] The federal government administers these acts without the need for state and local governmental assistance and the constitutionality of none of these acts was questioned until 1998.

The Sonny Bono act, however, was challenged in court on the ground the extension of copyright protection violated the constitutional authority of Congress to protect the exclusive rights of authors "for limited times." The issue in the court challenge was the extension of copyright protection for cultural works for an additional twenty years. This extended copyright protection to seventy years after the death of the author and ninety-five years from publication of works created for or by corporations.[28] A prime beneficiary of the extension is the Walt Disney Company, whose copyrights, among others, include Cinderella, Mickey Mouse, and Snow White. Critics maintained the extension act is ultra vires because it violates the "limited times" constitutional provision and the First Amendment to the U.S. Constitution.[29] The U.S. Supreme Court in 2003 in *Eldred v. Ashcroft* sustained the act by explaining "the copyright clause empowers Congress to determine the intellectual property regimes that, overall, in that body's judgment, will serve the ends of the clause" and "[t]he wisdom of Congress' action...is not within our province to second-guess."[30] The *New York Times* editorialized, "the Supreme Court's decision makes it likely that we are seeing the beginning of the end of the public domain and the birth of copyright perpetuity."[31]

Although no state has enacted a copyright act that would be preempted by congressional copyright acts, the common law or statutes in twenty-five states provide for the right of publicity which allows individuals, primarily celebrities, to control the commercial use of their names. Such protection bears a similarity to the protection offered by congressional copyright and trademark statutes. The U.S. Supreme Court has addressed only once the question whether state right of publicity provisions are preempted. In 1977, the court in *Zacchini v. Scripps-Howard Broadcasting Company* ruled in favor of the "human cannonball" whose fifteen-second performance was videotaped without his permission at an Ohio country fair and broadcasted on television.[32] Noting the Ohio state legislature could enact a statute privileging the press, the U.S. Supreme Court opined neither the First Amendment nor the Fourteenth Amendment requires such an enactment.[33]

Congress in 1898 preempted a judicial power of the states by assigning complete responsibility for adjudicating bankruptcies to the U.S. District Court and the Supreme Court of the District of Columbia.[34] By assigning this function to federal courts, Congress avoided the need to rely upon subnational governments for assistance in the performance of this governmental function. In 1933, Congress enacted a statute creating the U.S. Bankruptcy Court to handle all bankruptcy filings in the United States.[35]

On occasion, the Bankruptcy Act and the Copyright Act have become the subject of a lawsuit. The question has been raised, for example, whether the latter act preempts the Uniform Commercial Code, enacted by all state legislatures, with respect to the unregistered copyrights of a company in the U.S. Bankruptcy Court. A buyer of unregistered copyrights from the trustees of a bankrupt company brought a proceeding to void a bank's security interests in copyrights and its attempt to recover them or their value. The bank had filed the required financing statements under Article 9 of the Uniform Commercial Code enacted by the California State Legislature. The U.S. Bankruptcy Court granted summary judgment for the bank in 1999.[36] An appeal was made.

The owner of the unregistered copyrights maintained the Copyright Act completely preempted the Uniform Commercial Code enacted by the California state legislature. The U.S. Court of Appeals for the Ninth Circuit in 2002 rejected this argument by opining the code was not preempted by the Copyright Act, was the only system available for filing unregistered copyrights, and holding the code to be preempted would make unregistered copyrights of no value as collateral.[37] The court noted, "the Copyright Act doesn't provide for the rights of secured parties to unregistered copyrights; it only covers the rights of secured parties in registered copyrights."[38] The court added the act does not mandate that copyrights must be registered because it provides copyrights "may" be registered.

The origin of another complete preemption statute is traceable to state legislatures commencing to regulate emissions from motor vehicles in the 1960s to reduce air pollution. The motor vehicle industry immediately became concerned it might have to develop fifty specialized emission control systems to meet the different requirements of each state. It lobbied Congress to remove completely from states their authority to establish emission standards for new vehicles. Congress in 1967 responded to the lobbying by enacting the *Air Quality Act*, which totally preempts responsibility for the establishment of emission standards for motor vehicles commencing with 1968 models.[39] A new approach to the motor vehicle air pollution problem was initiated by Congress when it enacted the *Clean Air Act Amendments of 1970*, which did not consider the economic and technical feasibility of achieving the mandated 90 percent reductions in emissions of carbon monoxide, hydrocarbons, and nitrogen oxides by 1975 model vehicles.[40]

No state and local government assistance is needed by the federal government to ensure emissions from new motor vehicles meet national air quality standards. The federal government is dependent, however, upon state inspection of on-highway vehicles to determine whether they meet the standards in states which have applied for and received regulatory primacy authority under the Clean Air Act's minimum standards provision (see chapter 5).

The *Religious Freedom Restoration Act of 1993* preempts any state or local government law placing a substantial burden on an individual's exercise of religion and grants standing to any "person whose religious exercise has been burdened" by a government to seek a judicial remedy.[41] In 1997, the U.S. Supreme Court invalidated the act on the ground the act exceeded the power granted to Congress by Section 5 of the Fourteenth Amendment to the constitution to enforce the amendment's guarantees.[42]

Various preemptive tax statutes require no assistance by subnational governments as illustrated by the 1996 act prohibiting state taxation of specified income sources or pension income or state or local governmental taxation of sales of products on the Internet.[43] The *Needlestick Safety and Prevention Act of 2000* is a most unusual complete preemption statute requiring no subnational governmental assistance because its bloodborne pathogen standard only remains in effect until it is "superseded in whole or in part by regulations promulgated by the Secretary of Labor under section 6(b) of the Occupational Safety and Health Act of 1970.... "[44]

Economic Deregulation Statutes

An economic deregulation movement, particularly for the transportation industry, gained strength in Congress in the 1970s. Proponents contended increased competition would be a product of deregulation, and competition would benefit consumers in terms of lower fares. Congress accepted this contention and enacted the *Airline Deregulation Act of 1978*, which stipulates "no State or political subdivision thereof and no interstate agency or other political agency of two or more States shall enact or enforce any law, rule, regulation, standard, or other provision having the force and effect of law relating to rates, routes, or services of any air carriers having authority...to provide interstate air transportation."[45]

The *Motor Carrier Act of 1980* forbids subnational governments to engage in economic regulation of the motor carrier industry and the *Bus Regulatory Reform Act of 1982* contains an identical prohibition with respect to buses.[46] States, however, may exercise their police power to ensure the safety of trucks and buses. The former act did not induce additional expenditures by state governments, but the restraint contained in the latter act did. Prior to the 1982 act, a state government would grant a franchise to a bus company to operate buses between major cities provided it agreed to serve specified small municipalities; such service typically produced a deficit. Today, states desiring to ensure buses will serve smaller municipalities must contract for and pay bus companies providing the service.

A number of state legislatures during the Great Depression enacted price maintenance laws, termed "fair trade laws." These stipulated an agreement signed by a manufacturer with one retailer in the state providing a fixed price for an article was binding upon all retailers in the state. When these laws came under attack as violating the interstate commerce clause, Congress validated them by enacting the *Miller-Tydings Act of 1937* exempting such agreements from the *Sherman Antitrust Act of 1890*.[47] Congress in 1975 became more protective of consumer interests and repealed the authorization for the enactment of fair trade laws by state legislatures because they resulted in higher consumer prices.[48]

No Mandatory Retirement Age

In the 1960s Congress decided action was needed to protect older citizens against employment discrimination and it enacted the *Age Discrimination in Employment Act of 1967*.[49] In 1982, Congress amended the act to prohibit private and public employers from requiring their employees to retire because of advanced age.[50] State and local governments protested strongly that the amendment should not apply to firefighters and police, who must be in prime physical condition to perform their duties in the most effective manner.

The relief the subnational governments were seeking was not provided until 1986 when Congress enacted the *Age Discrimination in Employment Amendments* stipulating it is not unlawful for a state or a political subdivision

> To fail or refuse to hire or to discharge any individual because of such individual's age if such action is taken—
> > (1) with respect to the employment of an individual as a firefighter or as a law enforcement officer and the individual has attained the age for hiring or retirement in effect under applicable State or local law on March 3, 1983, and

(2) pursuant to a bonafide hiring or retirement plan that is not a sub-
terfuge to evade the purposes of this Act.[51]

Subnational Assistance Needed

Note has been made of the fact the *Atomic Energy Act of 1946* completely removed authority from state and local governments to regulate
ionizing radiation. Lack of resources, however, makes the U.S. Nuclear
Regulatory Commission (NRC) dependent upon state and local governments for emergency response personnel and equipment to protect
public health and safety in the event of a radioactive discharge at a
nuclear facility. A major controversy, described in a subsequent section,
swirled around attempts to have the commission repeal a regulation that
requires emergency planning around new civilian nuclear power plants,
including establishment of ten-mile evacuation zones, prior to the plants
being allowed to operate at full power (see below).[52]

The *Commercial Motor Vehicle Safety Act of 1986* was enacted at
the request of states unable to solve the regulatory problem caused by
numerous drivers of such vehicles, holding operator licenses from several states, who continued to drive after a license was revoked by a state
for a serious motor vehicle infraction.[53] The act allows states to continue
to issue commercial drivers licenses under federal standards and makes
possession of more than one commercial driver license a federal crime.
The *Motor Carrier Safety Improvement Act of 1999* mandates that if a
motor vehicle violation (other than a parking violation) has occurred, the
state in which it occurred must notify the state that issued the commercial motor vehicle operator license, and the issuing state must cancel,
revoke, or suspend the license in accordance with regulations promulgated by the secretary of transportation.[54]

Congress, in enacting the *Safe Drinking Water Act Amendments of
1986*—banning use of lead pipes, solder, and flux in public water systems—immediately became dependent upon subnational governments
for enforcing the prohibition.[55] Each state may determine the best means
of enforcing the ban, but failure to enforce the ban may result in the loss
of 5 percent of the federal safe drinking water grants-in-aid authorized
by the amendments.

State-Activities Exception

Congress, with one stipulated exception, preempted completely responsibility for establishing motor vehicle safety standards by enacting the
National Traffic and Motor Vehicle Safety Act of 1966.[56] The exception

applies to motor vehicles operated by state and local governments and allows these governments to procure special safety equipment for the vehicles provided it accords occupants a higher degree of safety.

The complete preemption of all other motor vehicle safety standards has been controversial because of court decisions holding the act preempts the tort claims statutes of the fifty states.

Grandfather Clause Exception

The *Professional and Amateur Sports Protection Act of 1992* forbids "a governmental entity to sponsor, operate, advertise, promote, license, or authorize by law or compact…a lottery, sweepstakes, or other betting, gambling, or wagering scheme based, directly or indirectly (through the use of geographical references or otherwise), on one or more competitive games in which amateur or professional athletes participate, or are intended to participate, or on one or more performances of such athletes in such games."[57] A grandfather clause stipulates the prohibition does not apply to the named sports gambling activities if they were in operation during specified dates.[58]

Limited Regulatory Turn-backs

Several complete preemption statutes authorize a federal officer or agency to delegate limited regulatory responsibilities to states. As noted, the *U.S. Grain Standards Act* completely preempts responsibility for determining grain quality standards but allows the administrator of the Federal Grain Inspection Service to delegate to state agencies authority to perform official inspection and weighing. Seven states presently inspect and weigh grain at export-port locations for foreign markets, and an additional seven states perform these functions at interior locations for domestic markets.[59] States are not fiscally burdened by performing these regulatory functions for the federal government since the states provide the services on a fee-for-service basis.

The *Resource Conservation and Recovery Act of 1976* preempts in part the authority of states to regulate hazardous waste and also permits a turn-back of regulatory authority.[60] Forty-nine states and territories currently have assumed responsibility for such programs. The *Hazardous and Solid Waste Amendments of 1984*, however, allow states to assume responsibility for the U.S. Environmental Protection Agency's (EPA) hazardous waste program. Fifty states and territories have assumed responsibility for the initial or basic program and many states have assumed responsibility for other parts of the program, such as land disposal restrictions.[61]

The completely preemptive *Federal Railroad Safety Act of 1970* authorizes state officers to inspect railroads to ensure that trains and tracks comply with national safety standards.[62] Currently, thirty states participate in the state safety program, funded in part by the Federal Railroad Administration.[63] The high rate of state participation in the program is reflective of the concern federal safety inspections are not carried out as frequently as they should be to ensure all trains and tracks meet the national safety standards.

As noted, the *Safe Drinking Water Act Amendments of 1986* ban the use of lead pipes, solder, and flux in any public drinking water system.[64] All states, except Wyoming, have been authorized by EPA to enforce the ban.

There is general agreement that the most successful major program involving states voluntarily administering federal inspection laws and regulations is the Nuclear Regulatory Commission's (NCR) agreement states program. Congress in 1959 amended the *Atomic Energy Act of 1946* to authorize the Atomic Energy Commission (now Nuclear Regulatory Commission) to sign agreements with states providing for them to assume designated regulatory responsibility for certain byproducts, source, and small quantities of special nuclear materials.[65] As of 2004, thirty-two states had signed agreements with the commission and three additional states were in the process of becoming agreement states.[66] NRC assists states in becoming agreement states and provides technical assistance to signatory states. These states and NRC jointly develop new regulations, regulatory guidance, and other regulatory initiatives.

In contrast to minimum standards preemption statutes, described in chapter 5, the agreement states program's only condition is that a state radiation-control program be compatible with, and not necessarily identical to, the commission's regulatory program.

The National Governors' Association's Committee on Energy and Environment in 1983 released the first comprehensive report on the agreement states program and concluded the "program is one of the most successful state/federal partnerships yet established in terms of (1) the flexibility provided States in assuming regulatory responsibility, (2) successful state performance of regulatory duties, and (3) consultation with States in the preparation of new regulations."[67]

My survey of agreement states produced a similar conclusion: All respondents reported excellent experience with the program, and no state had considered abandonment of the program. A few respondents referred to the lack of federal financial assistance for the program as a disadvantage. In particular, respondents were convinced state regulation is preferable to NRC regulation because state personnel are more readily available to licensees who have questions, licensing action is completed more rapidly; licensees' facilities are inspected more frequently and minor problems are corrected before they become major problems; state personnel spend less time in travel, thereby reducing inspection costs; and state and local governmental emergency personnel can respond to an incident more rapidly than NCR personnel.

It should be noted, however, that New Mexico in 1986 returned responsibility to the commission for the uranium-mill licensing program. It did so primarily because program costs diverted Radiation Protection Bureau personnel from other licensing responsibilities.[68]

Mandated State Action and Restraints

A number of complete preemption statutes mandate states to initiate a specified action or prohibit states to continue or initiate a specified action. The *Equal Employment Opportunity Act of 1972* and similar laws direct state legislatures to enact state laws complying with federal laws subject to the threat of civil or criminal penalties.[69] The *Fair Labor Standards Amendments of 1974* extend federal minimum wage and overtime pay provisions to nonsupervisory employees of state and local governments.[70] The National League of Cities challenged the constitutionality of the amendments by maintaining Congress exceeded its delegated powers and hence the amendments were ultra vires. The U.S. Supreme Court in 1976 agreed and invalidated them on the ground the extension violated the Tenth Amendment to the U.S. Constitution and threatened the "separate and independent existence" of subnational governments.[71] The Court in 1985, however, reversed the above decision and subnational governments became subject to the amendments (see chapter 6).[72]

The *Armored Car Industry Reciprocity Act of 1993* requires each state to recognize the license issued by a sister state to an armored car crew member to carry a weapon.[73] The *National Child Protection Act of 1993* directs each state criminal justice agency to "report child abuse crime information to, or index child abuse information in, the national criminal history background check system."[74] The *Full Faith and Credit for Child Support Orders Act of 1994* mandates procedures for child support orders when parents live in different states.[75] The *Violence Against Women Act of 2000* requires states to certify "its laws, policies, and practices do not require, in connection with the prosecution of any misdemeanor or felony domestic violence offence, or service of a protection order, or a petition for a protection order to protect a victim of domestic violence, stalking, or sexual assault, that the victim bear the costs associated with the filing of criminal charges against the offender" and other associated costs.[76] And the *Campus Sex Crimes Prevention Act of 2000* mandates states to have procedures ensuring "updated information" on sexually violent offenders who are students or employees of institutions of higher education "is promptly made available to a law enforcement agency having jurisdiction where" the institution is located and is entered into the state data system.[77]

State governments administer federal elections as well as state elections. The *Help America Vote Act of 2002* contains mandatory "uniform and nondiscriminatory election technology and administration requirements" for federal elections and amends the *National Voter Registration Act of 1993* by authorizing states to remove from the voting rolls an individual who failed to respond to a notification from the registrar of voters or vote in two or more consecutive federal elections.[78]

Relative to preemption restraints, the *Ocean Dumping Ban Act of 1988* prohibits the disposal of sewage sludge in an ocean.[79] Various municipalities have been fined for violating the act and have also incurred significantly increased disposal costs since expensive alternatives, such as incineration, have to be employed. Another important federal restraint, contained in the *Driver's Privacy Protection Act of 1994*, prohibits the release and use of certain personal information contained in state motor vehicle records.[80] A state motor vehicle department found to have a policy or practice not in compliance with the act is subject to a civil penalty of $5,000 for each day of noncompliance.[81]

Interstate Compact Formation Promotion

Each state is responsible, according to the *Low-Level Radioactive Waste Policy Act of 1980*, "for providing for the availability of capacity either within or outside the State for the disposal of low-level radioactive waste generated within its borders," except wastes generated by federal defense and/or research facilities.[82] In enacting this statute Congress explicitly encouraged states to form low-level radioactive waste interstate compacts for a period of five years, subject to congressional consent for each compact.[83] Ten compacts, involving forty-four states, have been enacted into law by state legislatures. Compacts typically involve only contiguous states, but one low-level radioactive waste compact was enacted into law by the Maine, Texas, and Vermont state legislatures.[84] Each commission, created by a compact, has been authorized by the act since 1986 to exclude wastes from nonmember states from its disposal site.

No compact commission had developed a new disposal facility by 1999, according to the U.S. General Accounting Office, because of exceptionally strong opposition by elected political leaders and citizens.[85] The office also explained the failure to establish a new facility was attributable to the availability of other disposal facilities, the high cost of a new facility, and a reduction in the volume of such wastes. To date, no such facility is operational.

Preemption Removal Petition

A controversy arose in New York City over the placement of toll booths for a bridge when a decision was made by the Triborough Bridge and Tunnel Authority to double tolls but collect them only at one end of toll bridges and tunnels. The argument involved the Verrazano Narrows Bridge which connects Brooklyn and Staten Island in New York City. U.S. Representative Guy V. Molinari of Staten Island attached a rider to a congressional appropriations act stipulating tolls can be collected only as vehicles exit the bridge in Staten Island.[86] This requirement enables Staten Island residents to travel on the bridge to Brooklyn without paying a toll and to return to their homes by way of the Holland and Lincoln Tunnels under the Hudson River and a New Jersey to Staten Island bridge which initially was not tolled. This preemption statute causes increased congestion and air pollution at the entrance to the tunnels and reduces revenues for the Triborough Bridge and Tunnel Authority. Although the act authorizes the New York governor to petition the secretary of transportation to remove the toll booths' location requirement, no governor has filed a petition.

State Veto of a U.S. Administrative Decision

The U.S. secretary of energy is authorized by the *Nuclear Waste Policy Act of 1982* to select a site where a high-level radioactive waste facility will be built, but the site is subject to a veto by the governor or the state legislature of the concerned state.[87] The act also provides Congress may override the state veto.

Congress in December 1987 ignored the procedure for selecting the site outlined in the act and included in the *Omnibus Budget Reconciliation Act of 1988* an amendment to the 1982 act removing sites in Texas and Washington, two of the three sites under consideration by the Department of Energy as a location for the facility.[88] The amendment in effect selected the Yucca Mountain site in Nevada, subject to tests for suitability. Congress formally overrode the notice of disapproval of the Yucca Mountain site submitted by the governor of Nevada on April 8, 2002.[89]

Contingent Complete Preemption

The presence of two conditions within a state or local government triggers the application of the *Voting Rights Act of 1965*, as amended to a subnational unit.[90] The conditions are: a test or device employed to abridge the rights of citizens to vote because of race or color as of November 1, 1964; and a determination by the director of the U.S. Bureau of the Census that fewer than 50 percent of persons of voting age were registered to vote on the same date or less than 50 percent of persons of voting age exercised the franchise in the 1964 presidential election.

Should a determination be made that the act applies to a state or a political subdivision, the covered unit automatically becomes subject to the act's preclearance requirements prohibiting the unit to enact or administer any change, no matter how minor, in its election system unless the attorney general of the United States, within sixty days of submission of a proposed change to her/him, fails to register an objection. A covered unit has an alternative; that is, to seek a declaratory judgment by the District Court for the District of Columbia holding the proposed change would not abridge the right to vote of protected citizens.

This act has been amended on several occasions and the latest amendments in 1992 require covered jurisdictions must provide bilingual voting materials if any protected language minority—Alaskan Natives, Asiatic Americans, American Indians, or persons of Spanish heritage—constitutes 5 percent or more of the voting-age population.[91]

A slightly different type of contingent preemption, authorized by the *Prescription Drug Amendments of 1992*, provides any person engaged in the wholesale distribution of drugs in interstate commerce must register with the secretary of health and human resources unless the state has "a program that meets the guidelines" established by the secretary.[92] This act contains a sunset provision effective September 14, 1994.

Contingent Fishing Moratorium

The *Atlantic Striped Bass Conservation Act Amendments of 1986* were designed to encourage states to comply with the fisheries management plans developed by the interstate-compact–created Atlantic States Marine Fisheries Commission which lacks enforcement powers.[93] Failure of a state to comply with a commission plan results in a striped-bass fishing moratorium imposed by the U.S. Fish and Wildlife Service

and the Marine Fisheries Service in the coastal waters of the noncomply-
ing state.

National Title Assertion

A complete preemption statute paradoxically can be state friendly.
Technological developments by the early 1980s were aiding searchers to
locate shipwrecks, but a legal question was raised: Who holds title to a
shipwreck? Congress answered this question by enacting the *Abandoned
Shipwreck Act of 1987*, asserting a national title to each historic abandoned shipwreck and directing the title be transferred automatically to
the state within whose waters the shipwreck is located.[94]

Cooperative Enforcement

In contrast to the limited turn-back to states of regulatory authority
described above, the *Age Discrimination in Employment Amendments of
1986* grant the Equal Employment Opportunity Commission authority
to sign cooperative enforcement agreements with state or local government fair employment agencies.[95]

The *Oil Pollution Act of 1990* authorizes states to enforce on their
respective navigable waters only "the requirements for evidence of
financial responsibility" of the party responsible for a ship carrying oil
as cargo or fuel.[96]

The *Anti Car Theft Act of 1992* is a complete preemption statute
establishing a national motor vehicle title information system and theft
prevention standards relative to motor vehicle parts.[97] The act also provides grants-in-aid to state and local governments to help them curb
motor vehicle thefts and related violence, and directs the U.S. attorney
general and U.S. attorneys "to work with State and local officials to
investigate car thefts, including... armed carjacking...."[98]

In 1994, Congress enacted the *Telemarketing and Consumer Fraud
and Abuse Prevention Act*, a complete preemption statute. It authorizes
each state, as *parens patriae*, to "bring a civil suit in an appropriate
District Court of the United States to enjoin such telemarketing, to
enforce compliance with such rule of the [Federal Communications
Commission], to obtain damages, restitution, or other compensation on
behalf of" its residents.[99]

The *Consumer Credit Reporting Reform Act of 1996* also grants
authority to the chief law enforcement officer of each state to bring an
action in the U.S. district court to enjoin a violation of the act, and also
exempts from preemption any state law "relating to the prescreening of

consumer reports" and other specified state laws in effect in 1996, including "section 54A(a) of chapter 93 of the Massachusetts Annotated Laws...."[100]

In addition, the *Antiterrorism and Effective Death Penalty Act of 1996* authorizes state and local government law enforcement officers to arrest an illegal alien or a person convicted of a felony in the United States who was deported or left the country after conviction subject to obtaining information from the Immigration and Naturalization Service on the status of any such person.[101]

The *Children's Online Privacy Protection Act of 1998* grants the attorney general of a state authority to bring a *parens patriae* civil suit in the U.S. District Court if he or she believes "an interest of the residents of that State has been or is threatened, or adversely affected by the engagement of any person in a practice that violates any regulation of the Commission" [Federal Trade Commission].[102]

The *State and Local Enforcement of Federal Communications Commission Regulations on Use of Citizens Band Radio Equipment Act of 2000* takes a different approach to enforcement by allowing a state legislature or a local government legislative body to enact a law prohibiting a violation of specified regulations promulgated by the Federal Communications Commission.[103]

A partial preemption statute also may authorize state enforcement. The *Telephone Disclosure and Dispute Resolution Act of 1992*, for example, authorizes a state to bring a civil action on behalf of its citizens in the U.S. District Court to enforce compliance with rules and regulations promulgated under the act by the Federal Communications Commission.[104]

Uniform Law Exemption

The *Electronic Signatures in Global and National Commerce Act of 2000* preempts the electronic signatures laws and regulations of forty-four states, but provides an exception if a state legislature enacts "the Uniform Electronic Transactions Act as approved and recommended for enactment in all the States by the National Conference of Commissions on Uniform State Laws in 1999."[105] If a state legislature in enacting the uniform law approves an amendment to the law, the amendment is preempted to the extent it is inconsistent with the congressional act.

This act also respects the semi-sovereign status of states by providing exceptions for their actions taken as market participants by stipulating the act "shall not apply to the statutes, regulations, or other rules of law governing procurement by any State or any agency or instrumentality thereof."[106]

Minimum Training Requirements

The *Food Quality Protection Act of 1996*, a complete preemption statute, amends the *Federal Insecticide, Fungicide, and Rodenticide Act of 1975*. It authorizies states to establish minimum requirements for the training of applicators and service technicians who deposit pesticides to control pests which damage structures and lawns, and limits the authority of the Environmental Protection Agency administrator "to ensuring that each State understands the provisions of this section."[107]

Nuclear Evacuation Plans and Truck Size and Weight

As explained above, Congress has assigned certain federal regulatory commissions, departments, or agencies responsibility for a preempted function, yet these commissions or agencies lack essential complementary powers and resources to ensure the full implementation of their assigned responsibilities. Protection of the public from radioactive discharges by nuclear power plants is an example of a governmental function that requires the cooperation of subnational governments with the federal government if the protection is to be effective. Congressional highway preemption statutes also are dependent heavily upon the cooperation of state and local governments for their implementation.

Nuclear Evacuation Plans

The federal government's dependence upon a state and several of its political subdivisions for the successful implementation of a completely preempted function is revealed by the experience with nuclear power plants and other major nuclear facilities. Governor Mario M. Cuomo of New York requested the assistance of U.S. Senator Daniel P. Moynihan of New York in a 1983 letter: "I am writing to request that you initiate a hearing process to: (1) achieve a clarification and a precise specification of the respective responsibilities of local, state, and federal governments for off-site emergency plans at our nation's nuclear plants, and (2) devise a federal system for the administration and funding of the extensive activities undertaken by all three levels of government in the implementation, and (3) examine the consequences of decisions required by this off-site emergency planning process."[108]

The continuing controversy involving the under construction Shoreham nuclear power plant on Long Island induced Governor Cuomo to register his objections with U.S. Secretary of Energy John S. Herrington. Governor Cuomo objected to the Department of Energy's support of the evacuation plans drafted by the Long Island Lighting Company (LILCO):

> The emergency preparedness situation concerning the Shoreham plant is the result of scrupulous and deliberate decisions of the County of Suffolk and New York State not to adopt or implement an off-site emergency plan for Shoreham. These governmental decisions were reached through the exercise of police powers which are vested inherently in the state government and the local government to which the State has delegated those powers. The efforts of your Department to promote LILCO's emergency plan over constitutionally sound objections of the State and local governments is an affront to the sovereignty of New York State and an injury to the people of New York.[109]

The governor buttressed his statement by quoting President Ronald Reagan's statement that "this Administration does not favor the imposition of Federal Government authority over the objections of State and local governments in matters regarding the adequacy of an emergency evacuation plan for a nuclear power plant such as Shoreham." This controversy ultimately was settled when New York State negotiated an agreement with LILCO for the termination of the construction of the nuclear power plant.

A similar controversy raged over the February 26, 1986, test of the evacuation procedures at the Seabrook nuclear power plant under construction in New Hampshire. Massachusetts and seven New Hampshire towns refused to participate in a proposed evacuation of nearby residents exercise because of safety considerations. Chairman John Walker of the Hampton, New Hampshire, Board of Selectmen emphasized "[t]here just isn't a highway structure in place to handle the traffic, yet they have known for seven years—since Three Mile Island—that they needed an evacuation plan."[110]

The plan was tested and the Federal Emergency Management Agency identified several major problems. Sixty percent of the evacuation buses failed to report to their proper sites, and the backup plan was inadequate to compensate for local governments that refused to participate.[111] Furthermore, a telephone number provided on radio broadcasts as an emergency information number was the number of the commercial loan department of a bank in nearby Portsmouth, New Hampshire.[112]

Governor Michael S. Dukakis of Massachusetts announced on September 20, 1986, he would not submit evacuation plans for the Massachusetts portion of the evacuation zone and suggested that consideration be given to converting the Seabrook facility into a fossil-fuel burning plant.[113] Six days later, Senior Vice President Derrickson of New Hampshire Yankee informed the Nuclear Regulatory Commission's (NCR) Advisory Committee on Reactor Safeguards that the risk posed by the plant was lower than was estimated in 1983 and the evacuation zone should be reduced to a two-mile radius.[114]

These controversies persuaded NRC in 1980 to promulgate a rule providing for a ten-mile radius emergency evacuation zone around a nuclear power plant and in 1987 to promulgate a rule allowing the licensing of a nuclear power plant even though subnational governments do not participate in the emergency evacuation plans.[115] The commission referred to the serious financial problems that would befall a utility company which had constructed and was forced to abandon a nuclear power plant and issued a statement highlighting its preemptive authority: "...at least in situations where non-cooperation in offsite emergency planning is motivated by safety issues, vesting state or local governments with *de facto* veto authority over full-power operation is inconsistent with the fundamental thrust of the Atomic Energy Act whereby the Commission is given exclusive *de jure* authority to license nuclear power plants and to impose radiological safety requirements for their construction and operation."[116]

The NRC's Atomic Safety and Licensing Board on April 22, 1987, rejected the application of the Public Service Company of New Hampshire for a reduction in the emergency evacuation zone from a ten-mile radius to a one-mile radius extending inland from the Seabrook nuclear power plant.[117] However, NRC on October 29, 1987, amended its rules to permit the operation of nuclear power plants in the absence of state and/or local governmental participation in off-site emergency planning.[118] And NRC in 1990 unanimously voted to license the Seabrook nuclear power plant, the U.S. Court of Appeals for the District of Columbia Circuit rejected a Massachusetts petition for a stay of the license pending a ruling in a suit brought by Massachusetts and other plant opponents.[119]

The Seabrook nuclear power plant case reveals the preemptive power of the federal government and its lack of administrative capacity to guarantee public safety in the event of a radioactive discharge at such a plant. The cooperation of state and local governments is essential if residents in the area of a nuclear facility need to be evacuated. Cooperation and not compulsion is the key. The federal government probably could secure greater cooperation by subnational governments if grants-in-aid were offered to them and they were allowed to exercise a limited degree of regulatory authority.

The September 11, 2001, terrorists' attacks upon the United States ignited fears that such attacks in the future may involve nuclear generating plants. Emergency plans for protecting citizens against an accidental radioactive discharge from the Indian Point nuclear power plant in Westchester County, located approximately thirty-five miles north of Manhattan, have been criticized for years as inadequate. The controversy reached a new height when a 500-page draft report, prepared by a former Federal Emergency Management Agency director, was released and detailed the inadequacies of the response plans.[120] In common with the Seabrook nuclear power plant emergency plans, the Indian Point plans cover only a ten-mile radius, encompassing 298,013 persons. While the NRC in November 2002 concluded a September 24, 2002, emergency exercise revealed the evacuation plans were adequate, the report, noted Putnam County officers in the field were unable to radio radiation readings because the frequency was jammed, a number of sirens did not function, and a few area fire chiefs were skeptical that volunteer firemen would respond because they would be protecting the safety of their families.

The New York State Emergency Management Office annually decides whether to certify the adequacy of the emergency evacuation plans. In January 2003, three of four neighboring county executives announced they would refuse to certify the adequacy of the plans, and subsequently the director of the State Emergency Management Office notified the Federal Emergency Management Agency (FEMA) the state would not certify the plan.[121] Local opposition to the plans was increased by a July 2003 report, prepared by the plant's owner, which concluded nine hours and twenty-five minutes would be required to evacuate all residents within the ten-mile zone around the plant, in contrast to a 1994 report indicating the required time would be five and one-half hours.[122]

In February 2003, FEMA released a 500-page preliminary findings report and announced it could not provide "reasonable assurance" the emergency evacuation plans were adequate. It nevertheless found the plans adequate in July 2003 and NRC approved them.[123] In August 2003, NRC chairman Nils J. Diaz posted a letter to concerned local government officers asserting "Indian Point has a 'strong defensive strategy and capability,'" and that the plant's security unit "successfully protected the plant from repeated mock-adversary attacks."[124] The Union of Concerned Scientists on September 7, 2003, revealed that NRC in 1996 had categorized as serious the problem of corrosive pipes in the emergency cooling systems at nuclear power plants. The systems are designed to prevent the reactors from melting should a water pipe rupture.[125]

Controversies continue relative to the adequacy of emergency evacuation plans for other nuclear power plants. In 2003, local government officers decryied the inadequacy of such plans for the Yankee nuclear power plant in Vernon, Vermont. The boards of selectmen in Brattleboro and Marlboro, Vermont, have questioned the adequacy of the plans that have been rejected by the latter board.[126] Hinsdale, New Hampshire, located across the Connecticut River from the plant, refused to participate in an emergency evacuation drill on April 8, 2003, and stressed the town's public schools are less than one mile from the plant.[127]

These brief nuclear power plant case studies reveal the lack of congressional response to the legitimate complaints of subnational governments and suggest the political safeguards theory is invalid (see chapter 7). The following case study examines congressional responsiveness to complaints on other subjects by elected state and local government officers.

Truck Size and Weight

Congress created confusion relative to responsibility for public safety when the *Surface Transportation Assistance Act of 1982* (STAA) was enacted. The provisions of STAA allow heavy trucks, including tandem trailers, to operate on interstate highways, certain federally aided primary routes designated by the secretary of transportation, and local "access" roads to motels, restaurants, service stations, and terminals.[128] This preemption statute, however, contains no criteria for determining whether sections of interstate designated highways constructed prior to the *National Interstate and Defense Highways Act of 1956* and federally aided primary routes are capable of accommodating larger and heavier trucks safely or for determining which local roads are bona fide "access" routes. It is apparent Congress enacted this preemption statute in response to the powerful trucking industry, a major contributor to congressional election campaigns, and failed to consider adequately the safety problems subnational governments would not be allowed to address.

This act specifically stipulates that "No State shall establish, maintain, or enforce any regulation of commerce which imposes a vehicle length limitation of less than forty-eight feet on the length of the semi-trailer unit operating in a truck tractor-semitrailer-trailer combination, on any segment of the National System of Interstate and Defense Highways and those classes of qualifying Federal-aid Primary System highways as designated by the Secretary."[129]

The act also forbids a state to enact or enforce a law prohibiting large trucks to travel "to and from the Interstate Highway System to terminals and facilities for food, fuel, repairs, and rest."[130] Interestingly, the act employs conditional federal highway grants-in-aid, a type of informal preemption, to induce states to allow heavier trucks to be driven on interstate highways.

The trucking industry had a legitimate complaint against the patchwork quilt of conflicting state truck size and weight limits, and Congress responded favorably to their complaint because states had failed to engage in negotiations leading to the enacting of harmonious truck size and weight limits. The driver of a triple rig, for example, would have to decouple one or two trailers at the border of certain states prior to entering them. Nevertheless, Congress can be faulted for its failure to investigate or to direct the secretary of transportation to employ safety criteria in determining whether segments of interstate and other highways could accommodate large trucks safely.

New York State Executive Deputy Commissioner of Transportation John Mladinov testified at a state legislative public hearing on August 9, 1983, that traffic congestion and the substandard condition of New York City metropolitan area highways necessitated the prohibition of tandem trucks in the city and on Long Island because "many of the designated highways have serious geometric, safety, and capacity problems."[131] In 1983, the New York State Department of Transportation (NYSDOT) identified 88.46 miles of federally designated highways with substandard lane widths for a portion of the total length of the routes.[132] The Federal Highway Administration (FHWA) was partially responsive to the New York State complaint and on May 3, 1983, removed several of the routes from the federally designated highway system; the removed routes generally were parallel to interstate highways meeting all safety standards.[133] Nevertheless, fourteen of the non–New York City–Long Island highways classified by NYSDOT as substandard were not removed by FHWA from the designated system.

An additional national-state controversy was generated when Congress amended STAA in 1983, mandating all states, with the exception of Hawaii, to permit 102-inch-wide trucks on all federally designated highways if lane widths exceed twelve feet.[134] Expressing opposition to the new mandate, Sean Tisdale of the Idaho transportation department stressed: "We are not against trucks out here—after all, we allow double trailers and even triple trailers on our interstates and many other roads. But this plan simply did not put enough emphasis on the safety factor on mountain roads."[135] Vermont Attorney General John H. Easton, Jr. reacted to the new statute by stating, "it looks like some guy with a Rand McNally map sat in an office here and drew the whole thing up and he simply forgot that Vermont has hills."[136]

Congressional Response

Strong protests by state government officers against STAA and its amendment led to congressional responses to state safety concerns in the form of the *Tandem Truck Safety Act of 1984* and the *Motor Carrier Safety Act of 1984.*[137]

The first act established a procedure authorizing the governor of a state, subsequent to consulting concerned local governments, to notify the secretary of transportation that the governor has determined a specific segment(s) "of the national System of Interstate Highways is not capable of safely accommodating motor vehicles" of the length permitted by STAA or 102-inch-wide vehicles other than buses.[138] The act also addressed state officers' safety concerns with respect to local access roads by providing "nothing in this section shall be construed as preventing any State or local government from imposing any reasonable restriction, based on safety considerations, on any truck tractor-semitrailer combination in which the semitrailer has a length not to exceed 28 1/2 feet and which generally operates as part of a vehicle combination" as described in the act.[139]

The *Motor Carrier Safety Act of 1984* directed the secretary of transportation, within eighteen months of the enactment date, to promulgate regulations establishing minimum safety standards for commercial motor vehicles ensuring that

(1) commercial motor vehicles are safely maintained, equipped, loaded, and operated;
(2) the responsibilities imposed upon operators of commercial motor vehicles do not impair their ability to operate such vehicles safely;
(3) the physical condition of operators of commercial motor vehicles is adequate to enable them to operate such vehicles safely; and
(4) the operation of commercial motor vehicles does not have deleterious effects on the physical condition of such operators.[140]

In addition, the statute created a safety panel to advise the secretary of transportation with respect to whether a "state law or regulation is additional to or more stringent than a regulation issued by the Secretary."[141] Any such law or regulation may be enforced commencing five years after the enactment date of the national statute unless the secretary determines "(A) there is no safety benefit associated with such state law or regulation; (B) such state law or regulation is incompatible with the regulation issued by the Secretary;...or (C) enforcement of such state law or regulation would be an undue burden on interstate commerce."[142]

The act also authorizes any individual to petition the secretary of transportation for the issuance of a waiver from a determination of the secretary that a state law or regulation is preempted.[143] The Blackmun thesis is supported by this case study.

Summary and Conclusions

The U.S. Supreme Court generally has accorded Congress broad discretion relative to the enactment of statutes explicitly removing regulatory authority from states and their political subdivisions and has held many statutes lacking a preemption provision to be preemptive.

Our typology of complete federal preemption statutes is helpful in determining whether the stated goals of a preemption statute can be achieved without the assistance of subnational governments. The case studies of emergency evacuation plans for a ten-mile evacuation area around nuclear power electric-generating plants reveal the national government is incapable of protecting the safety of citizens residing in the evacuation area, emergency assistance by state and local governments is essential, and the required plans are inadequate. These studies also demonstrate the unresponsiveness of Congress to the complaints of the concerned two states and their concerned local governments to the inadequacies of the evacuation plans.

The case study of complete congressional preemption of truck size and weights on certain highways highlights the concerns of state and local government officers relative to the failure of Congress to include criteria in STAA for determining whether pre-1956 highways can accommodate larger and heavier trucks. This case study reveals Congress will respond affirmatively to the complaints of subnational governmental officers. Congressional responsiveness to this public safety problem, in contrast to the evacuation plans case study, may be attributable to the fact STAA and its amendments impact all states, whereas the evacuation plans affect only two state governments and a small number of local governments.

Chapter 5 contains typologies of *imperium in imperio* federalism and partial congressional preemption statutes. One such statute—*Air Quality Act of 1967*—also contains a section that completely preempts state regulation (this is of emissions from new motor vehicles.)

Chapter 5

IMPERIUM IN IMPERIO AND LIMITED PREEMPTION

The undesirability of a static distribution of political powers between the national government and the states was recognized fully by the drafters of the U.S. Constitution, who included in the fundamental document procedures for formally amending it and authorization for Congress to employ its delegated powers to remove concurrent regulatory powers from the states. The Bill of Rights, demanded by persons fearing an omnipotent and abusive national government, placed limitations only upon congressional powers; no limitations were imposed upon state powers by amendments until ratification of the Fourteenth Amendment in 1868. This amendment laid the constitutional basis for enlarged judicial preemption, including judicial receivership of certain state government institutions and local governments, a subject examined in chapter 6.

Congressional preemption of state regulatory powers, as explained in chapter 1, generally was not a common occurrence and involved primarily limited preemption until 1965. State legislatures in the post–World War II period on a number of occasions enacted a uniform state law or an interstate compact in an attempt to forestall threatened congressional preemption. An example of an unsuccessful attempt to create a regional regulatory commission by an interstate compact is the Mid-Atlantic States Air Pollution Control Compact. Enacted by the state legislatures in Connecticut, New Jersey, and New York, this compact was a response to President Lyndon B. Johnson's air pollution message to

Congress urging enactment of a law completely preempting responsibility for air pollution abatement.[1] Similarly, the National Association of Insurance Commissioners in 2002 drafted the Insurance Product Regulation Compact in response to the threat of further congressional preemption of state authority to regulate the business of insurance.[2]

The great increase in the number of post-1965 limited preemption statutes enacted by Congress can be attributed to the following seven principal factors. First, the inadequacy of interstate cooperation as a mechanism for addressing effectively many multistate problems was evident to the president and many members of Congress.

Second, the increasing use of motor vehicles and continuing industrialization of the nation magnified the air pollution problem and its associated deleterious impact on the health of citizens. Airsheds are national and international in nature, respect no state or national boundary, and necessitate national and international remedial action.

Third, the failure of individual states to initiate corrective action to solve serious public problems within their respective boundaries generated pressure for congressional action. A U.S. representative wrote to the author in 1986 and attributed the increased pace of enactment of preemption statutes to "the failure of local governments to do what the Federal Government believes should be done." A western state governor in the same year informed the author there is congressional reluctance "to rely on the States due to special interest group influence."

Fourth, manufacturing industries were burdened by nonharmonious state regulatory standards that increased their costs significantly. The motor vehicle industry in particular lobbied Congress to enact a statute completely removing state authority to establish new motor vehicle emission standards. A second U.S. representative wrote to the author in 1986 and reported "industry has gradually decided a single standard, though tough, is likely to be better than fifty standards, some loose, some very tough." Another governor wrote to the author in the same year and supported congressional preemption because "industry can function more efficiently when state to state differences in product regulation are eliminated."

Fifth, a majority of the members of Congress became convinced a number of expensive federal grants-in-aid had failed as incentives to persuade many state legislatures to enact harmonious regulatory statutes. A third governor informed the author in 1986 that preemption is employed more frequently because "the federal government does not have the resources to buy compliance with national goals through a grant."

Sixth, newly formed environmental and other public interest groups encouraged citizens to write to their U.S. representatives and senators and urge them to enact preemption statutes and also lobbied Congress effectively for the enactment of such statutes.

Seventh, a new type of member of congress was elected commencing in the 1960s. Many had never held a state or local government elected office and lacked an in-depth understanding of the reasons why the drafters of the U.S. Constitution devised the world's first federal system rather than providing for a unitary system with all regulatory powers confided to Congress. A U.S. senator wrote to the author in 1986 and attributed the very significant increase in the number of preemption statutes during the previous two decades to "Democratic control of the Congress." A second U.S. senator in the same year assigned responsibility for the explosion in preemption statutes to "Congressmen not living up to the spirit of the Constitution."

The foci of this chapter are the exercise of concurrent powers by state legislatures and Congress under the original *imperium in imperio* system established by the U.S. Constitution, enactment of various types of limited preemption statutes by Congress, and the impact of certain of these statutes on gubernatorial-legislative relations in the typical state.

Imperium in Imperio

The heart of the federal system is an *imperium in imperio*, or an empire within an empire, with each possessing substantial powers. There would be no federal system without the exercise of relatively autonomous political powers by a national legislature and subnational legislatures as political powers otherwise would be centralized in the national plane (a unitary system) or in the subnational plane (a confederate system).

As described earlier, Alexander Hamilton, John Jay, and James Madison wrote a series of letters to editors of New York City newspapers, between September 1787 and August 1788, explaining the major provisions of the proposed U.S. Constitution. These letters remain the best explanation of why various provisions were included in the fundamental document. In "The Federalist Number 32, Hamilton explained there were three types of national powers: "where the Constitution in express terms granted an exclusive authority to the Union; where it granted in one instance an authority to the Union, and in another prohibited the States from exercising the like authority; and where it granted an authority to the Union to which a similar authority in the States would be absolutely and totally contradictory and repugnant."[3] He cited the power to establish a uniform rule of naturalization as an example of the third type of exclusive power.

Available evidence suggests the drafters of the Constitution operated under the assumption Congress would confine its attention and activities in the foreseeable future almost exclusively to foreign affairs, national defense, major public works projects such as river and harbor projects, and regulation of interstate commerce. They, of course, recognized Congress would exercise its preemption powers to prevent the enactment of certain state laws and to nullify state actions when necessary to perfect the economic and political union, and included the supremacy of the laws clause (art. VI) to ensure a congressional statute based upon a delegated power would prevail whenever there was a conflict with a state law or constitutional provision.

The drafters observed the undesirable impact of state-erected mercantilistic trade barriers during the confederation and sought to ensure no such barriers would exist in the new federal system by including a provision in the Constitution (art. I, §8) delegating blanket power to Congress to regulate commerce among the several states. Justice Robert H. Jackson of the U.S. Supreme Court in 1949 described the interstate commerce clause's dormant nature in the following terms:

> The commerce clause is one of the most prolific sources of national power and an equally prolific source of conflict with legislation of the States. While the Constitution vests in Congress the power to regulate commerce among the States, it does not say what the States may or may not do in the absence of congressional action, nor how to draw the line between what is and what is not commerce among the States. Perhaps even more than by interpretation of its written word, this Court has advanced the solidarity and property of this nation by the meaning it has given to these great silences of the Constitution.[4]

Congress and state legislatures are authorized by the Constitution to exercise two types of concurrent powers. The first type includes the power to tax. Congress may not preempt the taxing powers of states unless they are employed to place an undue burden on interstate commerce or discriminate against a person or group in violation of the equal protection of the laws clause of the Constitution's Fourteenth Amendment. Second, ratification by the states of the Constitution did not restrict the authority of state legislatures to determine the nature of electoral systems and to prescribe voter qualifications, and the Constitution specifically stipulated electors of members of the U.S. House of Representatives "shall have the qualifications requisite for electors of the most numerous branch of the State Legislature" (art. I, §2).

The Fifteenth Amendment to the U.S. Constitution, ratified in 1870, guarantees "the right of citizens of the United States to vote shall not be denied or abridged by the United States or by any State on Account of race, color, or previous condition of servitude" and empowers Congress to enforce the guarantee "by appropriate legislation."

Congress in 1870 exercised this new power by enacting a law making private or public obstruction of the right to vote a federal misdemeanor punishable by imprisonment for no less than one month and not longer than one year.[5] This act was amended in 1871 to authorize federal oversight of the election of U.S. representatives in every city and town with a population over 20,000 "whenever...there shall be two citizens thereof who...shall make known, in writing to the Judge of the Circuit Court of the United States for the Circuit wherein such city or town shall be, their desire to have said registration, or said election, or both, guarded and scrutinized."[6]

The constitutionality of the act and its amendment were challenged and the U.S. Supreme Court in 1875 invalidated sections not limited solely to the protection of the voting rights of black citizens, since the act also provided for the punishment of those who interfered with the voting rights of white citizens.[7] Congress in 1894 repealed the most important remaining sections of the two acts and states became relatively free of direct federal supervision of the conduct of elections until the congressional enactment of the *Voting Rights Act of 1965*, a suspensive complete preemption statute described in chapters 4 and 6.

This chapter identifies seven types of *imperium in imperio*, which can be contrasted with limited congressional preemption statutes, the subject of the latter part of this chapter.

State Powers Not Subject To Preemption

The taxation powers of states, as noted above, are not subject to congressional preemption unless their exercise is based on mercantilistic principles imposing an inordinate burden upon interstate commerce or denies equal protection of the laws. Section 10 of Article I of the U.S. Constitution stipulates: "No State shall, without the consent of the Congress, lay any imposts or duties on imports or exports, except what may be absolutely necessary for executing its inspection laws." This provision, known as the import-export clause, applies also to political subdivisions of states.

Gwinnett County, Georgia, imposed an ad valorem property tax on imported Michelin tires. The Superior Court for Gwinnett County issued a permanent injunction against the collection of the tax, but this decision was reversed in 1975 by the Georgia Supreme Court on the ground the tires had lost their status as imports.[8] In 1975, the U.S.

Supreme Court ruled the constitutional prohibition of levying such a tax on imports without the consent of Congress does not apply to the ad valorem property tax because the tires in question were not in transit, were stored with other tires in a warehouse "operated no differently than...a distribution warehouse dealing solely in domestic goods."[9] In contrast, the U.S. District Court for the Northern District of California in 1982 opined that "as a matter of federal supremacy, the power of the State to discriminate against rail transportation property for purposes of applying tax rates was preempted by the passage of the RRR Act in 1976."[10]

Must states secure the consent of Congress prior to entering into interstate compacts? Section 10 of Article I of the U.S. Constitution stipulates: "No State shall, without the consent of Congress,...enter into any agreement or compact with another state." A literal reading of the compact clause leads to an affirmative answer to the question raised. Nevertheless, the U.S. Supreme Court in 1893 in *Virginia v. Tennessee*, issued an opinion holding such consent is required only for "political" compacts affecting the balance of power between states and the Union.[11]

Constitutional authority has not been delegated to Congress to preempt directly the vast array of powers the states possess to deliver services to their citizens, unless the services are provided in a discriminatory manner. Similarly, Congress lacks the power to preempt state regulation of business firms and individuals unless such regulations violate the interstate commerce clause, or the due process, equal protection, or privileges and immunities guarantees of the Fourteenth Amendment. Chapter 3 explains that the national legislature has gained considerable influence over the states' reserved powers by means of conditional grants-in-aid and crossover sanctions.

Direct and Positive Conflict of Laws

To reduce the preemptive impact of its legislation, Congress frequently includes a savings provision in a law which stipulates a state law on the same subject is valid absent a direct and positive conflict between the two laws, in which event the supremacy of the laws clause of the Constitution provides for the invalidation of the state law. Such a proviso dates to at least 1911 when Congress enacted a corrupt practices act with the proviso it "shall not be construed to annul or vitiate the laws of any State, not directly in conflict herewith, relating to the nomination or election of candidates for the offices herein named, or to exempt any such candidate from complying with such State laws."[12]

A more recent example of such a proviso is found in the *Civil Rights Act of 1964*: "Nothing in this Act shall be construed as indicating an intent on the part of Congress to occupy the field in which any such title operates to the exclusion of state laws on the same subject matter, nor shall any provision of this Act be construed as invalidating any provision of state law unless such provision is inconsistent with any of the purposes of this Act, or any provision thereof."[13] An almost identical provision is contained in the *Drug Abuse Control Amendments of 1965*.[14] A similar section is found in the *Gun Control Act of 1968*: "No provision of this chapter shall be construed as indicating an intent on the part of the Congress to occupy the field in which such provision operates to the exclusion of the law of any State on the same matter, unless there is a direct and positive conflict between such provision and the law of the State so that the two can not be reconciled or consistently stand together."[15] The *Truth in Lending Act of 1968* declares it "does not annul, alter, or affect, or exempt any creditor from complying with the laws of any State relating to the disclosure of information in connection with credit transactions, except to the extent that those laws are inconsistent with the provisions of this title or regulations thereunder, and then only to the extent of the inconsistency."[16] And the *Federal Election Campaign Act of 1971* provides: "Nothing in this Act shall be deemed to invalidate or make inapplicable any provision of any State law, except where compliance with such provision of law would result in a violation of a provision of this Act." The act also includes a restraint stipulating "no provision of State law shall be construed to prohibit any person from taking any action authorized by this Act or from making any expenditures...which he could lawfully make under this Act."[17]

A minimum preemption standards provision is included in the *Federal Railroad Safety Act of 1970*, which authorizes states to adopt laws, rules, regulations, orders, and standards relative to railroad safety more stringent than the counterpart federal ones "when necessary to eliminate or reduce an essentially local safety hazard, and when not incompatible with any federal law, rule, regulation, order, or standard, and when not creating an undue burden on interstate commerce."[18]

The *Occupational Safety and Health Act of 1970* contains slightly different language: "Nothing in this Act shall prevent any State agency or court from asserting jurisdiction under State law over any occupational safety or health issues with respect to which no [federal] standard is in effect."[19] The *Federal Election Campaign Act of 1971* intentionally seeks to reduce the preemptive impact of the act by declaring "[n]othing in this Act shall be deemed to invalidate or make inapplicable any provision of any State law, except where compliance with such provision of law would result in a violation of a provision of this Act."[20]

In 1991, Congress enacted the *Truth in Savings Act,* regulating deposit accounts, but exempted from preemption "the law of any State relating to the disclosure of yields payable or terms for accounts to the extent such State law requires the disclosure of such yields or terms of account, except to the extent that those laws are inconsistent with the provisions of this Act, and then only to the extent of the inconsistency."[21] Similarly, the *Telephone Disclosure and Dispute Resolution Act of 1992* stipulates state laws on the same subject are valid unless inconsistent with the act.[22]

The *Interstate Commerce Commission Termination Act of 1995* is a broad preemption statute containing two savings provisions—a subnational governmental law or regulation that "is no more burdensome than compliance with, a provision of this part or a regulation issued by the Secretary or the Board under this part..." and a state requirement that a motor carrier must register with the State provided the requirement "is not an unreasonable burden on transportation."[23]

Congress enacted the *National Securities Markets Improvement Act of 1996* and included a section declaring "[n]othing in this title shall affect the jurisdiction of the securities commissioner (or any agency or officer performing like functions) of any State over any security or any person insofar as it does not conflict with the provisions of this title or the rules and regulations thereunder."[24]

The *Health Insurance Portability and Accountability Act of 1996* contains two provisions exempting state statutes from preemption provided they do not prevent the application of a federal requirement.[25] The act also waives preemption with respect to the guarantee of availability of individual health insurance coverage in a state with an "alternative mechanism," and authorizes the secretary of health and human resources to waive other preemption provisions relating to fraud and abuse prevention if he or she finds it is necessary "(I) to prevent fraud and abuse; (II) to ensure appropriate State regulation of insurance and health plans; (III) for State reporting on health care delivery or costs, or (IV) for other purposes."[26]

The *Intercountry Adoption Act of 2000* incorporates the Convention on Protection of Children and Cooperation in respect of Intercountry Adoption, prepared at The Hague on May 29, 1993, and declares the relationship of the act and convention to other laws as follows: "The Convention and this Act shall not be construed to preempt any provision of the law of any State or political subdivision thereof, or prevent a State or political subdivision thereof from enacting any provision of law with respect to the subject matter of the Convention or this Act, except to the extent that such provision of State law is inconsistent with the Convention or this Act, and then only to the extent of the inconsistency."[27]

The *Mobile Telecommunications Sourcing Act of 2000* is a preemption statute containing the following stipulation: "Notwithstanding the law of any State or political subdivision of any State, mobile telecommunications services provided in a taxing jurisdiction to a customer, the charges for which are billed by or for the customer's home service provider, shall be deemed to be provided by the customer's home service provider."[28] The act, however, exempts "the determination of the taxing situs of prepaid telephone calling services," the initial or subsequent resale of mobile telecommunications services, and "the determination of the taxing situs of air-ground radiotelephone service."[29]

Exclusive State Jurisdiction

Congress is free to devolve some of its delegated powers to states and first did so in a 1789 statute authorizing states to regulate marine port pilots, thereby establishing an *imperium in imperio* relative to regulation of pilots.[30] The current *Shipping Statute*, revised in 1983, contains a clause almost identical to the one in the 1789 statute: "Pilots in the bays, rivers, harbors, and ports of the United States shall be regulated only in conformity with the laws of the States."[31]

This statute, however, exempts a pilot of a "coastwise seagoing vessel" licensed by the federal government from subnational governmental regulation by forbidding states and their political subdivisions to "impose on a pilot licensed under this subtitle an obligation to procure a State or other license, or adopt any other regulation that will impede the performance of the pilot's duties under the laws of the United States."[32]

State Standard Adoption

Congress inserted a section in the *Coast Guard Authorization Act of 1984* directing the secretary of transportation to develop standards for determining whether an individual is intoxicated while operating a marine recreational vessel.[33] The Coast Guard, at the time a unit of the Department of Transportation, promulgated a final rule defining operation of a vessel while intoxicated. The rule adopts as the national standard the individual state blood alcohol content (BAC) standard, if it exists, but also establishes a federal BAC standard of 0.10 percent for states lacking a BAC standard. Should a state without a BAC standard adopt one, the Coast Guard automatically adopts the state standard as the federal standard for that state. The Coast Guard sought to encourage states to adopt a BAC standard and to make existing ones more stringent.

State License Adoption

The *Port and Tanker Safety Act of 1978* similarly grants authority to the secretary of transportation to require federally licensed pilots on all domestic and foreign self-propelled vessels "engaged in foreign trade while operating in the navigable waters of the United States in areas and under circumstances where a pilot is not otherwise required by state law."[34] This requirement is terminated immediately upon a state, with jurisdiction over the area, requiring a state-licensed pilot and notifying the secretary.

Preemption Precluded by Ruling

The *Voting Rights Act of 1965*, described in chapter 4, is a complete preemption statute with respect to the electoral system of a state or local government if two conditions are met: a voting device such as a literacy test had been employed in 1964 and less than 50 percent of the registered voters cast ballots in the preceding presidential election.[35] The purpose of the act, based upon the Fifteenth Amendment to the U.S. Constitution, is to prevent the abridgment of the voting rights of citizens on grounds of race or color. The 1975 amendments to the act extended its coverage to language minorities—"persons who are American Indian, Asian American, Alaskan Natives, or of Spanish heritage"—and cited the Fourteenth Amendment and the Fifteenth Amendment as the constitutional authority for the act.[36]

The language minorities provision applies to a state or a local government if in excess of 5 percent of the citizens of voting age are members of one language group and less than 50 percent of all citizens of voting age cast ballots in the 1972 presidential election. A subnational government unit also is covered by the amendments if in excess of 5 percent of the citizens of voting age are members of one language minority and the illiteracy race of the group exceeds the national literacy rate.

A state or local government covered by the act may make no change, no matter how minor, in its election systems unless the United States attorney general, within sixty days of submission of a proposed change to her or him, fails to register an objection or the U.S. District Court for the District of Columbia issues a declaratory judgment to the effect the proposed electoral system change would not abridge the right to vote of citizens protected by the act.[37]

In contrast to the *Voting Rights Act of 1965*, which provides for either an administrative or judicial ruling precluding congressional preemption, the *Hazardous Materials Transportation Safety Act of 1974* (HMTSA) authorizes only an administrative preclusion. The Materials Transportation Bureau of the Department of Transportation may issue an administrative ruling addressing the question whether a congressional statute precludes a state law or rule on the same subject.[38]

The Research and Special Programs Administration of the U.S. Department of Transportation in 1984 introduced the bureau's consistency rulings by noting Congress in effect intended to establish a type of *imperium in imperio*:

> Despite the dominant role that Congress contemplated for departmental standards, there are certain aspects of hazardous materials transportation that are not amenable to exclusive nationwide regulation. One example is traffic control. Although the Federal Government can regulate in order to establish certain national standards promoting the safe, smooth flow of highway traffic, maintaining this in the face of short-term disruptions is necessarily a predominantly local responsibility. Another aspect of hazardous materials transportation that is not amenable to effective nationwide regulation is the problem of safety hazards which are peculiar to a local area. To the extent that nationwide regulations do not adequately address an identified safety hazard because of unique location conditions, State or local governments can regulate narrowly for the purpose of eliminating or reducing the hazard. The mere claim of uniqueness, however, is insufficient to insulate a non-Federal requirement from the preemption provisions of the HMTSA.[39]

The National Assurance Corporation's request for an administrative ruling by the bureau is an example of the type of consistency questions raised. The corporation sought a determination whether the New York State Thruway Authority's prohibition of the transportation of radioactive materials on its facilities is inconsistent with and consequently preempted by HMTSA. The key question involved whether the corporation could comply with both a rule of the authority and a federal administrative rule. The bureau issued an administrative ruling holding the authority's "rule is not based upon any finding that transportation of highway route controlled quantity radioactive materials over the Thruway would present an unacceptable safety risk," and hence the "rule thus stands as a repudiation of the Department's rule of national applicability on highway routing of radioactive materials."[40]

Congress included in the *USA Patriot Act of 2001* a preemption provision forbidding a state to issue a motor vehicle license to any individual "transporting in commerce a hazardous material unless the secretary of transportation has first determined, upon receipt of a notification under subsection (c)(1)(B) that the individual does not pose a security risk warranting denial of the license."[41]

Remand of Removed Actions

The United States has a dual judicial system as well as dual executive and legislative systems. Litigants, depending upon the nature of the case, often have the choice of bringing a civil suit in a state or a United States court. To protect certain respondents in state suits, Congress enacted the *Removal of Causes Act of 1920*, allowing the removal of a case from a state court to the U.S. District Court because the former court "... might conceivably be interested in the outcome of the case.... [42]

Congress enacted the *Private Securities Litigation Reform Act of 1995* to reduce abusive class action private securities fraud litigation.[43] Within three years, Congress found the act was not achieving its goal and explained it had been presented with considerable evidence that revealed a significant number of such lawsuits had been shifted from U.S. courts to state courts. In consequence, Congress enacted the *Securities Litigation Uniform Standards Act of 1998*, which established national standards for such class action lawsuits, placing additional limitations on remedies, but also mandating a U.S. District Court must remand such a suit to the state court from which it was removed "if the federal court determines that the action may be maintained in State court pursuant to this subsection."[44] The act also preserves the right of a state, local government, or a state pension plan to bring "an action involving a covered security on its own behalf, or as a member of a class comprised solely of other States, political subdivisions, or State pension plans that are named plaintiffs, and that have authorized participation, in such action."[45]

Limited Congressional Preemption

Congress has employed two types of limited preemption of the regulatory powers of states. The first type is the product of Congress enacting a statute that removes the authority of subnational governments to engage in regulatory actions affecting a specified portion of a regulatory field. The preemption's scope may be very narrow, as illustrated by a provision in the *Department of Transportation and Related Agencies Appropriation Act of 1997* that stipulates "[n]o State or local building, zoning, subdivision, or similar or related law ... shall apply in connection with the construction, ownership, use, operation, financing, leasing, conveying, mortgaging, or enforcing a mortgage of (i) any improvement undertaken by or for the benefit of Amtrak as part of, or in furtherance of, the Northeast Corridor Improvement Project...or (ii) any land (and right, title or interest created with respect thereto) on which such improvement is located and adjoining, surrounding, or any related land."[46]

States historically regulated the business of insurance, and the U.S. Supreme Court in 1868 confirmed such regulation when it ruled the business of insurance was not commerce.[47] The court in 1944, however, reversed its earlier decision.[48] States successfully lobbied Congress to enact the *McCarran-Ferguson Act of 1945*, exempting states from congressional antitrust acts and devolving power upon them to regulate the business of insurance.[49] The resulting nonharmonious state regulation of the insurance industry gave rise to many complaints from insurance companies. They favored congressional preemption to establish a national uniform system of regulation. Congress responded to the complaints in part by enacting the *Gramm-Leach-Bliley Financial Modernization Act of 1999*, preempting thirteen specified areas of insurance regulation and threatening to impose a federal system of licensing insurance agents if twenty-six states did not adopt a uniform licensing system, certified by the National Association of Insurance Commissioners (NAIC), by November 12, 2002.[50] On September 10, 2002, NAIC certified thirty-five states had adopted a uniform licensing system, thereby averting a federal licensing system.

The terrorists' attacks on the World Trade Center in New York City and the Pentagon in Arlington, Virginia, on September 11, 2001, had a major impact on property and casualty insurance companies and raised the question of whether these firms would provide coverage for business firms and individuals against potential acts of terrorism. Congress addressed the problem by enacting the *Terrorism Risk Insurance Act of 2002*. This act establishes a temporary national government program to ensure the availability, at affordable premiums, of property and casualty insurance for terrorism risk.[51] This act preempts state authority by stipulating "State approval of any terrorism exclusion from a contract for property and casualty insurance that is in force on the date of enactment of this Act shall be void to the extent that it excludes losses that would otherwise be insurance losses."[52]

The U.S. Supreme Court in 2003 addressed the question of whether the "any willing provider" provisions of the *Kentucky Health Care Reform Act* were preempted by the *Employee Retirement Income Security Act of 1974*.[53] The court unanimously acknowledged its holdings in two earlier McCarran-Ferguson cases raise "more questions than they answer and provide wide opportunities for divergent outcomes."[54] The court made "a clean break from the McCarran-Ferguson factors" and opined the Kentucky law was constitutional because it satisfied the requirements that it "must be specifically directed toward entities engaged in insurance" and "must substantially affect the risk pooling arrangement between the insurer and the insured."[55]

The second type of limited preemption of states' regulatory powers is the product of a congressional act or an administrative rule establishing minimum national standards and granting states authority to continue to have primary responsibility for the preempted function provided its standards are certified by a supervising federal department or agency as being as stringent as the national ones and are enforced. This type allows an individual state to customize its regulatory program to address local problems.

It is apparent a limited preemption statute permits state regulation at the sufferance of Congress, which is free at any time to assume complete responsibility for a regulatory field. In contrast to the type of *imperium in imperio* inherent in the very nature of a federal system, a state under the first type of limited preemption may not exercise any authority in the congressionally preempted part of the regulatory field.

We identify below eleven types of limited congressional preemption of the regulatory authority of state and local governments, examine in greater detail minimum standards preemption acts, and describe the various powers granted by limited preemption statutes to governors of states.

Minimum Standards Preemption

The "gun behind the door" theory underlies this type of limited preemption. It also may be described as "contingent complete preemption," as states have the choice of enacting statutes and promulgating administrative rules and regulations establishing regulatory standards meeting or exceeding the national minimum ones or lose all regulatory authority in the field. A state desiring to exercise regulatory authority in the field must submit a detailed plan containing minimum national standards or higher, and evidence of possession of necessary technical equipment and qualified enforcement personnel. If the plan is determined by the supervising national department or agency to be adequate, it is directed by statute to delegate enforcement "primacy" to the state, which means all inspections and other regulatory actions will be carried out only by the state and the role of the department or agency will be a scrutinizing one. This type of partial preemption has had the most major impact of all preemption statutes on the federal system and in effect generally has resulted in a federal-state partnership designed to solve critical problems.

The prevalence of a series of nationwide problems, including ones that were becoming more serious, led Congress by the mid-1960s to conclude it was improbable these problems could be solved through interstate cooperation supported by federal grants-in-aid. Congress drew the obvious conclusion that only direct national assumption of regulatory responsibility, particularly in the environmental field, could eliminate or mitigate to a large extent the problems.

It is not difficult to discern why a state legislature, in the absence of mandated minimum national regulatory standards, would be hesitant to initiate a major corrective action to solve a serious environmental problem—air and water pollution are examples—which has spillover costs affecting sister states and/or nations. States were concerned that the establishment and enforcement of stringent standards would encourage polluting industrial firms to leave the state and/or discourage new firms from locating facilities in the state. States inherently tend to act in a mercantilistic manner to protect their industrial firms, thereby ensuring employment opportunities for their citizens. Minimum standards preemption eliminates the option for polluting industrial firms to relocate facilities to an "asylum" state with no or low environmental standards. This type of preemption also allows a state legislature to enact a statute superseding the corresponding national law if state standards meet or exceed the national minimum standards.

Do all state and local government officers oppose congressional minimum standards preemption? The answer is a resounding no. Many subnational governmental officers are fully aware of the benefits of such a statute, which can eliminate industrial haven states that otherwise would permit industrial firms to pollute the environment. This type of limited preemption also has a second advantage for states. A downstream state, for example, can pressure the U.S. Environmental Protection Agency (EPA) to require the upstream states to curtail the discharge of pollutants into a river. Prior to the *Water Quality Act of 1965*, the downstream state had two options regarding a polluting upstream state—seek to persuade the polluting state to initiate remedial action or sue the state in the U.S. Supreme Court. The first option generally proved to be of very limited value in terms of positive results. The second option often involves considerable expense and the problem may not be remedied for many years.

An interviewed New York state officer reported Governor Nelson A. Rockefeller in the early 1960s was convinced congressional involvement was essential for solution of the water pollution problem in his

state because New York lacked the financial resources to solve the problem.[56] The officer added that New York embarrassed the U.S. government by publicizing the water pollution facilities in the state in an effort
to obtain more federal remedial funds.

Water Quality. The first minimum standards preemption statute was
the *Water Quality Act of 1965*, which notified each state it must adopt
"water quality standards applicable to interstate waters or portions
thereof within such State," as well as an implementation and enforcement plan, if the state desires to be responsible for water pollution
abatement.[57] The act directed the secretary of the interior (now EPA
administrator) to promulgate interstate water quality standards which
became effective at the end of six months if a state failed to establish
standards meeting or exceeding the national ones.

Other congressional acts, particularly the *Federal Water Pollution
Control Act Amendments of 1972*, subsequently strengthened the state
role in identifying geographical areas with water quality control problems and designating "a single representative organization, including
elected officials from local governments or their designees, capable of
developing effective area waste treatment management plans" for each
area.[58] On September 14, 1973, EPA promulgated regulations that
granted governors until March 14, 1974, to designate or non-designate
such areas and agencies.[59] A New York state officer stated "the 1972 federal approach is what has been called the 'idiots' approach in the 1960s;
i.e., national uniformity. The proper approach was a stream classification
approach."[60]

The *Clean Water Act of 1977* expanded the coverage of the 1972
amendments and declared "it is the policy of Congress that the States
manage the construction grant program under this Act and implement
the permit programs under sections 402 and 404 of this Act."[61] California in 1983 returned its primacy for the construction grant program
to EPA "because state officials believed the EPA required more of primacy States than it did of its own regional officers who served as imple-
menters in States that did not accept primacy."[62]

EPA by 2003 had delegated regulatory primacy to only Michigan
and New Jersey for the Section 404 permit program relating to protection of wetlands, but had delegated regulatory primacy to forty states for
the underground injection control program.

The farm lobby is a powerful one in Washington, D.C., and its
influence is revealed by the successful insertion of the following provision in the 1977 act: "(1) The Administrator shall not require a permit
under this section for discharges composed entirely of return flows from

irrigated agriculture, nor shall the Administrator directly or indirectly require any State to require such a permit."[63]

Air Quality. Chapter 4 explains that the *Air Quality Act of 1967* is a complete preemption relative to exhaust emissions from 1968 and subsequent-model motor vehicles.[64] Additionally, the act provides for limited preemption of other air pollution abatement activities of state and local governments by incorporating minimum standards preemption procedures identical to those in the *Water Quality Act of 1965*. The 1967 act encouraged states to assume regulatory primacy, but also authorized direct national governmental action if a state failed to apply for or returned primacy or if its regulatory program in practice proved to be inadequate. Forty-five states had been delegated regulatory primacy as of 2003.

Congress made a dramatic break from its previous approach—reliance upon states to provide the necessary leadership and to take into consideration the technical feasibility of various types of abatement controls—by enacting the *Clean Air Act Amendments of 1970*.[65] Direct national action to protect public health became a national policy and explicit dates were set for the adoption by states of air quality standards and abatement plans. For example, it was required that 1975 model automobiles to achieve a 90 percent reduction of the 1970 standard for carbon monoxide emissions. The new standards were mandated without consideration of the technical feasibility of pollution abatement systems.

The amendments also created problems for the EPA because the U.S. Supreme Court in 1973 denied a petition for a writ of certiorari and let stand a U.S. District Court decision interpreting the amendments as forbidding states to permit significant deterioration of air quality.[66] The petition denial contained no opinion and the lower court did not elaborate on its ruling. As a result, EPA was forced to execute a nondegradation policy without judicial guidelines and the execution posed problems for states.[67]

The EPA is authorized to delegate responsibility for prevention of significant deterioration (PSD) of air quality to states. On November 24, 1976, for example, EPA responded to a North Carolina request by granting a partial delegation of PSD authority to the state and on September 21, 1984, expanding the state's authority by authorizing it to modify EPA issued permits in the state.[68]

Idaho in 1981 returned its air quality regulatory primacy authority to EPA, but reaccepted the authority in 1983 after EPA "assured stringent enforcement within Idaho by contracting out supervision to a private firm. This incident illustrates that States will rescind their acceptance of primacy if it suits their political interests."[69] Figure 5.1 depicts the June 2003 PDS program status in the various states.

The *Clean Air Act Amendments of 1990* are contained in a 313-page congressional preemption statute and many of the amendments are important ones.[70] Five sections of the statute specifically authorize state governors to initiate actions, a subject examined below relative to the impact of such authorizations on gubernatorial-legislative relations. To cite one example, a governor who believes the interstate transport of air pollutants causes a violation of a national ambient air quality standard can petition the EPA administrator to establish a transport region and a transport commission composed of EPA and state officers.[71] The EPA administrator, at the request of states, established the Ozone Transport Commission composed of representatives of twelve northeastern states and the District of Columbia.[72] Commission members have signed a number of memoranda providing for cooperative action to solve particular air pollution problems.

Title II of the amendments is devoted to mobile sources of air pollutant emissions and many sections direct the EPA administrator to promulgate specific standards, enforceable by the agency, relating to such subjects as control of vehicle refueling emissions, misfueling, fuel volatility, and lead substitute additives. The *Air Quality Act of 1967*, as explained in chapter 4, completely preempted responsibility for regulating emissions from new motor vehicles with the exception of California. A significant 1999 amendment authorizes sister states to adopt California motor vehicle emission standards, which are stricter than EPA standards.[73]

Title IV of the amendments addresses the problem of acid rain, attributable primarily to emissions of nitrous oxide (NO_x) and sulfur dioxide (SO_2) from coal-burning electric-generating plants, by establishing a new control approach: authorization for a utility company whose plants release fewer sulfur dioxide emissions than the maximum allowed to sell sulfur dioxide air pollution credits to other utility companies needing the allowance to avoid exceeding the emissions limit.[74] The emission trading program, in contrast to the former command and control system, is a flexible market-based approach. It allows utility companies to avoid fines by tailoring their compliance plans to the unique needs of each plant. They can employ the option of low-sulfur coal, install emission abatement equipment, and/or purchase allowances. EPA reported in 2001 SO_2 during the period 1995 through 1999 had been reduced by more than 50 percent.[75] Similarly, the 2002 *Economic Report of the President* revealed the trading program "has lowered emissions substantially while yielding considerable costs savings, especially compared with the previous, command-and-control regime."[76]

Figure 5.1 Prevention of Significant Deterioration Status, June 2003

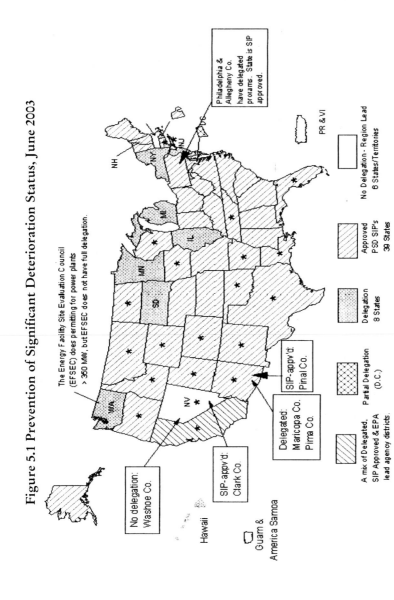

The Energy Facility Site Evaluation Council (EFSEC) does permitting for power plants > 350 MW, but EFSEC does not have full delegation.

No delegation: Washoe Co.

SIP-appv'd: Clark Co.

Delegated: Maricopa Co. Pima Co.

SIP-appv'd: Pinal Co.

Philadelphia & Allegheny Co. have delegated programs. State is SIP approved.

Hawaii

Guam & America Samoa

PR & VI

A mix of Delegated, SIP Approved & EPA lead agency districts.

Partial Delegation (D.C.)

Delegation 8 States

Approved PSD SIP's 39 States

No Delegation - Region Lead 6 States/Territories

* Denotes States with SIP-approved programs that also have Federal PSD program incorporated into the SIP for various reasons, e.g., Tribal Lands, previously issued EPA permits, etc.

Source: U.S. Environmental Protection Agency, June 2003.

Title V is devoted to permits for emission of air pollutants from stationary sources and requires a state issuing a permit or renewal of a permit to send a copy to the EPA administrator and a copy to each contiguous state to allow it to submit recommendations relative to the permit and its terms and conditions.[77]

A 2002 survey of state and local governmental air pollution program officers revealed twenty-six states have state restrictions preventing completely or partially the setting of air quality standards exceeding federal standards.[78]

Drinking Water. The minimum standards limited preemption approach also is embodied in the *Safe Drinking Water Act of 1974*, which stipulates "a State has primacy enforcement responsibility for public water systems" provided the EPA administrator determines the state "has adopted drinking water regulations which ... are no less stringent than" national standards."[79] Failure of a state to adopt or enforce such standards results in EPA assuming complete responsibility for regulating drinking water in the state.

Congress in 1986 extended the act's coverage by establishing national standards for underground drinking water sources.[80] Previously, EPA was forced to rely upon enforcement authority scattered in several sections of the *U.S. Code* and the *Code of Federal Regulations* to initiate action to protect subterranean sources of drinking water. The extension act contains schedules and precise dates by which the EPA administrator was required to establish maximum contaminant level goals and promulgate minimum drinking water quality standards to expedite action to improve and protect the quality of drinking water.[81]

These amendments also contained several expensive mandates whose implementation, particularly filtration requirements, imposed major costs on large cities. These amendments threatened to bankrupt many small local governments and placed a major financial burden on larger local governments, a subject examined in conjunction with federal mandates and the *Safe Drinking Water Act Amendments of 1996* in chapter 7.[82] The act provides for prompt federal enforcement if a state has not commenced action within thirty days of being notified by the administrator that a public water system must be made to comply with national standards.[83]

By 1987, regulatory primacy had been granted by EPA to all states except Indiana and Wyoming. Iowa was granted primacy in 1977, but returned it to EPA in 1981 because of the state's financial problems. When the problems were resolved, Iowa reaccepted primacy in 1982. All states except Wyoming in 2003 had been delegated regulatory primacy.[84] Wyoming and thirty other states have been delegated primacy for the underground injection control program under the *Safe Drinking Water Act* as amended.[85]

Congress updated the *Safe Drinking Water Act* by including a provision in the *Public Health Security and Bioterrorism Preparedness and Response Act of 2002* mandating "[e]ach community water system serving a population of greater than 3,300 persons" to "conduct an assessment of the vulnerability of its system to a terrorist attack or other intentional acts intended to substantially disrupt the ability of the system to provide a safe and reliable supply of drinking water" and to prepare an emergency response plan."[86]

Surface Mining. Another major minimum standards preemption law is the *Surface Mining Control and Reclamation Act of 1977.*[87] Each state with coal-mined land eligible for reclamation may submit to the secretary of the interior a reclamation plan and an annual list of projects to be carried out. No federal funds are granted to a state for its reclamation program unless the secretary approves it as meeting or exceeding the national standards.

This act was challenged as violating the Tenth Amendment to the U.S. Constitution, but the U.S. Supreme Court upheld the constitutionality of the act in 1981: "If a State does not wish to submit a proposed permanent program that complies with the Act and implementing regulations, the full regulatory burden will be borne by the federal government. Thus, there can be no suggestion that the Act commandeers the legislative process of the States by directly compelling them to enact and enforce a federal regulatory program."[88]

As of 2003, twenty-four states had been delegated regulatory primacy by the Office of Surface Mining of the U.S. Department of the Interior, which in 1984 initiated a full national regulatory program in Tennessee after its state legislature repealed its regulatory program.[89]

Combined Minimum Standards and *Imperium in Imperio*

The combination of minimum national standards preemption with the traditional *imperium in imperio* system is found in the *Occupational Safety and Health Act of 1970.*[90] It stipulates that "nothing in this Act shall prevent any state agency or court from asserting jurisdiction under state law over any occupational safety or health issue with respect to which no standard is in effect under section 6."[91]

Each state is authorized by the act to submit a plan to the secretary of labor for the assumption of responsibility for the regulatory function subject to a condition: State and local government employees must be extended protection equivalent to the protection extended to private employees.[92] Upon approval of a submitted plan by the secretary, the Occupational Safety and Health Administration (OSHA) will pay up to one-half of the program's operating costs.

Twenty-three states by 1990 were operating OSHA programs covering public sector and private sector employees, and Connecticut and New York were operating programs only for public employees.[93] Eight states with federal plan approval subsequently withdrew from participation under the act's provisions. In 2003, twenty-three states were operating regulatory programs covering private sector and state and local government employees, and Connecticut, New Jersey, and New York operated programs for public employees only.[94] Eight states—Colorado, Connecticut, Illinois, Montana, New Jersey, New York, North Dakota, and Wisconsin—at one time were approved as complete plan states but later withdrew their programs.

The Ohio Manufacturers' Association sued the city of Akron, Ohio, maintaining the *Occupational Safety and Health Act* preempted the city's "right to know" ordinance. The U.S. Court of Appeals for the Sixth Circuit in 1986 upheld the U.S. District Court's decision ruling in favor of the city, and emphasized "we cannot accept plaintiffs' contention that Congress expressly preempted local regulation by these provisions establishing a national standard. Furthermore, we agree with the trial court to the extent that express preemption, by definition, must be clearly manifested, especially when local health and safety provisions are endangered."[95]

In 1986 EPA promulgated a rule designed to protect subnational governmental employees from the potential hazards of asbestos-abatement work under the authority of the *Toxic Substances Control Act*.[96] While OSHA normally is responsible for promulgating regulations protecting workers, it lacks authority under the *Occupational Safety and Health Act of 1970* to extent its protection to subnational government employees. Twenty-three states, as noted above, had established protection standards for their employees as strict or stricter than OSHA's worker protection rules and regulations; OSHA has also determined four additional states—Idaho, Kansas, Oklahoma, and Wisconsin—have promulgated regulations comparable to or more stringent, in terms of worker protection, than OSHA's rules and regulations. As a consequence, the EPA rules and regulations apply only to the remaining states.

There are three principal differences between the OSHA standard and EPA regulations:

1. The EPA rule includes a provision, absent in the OSHA rule, that generally requires persons to report to EPA at least ten days prior to beginning an asbestos-abatement project using public employees.
2. EPA employs a different definition of asbestos in order to make the definition consistent with other EPA regulations. Its definition specifically does not include nonasbestiform tremolite fibers while the OSHA standard does.
3. The EPA rule does not include the OSHA provision indicating a preference for rotating employees in and out of the workplace to meet exposure limits in lieu of using respirators.

Opt-In and Opt-Out Provisions

Congress in enacting the *Riegle-Neal Interstate Banking and Branching Efficiency Act of 1994* accorded recognition to the long history of the dual banking systems in the United States by including several exemptions and savings provisions excluding state statutes, including tax ones, and regulations from preemption.[97] The act also contains an "opt-in" section that permits a state legislature to enact a law permitting interstate branching through *de novo* branches provided the law "applies equally to all banks; and expressly permits all out-of-state banks to establish *de novo* branches."[98] In addition, the act has an "opt-out" section allowing a state legislature to prohibit interstate branching within the state otherwise authorized by the act.[99] Only Montana and Texas have used the "opt-out" section.[100] A major study of the act concludes deregulation has "allowed banks to offer better services to their customers at lower prices."[101]

State Transfer of Regulatory Responsibility

The *Wholesome Meat Act of 1967* is another type of limited congressional preemption statute. It grants the secretary of agriculture authority to inspect meat and transfer responsibility for intrastate meat inspection to a state with a law requiring meat inspection and reinspection consistent with federal standards.[102] States are authorized by the act to transfer responsibility for inspection of meat for intrastate commerce to the U.S. Department of Agriculture, and eighteen states have effectuated such a transfer.

Similar provisions are contained in the *Poultry Products Inspection Act of 1968.*[103] A total of twenty-six states have shifted responsibility for inspecting intrastate poultry products to the U.S. Department of Agriculture.

Exceptions to Preemption in Certain States

The *Newborns' and Mothers' Health Protection Act of 1996* regulates group health insurance plans by mandating standards relating to benefits for mothers and newborns, but it also contains exceptions for health insurance coverage. Excepted are states which have a law requiring (a) "at least a 48-hour hospital length of stay following a normal vaginal delivery and at least a 96-hour hospital length of stay following a cesarean section" or (b) coverage "for maternity and pediatric care in accordance with guidelines established by the American College of Obstetricians and Gynecologists, the American Academy of Pediatrics, or other established professional medical association," or (c) "the hospital length of stay for such care is left to the decision of (or required to be made by) the attending provider in consultation with the mother."[104]

Administrative Preemption

State and local governments are permitted by the *Toxic Substances Control Act of 1976* to continue to regulate chemical substances or mixtures until the EPA administrator promulgates a rule or issues an order applicable to a substance or mixture designed to protect the health of the public.[105]

A degree of regulatory flexibility continues to exist after the administrator has promulgated a rule pertaining to a substance as he or she, upon the application of a state or a local government, may promulgate a rule exempting a chemical substance or mixture from the national requirements if the subnational requirements provide a higher degree of protection against injury to public health or the environment than the national requirements and do not "unduly burden interstate commerce."[106]

The *Needlestick Safety and Prevention Act of 2000* is a most interesting act. It stipulates that the bloodborne pathogens standard established by the act remains in effect "until superseded in whole or in part by regulations promulgated by the secretary of labor under section 6(b) of the *Occupational Safety and Health Act of 1970* (29 U.S.C. §655(b)."[107]

More Stringent State Standards

States are authorized by several congressional preemption statutes to impose standards stricter than national ones. The *Port and Tanker Safety*

Act of 1978, relative to bridges and other structures on or in navigable waters, explains that "nothing contained in this section with respect to structures, prohibits a State or political subdivisions thereof from prescribing higher safety equipment requirements or safety standards than those which may be prescribed by regulations hereunder."[108]

The *Natural Gas Policy Act of 1978* clarifies "nothing in this act shall affect the authority of any State to establish or enforce any maximum lawful price for the first sale of natural gas produced in such State which does not exceed the applicable maximum lawful price, if any, under title 1 of this act."[109]

A state is authorized by the *Telephone Consumer Protection Act of 1991* to impose, compared to federal requirements, "more restrictive intrastate requirements or regulations" pertaining to the use of electronic devices to send unsolicited advertisements, automatic telephone dialing systems, or artificial or prerecorded voice messages, and telephone solicitations.[110] In addition, a state attorney general may bring a civil action on behalf of state residents against any person violating the act and regulations promulgated under its authority.[111]

The *Gramm-Leach-Bliley Act of 1999* is a comprehensive financial reform statute exempting from its preemption provisions state laws affording greater protection against the disclosure of nonpublic personal information by financial institutions.[112]

These provisions are distinguishable from minimum standards limited preemption in that there is no congressional requirement that a state must submit its stricter standards to a federal department for approval prior to the standards becoming effective.

Additional Uses for a Federally Regulated Product

Two major provisions relating to state regulation of pesticides are found in the *Federal Environmental Pesticide Control Act of 1972*. The first provision grants authority to EPA to enter into cooperative agreements with states for enforcement of the act and to grant funds to states to cover part of their enforcement costs.[113] This provision is similar to the one in the *Federal Railroad Safety Act of 1970* that authorizes a limited federal turn-back of regulatory authority to allow state cooperation in railroad safety enforcement by means of state inspection of railroad equipment and facilities in accordance with national standards.[114]

The second provision is a distinctive approach to congressional structuring of national-state relations. The act authorizes a state to register "pesticides formulated for distribution and use within that State to meet special local needs if that State is certified by the Administrator as capable of exercising adequate controls to assure that such registration will be in accord with the purposes of this act and if registration for such use has not previously been denied, disapproved, or cancelled."[115] This act amends the *Federal Insecticide, Fungicide, and Rodenticide Act of 1947*, which completely preempts the registration of pesticides.[116]

Franchise Renewal Preemption

A new type of limited congressional preemption was established by the *Cable Communications Policy Act of 1984*. This act delegates power to state and general purpose local governments to issue and renew franchises for cable television subject to stringent congressional renewal standards requiring the subnational franchising authority to assess whether

    (A) The cable operator has substantially complied with the material terms of the existing franchise and with applicable law;

    (B) The quality of the operator's service, including signal quality, response to consumer complaints, and billing practices, but without regard to the mix, quality, or level of cable services or other services provided over the system, has been reasonable in the light of community needs;

    (C) The operator has the financial, legal, and technical ability to provide the services, facilities, and equipment as set forth in the operator's proposal; and

    (D) The operator's proposal is reasonable to meet the future cable-related community needs and interests, taking into account the cost of meeting such needs and interests.[117]

These franchise renewal standards make denial of a franchise renewal application exceptionally difficult.

Should a state or local franchising authority deny renewal of the franchise, the operator may seek relief in a state court or the U.S. District Court. Relief may be granted if the court finds "that the adverse finding of the franchise authority with respect to each of the factors...is not supported by a preponderance of the evidence."[118]

Title III of the *Telecommunications Act of 1996* amends the *Cable Communications Policy Act of 1984*, establishes new uniform standards, and further preempts the authority of subnational governments by freeing a cable operator providing telecommunications services from any requirement to obtain a franchise for the provision of such services.[119] The 1996 act also forbids a local government to levy a tax or impose a fee on a provider of direct-to-home satellite service, but contains a saving clause explaining the prohibition does not "prevent a local taxing jurisdiction from receiving revenue derived from a tax or fee imposed and collected by a State."[120]

Reverse Preemption

The findings section of the *Coastal Zone Management Act of 1972* declares "the key to more effective protection and use of the land and water resources of the coastal zone is to encourage the States to exercise their full authority over the lands and waters in the coastal zone."[121]

The act: (1) authorizes grants-in-aid to states for the development of a land and water resources management program to be submitted to the secretary of commerce for approval; (2) requires federal departments and agencies to ensure their development projects in coastal zones are consistent "to the maximum extent practicable" with federally approved state management programs; and (3) forbids federal departments and agencies to issue licenses or permits to a private applicant to undertake "an activity affecting land or water uses in the coastal zone" if the concerned state objects to the application.[122] In the event a state fails to act upon an application within six months of its receipt, the concerned federal department or agency may presume "conclusively" the state concurs with the application and issue the requested license or permit.

Should a state object to the issuance or a license or permit by a federal department or agency, the secretary may override the objection if "the activity is consistent with the objectives of this title or is otherwise in the interest of national security."[123]

The *Coast Guard Authorization Act of 1998* contains preemption sections and also includes a section stipulating:

> (a) Nothing in this title shall be interpreted to adversely affect existing State regulatory or enforcement power which has been granted to any State through the *Clean Water Act* or *Coastal Zone Management Act of 1972.*
>
> (b) Nothing in this title shall be interpreted to expand the regulatory or enforcement power of the Federal Government which has been delegated to any State through the *Clean Water Act* or *Coastal Zone Management Act of 1972.*[124]

Limited Preemption Mandates

Several congressional statutes preempting a limited area of state regulatory authority impose mandates on states to initiate specified actions. The *National Voter Registration Act of 1993* imposes several mandates, illustrated by the following requirements: "Each State shall include a voter registration application form for elections for Federal office as part of an application for a State motor vehicle driver's license" and "[e]ach State shall accept and use the mail voter registration application form prescribed by the Federal Election Commission."[125]

Congressionally Delegated Powers to Governors

Several congressional preemption statutes and implementing administrative rules and regulations delegate powers to governors not granted to them by their respective state constitution or statutes, thereby altering the balance of power between the governor and the state legislature. These delegated powers are designed to provide states with additional flexibility in solving problems, but also generate increased lobbying of governors by interest groups and are particularly important in states where the governor is weak in terms of formal constitutional powers. A governor of an eastern state wrote to the author in 1986 that "I don't think many students of federalism understand how important these changes are, not only in an intergovernmental sense, but to Governors themselves in the expansion of their responsibilities as chief executive within their respective States."

Thirteen major congressional preemption laws and one presidential executive order grant governors new powers, including several of great importance. There are thirteen types of these delegated powers.

The first type is a specific statutory authorization for a governor to submit a plan to a federal department or agency. The *Federal Environmental Pesticide Control Act of 1972* grants authority to the governor to submit a plan to the EPA administrator for state assumption of responsibility for certification of pesticides applicators.[126] The *Clean Air Act Amendments of 1977* direct the administrator, who is required to review each state implementation plan within eighteen months of their submission, to consult the governor prior to mandating a revision of the plan.[127]

The second type involves the annual certification of state plans. The *Federal Water Pollution Control Act Amendments of 1972* authorize only the governor or his or her designee annually to certify area-wide waste water treatment management plans if the state desires to retain regulatory primacy.[128]

Certification of state compliance with a national requirement is a third type of power granted by congressional statutes to governors. The *Emergency Highway Energy Conservation Act of 1974* required states to establish a maximum speed limit of fifty-five miles per hour as a condition for the receipt of federal highway grants-in-aid and directed the federal highway administrator to promulgate implementing regulations stipulating "each Governor shall submit to the Federal Highway Administrator...a statement that the State" is complying with the nationally established maximum speed limit.[129] Congress in 1987 overrode President Ronald Reagan's veto of the *Surface Transportation and*

Uniform Relocation Assistance Act of 1987, which authorizes states to increase the speed limit to a maximum of sixty-five miles per hour on rural interstate highways without suffering the loss of federal highway grants-in-aid.[130]

The fourth type is authority to request temporary permits. The *Safe Drinking Water Act of 1974* authorizes the EPA administrator, upon the application of a governor, to issue "one or more temporary permits each of which is applicable to a particular injection well and to the underground injection of a particular fluid."[131]

Authority to request the waiver of the federal single agency requirement, described in chapter 3, is the fifth type of power granted to governors. The *Federal Metal and Nonmetallic Mine Safety Act of 1966*, repealed in 1977, allowed the secretary of labor "upon request of the Governor, to waive the single state agency provision hereof and approve another state administrative structure or arrangement if the Secretary determines that the objectives of this Act will not be endangered by the use of such other state structure or arrangement."[132]

The sixth type is a provision in a preemption statute empowering the governor to request state assumption of responsibility for a function. Such a provision is contained in the *Wholesome Meat Act of 1967* and the *Poultry Products Inspection Act of 1968*.[133]

The seventh type empowers the governor to designate a state department or agency responsible for the preempted function. The *National Health Planning and Resources Development Act of 1974* grants a governor the authority to designate a state department or agency as the state health planning and development agency.[134]

Two somewhat similar provisions are found in the *Federal Water Pollution Control Act Amendments of 1972*, which authorize governors to identify areas with "substantial water quality control problems"; designate "a single representative organization, including elected officials from local governments or their designees, capable of developing effective areawide waste treatment management plans for such" areas; and designate "one or more waste treatment management agencies...for each area."[135] The *Clean Air Act Amendments of 1977* similarly empower governors, after consultation with elected local government officers in the affected area, to designate a state agency to prepare a remedial plan.[136] Many conditional grants-in-aid programs also authorize the governor to designate a state department or agency responsible for each such program. The *Surface Transportation Assistance Act of 1978*, for example, grants the governor authority to designate metropolitan planning organizations.[137]

The eighth type is a preemption statute authorizing governors to appoint members of a state council. *The National Health Planning and*

Resources Development Act of 1974, for example, stipulates the members of the Statewide Health Coordinating Council are to be appointed by the governor.[138]

A ninth type is illustrated by a provision in the *Highway Safety Act of 1966*: "The Secretary [of Transportation] shall not approve any state highway safety program under this section which does not provide that the Governor of the State shall be responsible for the administration of the program."[139] This authorization prevents the state legislature from placing responsibility for state highway safety programs in an agency independent of the governor. In 1973, Governor Nelson A. Rockefeller of New York used the authority granted by the act to establish by executive order an interdepartmental Traffic Safety Commission as the state agency in charge of state highway safety programs.[140]

The tenth type is very important during a period of time when there is a shortage of gasoline. A 1979 executive order, issued by President James E. Carter, grants authority to the governor of a state "to establish a system of end-use allocation for motor gasoline."[141]

The *Tandem Truck Safety Act of 1984* authorizes each governor, after consulting with concerned local governments, to notify the secretary of transportation that specified segments of the interstate highway system in the governor's state cannot safely accommodate motor vehicles of the length permitted by the *Surface Transportation Assistance Act of 1982* or 102-inch vehicles other than buses.[142]

The twelfth and potentially most important type is the grant of air pollution abatement powers by preemption statutes to the governor. As explained above, EPA was forced to develop and issue regulations forbidding states to permit significant deterioration of existing air quality by court decisions issued in 1972 and 1973.[143] To implement the courts' decisions, the agency promulgated in 1974 final rules and regulations for prevention of significant deterioration of existing air quality by establishing three classes of air zones.[144] New pollution, measured in terms of sulfur dioxide and total suspended particulate matters, is not allowed in Class I areas; a limited amount of development is allowed in Class II areas provided such development would not cause "significant deterioration of air quality;" and deterioration up to secondary standards is permitted in Class III areas. Primary ambient air quality standards are national ones designed to protect the health of susceptible citizens. Secondary standards generally are more stringent and are designed to prevent adverse environmental effects such as damage to animals, climate, vegetation, and water quality.

The 1977 amendments to the *Clean Air Act* added "Part C: Prevention of Significant Deterioration of Air Quality," which contains provisions similar to EPA regulations with one major exception:

Pollutants in Class III areas are limited to 50 percent of the amount allowed by secondary standards.[145] Each state governor is allowed to redesignate areas from Class I to Class II with certain specified exceptions, principally national parks and wilderness areas, provided the redesignation has been approved

> [a]fter consultation with the appropriate Committees of the Legislature if it is in session or with the leadership of the Legislature if it is not in session (unless State law provides that such redesignation must be specifically approved by state legislation) and if general purpose units of local governments representing a majority of the residents of the area so redesignated enact legislation (including for such units of local governments resolutions where appropriate) concurring in the state redesignation; (b) such redesignation will not cause, or contribute to, concentrations of any air pollutant which exceed any maximum allowable increase or maximum allowable concentration permitted under the classification of any other area; and such redesignation otherwise meets the requirements of this part.[146]

The EPA administrator may invalidate a redesignation only if procedural requirements were not followed. In effect, redesignation allows a governor to balance the need for economic development with preservation of air quality provided pollutants emanating from new developments do not exceed national standards.

The Clean Air Act Amendments of 1990 direct the governor of a state with regulatory primacy to submit to the EPA administrator "a list of areas (or portions thereof) in the State designated as nonattainment, attainment, or unclassifiable."[147] The governor, at any time, may submit a revised list to the administrator. An entire metropolitan statistical area or consolidated metropolitan statistical area is classified as a nonattainment area if the ozone or carbon monoxide air quality in any sub-area is classified as serious, severe, or extreme. If the governor can demonstrate to the administrator that sources of air pollution in "a portion of a metropolitan statistical area or consolidated metropolitan statistical area" do not contribute significantly to the violation of air quality standards, the administrator is directed to grant the application of the governor for exclusion of the portion from the area designated as nonattainment.[148]

The *Clean Air Act Amendments of 1977* grant authority to a governor, after a public hearing is held, to promulgate rules providing "that for purposes of determining compliance with the maximum allowable increases in ambient concentrations of an air pollutant," the concentration of the pollutant listed below will not be considered:

> (A) concentrations of such pollutant attributable to the increase in emissions from stationary sources which have been converted from the use of petroleum products, or natural gas, or both, by reason of an order

which is in effect under provisions of section 2(a) and (b) of the *Energy Supply and Environmental Coordination Act of 1974* (or any subsequent legislation which supersedes such provisions) over emissions from such sources before the effective date of such order.

(B) The concentrations of such pollutant attributable to the increase in emissions from stationary sources which have been converted from using natural gas by reasons of a natural gas curtailment pursuant to a natural gas curtailment plan in effect pursuant to the *Federal Power Act* over emissions from such sources before the effective date of such plan.

(C) Concentrations of particulate matter attributable to the increase in emissions from construction or other temporary emission-related activities, and

(D) The increase in concentrations attributable to new sources outside the United States over the concentrations attributable to existing sources which are included in the baseline concentration determined in accordance with section 169(4).[149]

The amendments also authorize a governor, subject to the agreement of the federal land manager, to grant a variance from the maximum allowable increase in sulfur dioxide by a proposed major emitting facility denied certification under the standard certification procedure for a Class I area provided the owner or operator of the proposed facility can convince the governor, after a public hearing, a variance "will not adversely affect the air quality related values of the area (including visibility)."[150]

In addition, the EPA administrator is directed to delete from a transportation control plan a requirement for the tolling of bridges upon the application of the governor of the concerned state.[151] This provision was inserted in the amendments after intense lobbying by New York City and New York State officers. Governor Hugh L. Carey of New York on October 19, 1977, notified the administrator that the requirement that East River bridges in New York City be tolled should be deleted from the transportation control plan, and the requirement was deleted.[152]

The coal industry is impacted by the amendments, and its influence is detectable in the section authorizing the governor, "with the written consent of the President or his designee," to "prohibit any such major fuel burning stationary sources (or class or category thereof) from using fuels other than locally or regionally available coal or coal derivatives to comply with implementation plan requirements."[153]

The thirteenth type of delegated power is authorization in the *Clean Air Act Amendments of 1990* for a governor to petition the EPA administrator to establish a transport commission if "the interstate transport of air pollutants from one or more States contributes significantly to a violation of a national ambient air quality standard in one or more other States.[154] The administrator established the Ozone Transport

Commission, whose members are representatives of twelve northeastern states and the District of Columbia.

Summary and Conclusions

The United States continues to have an *imperium in imperio* system as the fifty states possess important powers not subject to formal congressional preemption and other powers excluded from preemption acts by savings clauses in congressional statutes. For decades Congress generally was respectful of traditional state regulatory powers and it enacted few preemption statutes. The greatly increased mobility of citizens and business firms, and inventions and technological developments spurred enactment of congressional statutes that remove regulatory powers from states, but many of these statutes either cover only part of a field or contain exceptions and savings provisions preserving a degree of state regulatory authority.

A revolutionary new type of preemption statute, minimum standards preemption, dates to 1965 and allows states to exercise regulatory authority in the preempted field provided a state adopts and enforces standards meeting or exceeding the national minimum standards. Congress in enacting many preemption statutes recognized the inability of the national government to regulate effectively certain fields in a geographically large and diverse nation with special regional problems, the desirability of national-state cooperation, and the need for the implementation assistance of state and local governments. These statutes also provide states with a degree of flexibility in addressing special problems.

Congress has devolved significant powers upon governors by several preemption statutes and on occasion these powers have resulted in conflicts between a state legislature and a governor who is not granted the powers by the state constitution or statutes. The state legislature, of course, controls the purse strings and may be able to frustrate the governor's use of one or more devolved powers. It should be noted that federal department and agency promulgation of voluminous rules and regulations, authorized by preemption statutes, makes it difficult for the typical state legislator to keep informed about the changing roles of the governor under limited preemption statutes.

The subject matter of chapter 6 is judicial determination of whether a congressional preemption statute is constitutional and whether a statute lacking an explicit preemption provision removes regulatory authority completely or partially from the states. United States courts serve as an arbitrator of federal-state conflicts and a protector of the civil rights of citizens. Relative to the latter, the U.S. district court assumed complete control of the Boston public school system to remove racial discrimination.

Chapter 6

JUDICIALLY DETERMINED PREEMPTION

The U.S. Constitution established a dual judicial system as well as a dual legislative system. The former includes state courts with exclusive jurisdiction over certain matters and jurisdiction concurrent with U.S. courts over other matters. Similarly, federal courts have exclusive jurisdiction over specified matters and concurrent jurisdiction over other matters. Section 2 of Article III of the U.S. Constitution defines the judicial power of the United States; this definition has been supplemented by the *Judiciary Act of 1789*.[1] Plaintiffs often have the option of bringing a civil suit in a federal court or in a state court, with the result that forum shopping is relatively common, as described in a subsequent section.

The *Removal of Causes Act of 1920* updates the removal provision in the 1789 act and allows the defendant(s) in a civil suit filed in state court to have the case removed to a U.S. district court if a federal question is involved.[2] A case removed to the latter court can be remanded to the state court.[3] The 1920 act does not allow the removal of an interstate diversity case if any defendant(s) is a citizen of the state where the suit was filed.[4]

The delegation by the U.S. Constitution of specific powers to Congress in broad terms allows it wide latitude in determining when its statutes should displace completely or partially the concurrent regulatory powers of the states and their political subdivisions. Writers often cite the interstate commerce clause and the supremacy of the laws clause as the sources of authority for Congress to exercise preemption powers.

The former clause is not the only one employable to remove authority from states as Congress is delegated other preemption powers, including the power to enact copyright and patent acts. The latter clause is limited to "conflict preemption," that is, a court may invalidate a state constitutional or statutory provision if it conflicts with a congressional statute based upon a delegated power. The invalidation of a specific state statute on the ground of a conflict, however, does not deprive states of all concurrent powers to regulate in the given field. Subsequent state law enactments in the field, of course, may be subject to court challenges if they result in new conflicts. It is the courts, not Congress, that decide whether there is a direct conflict between a federal law and a state law of a magnitude triggering activation of the supremacy of the laws clause. Congress is not limited to conflict preemption, and prospectively can preempt completely or partially state regulatory authority in the absence of state constitutional and statutory provisions by exercising its delegated powers, including the necessary and proper clause, which allows enactment of preemption and other laws not based upon a specifically delegated power. Chief Justice John Marshall in *McCulloch v. Maryland* opined in 1819, "let the end be legitimate, let it be within the scope of the Constitution, and all means which are appropriate, which are plainly adapted to that end...are constitutional."[5] Consequently, Congress may enact a "field preemption" statute, which completely deprives state legislatures of authority to enact regulatory statutes in a specified field for the first time.

In invalidating state statutes, the U.S. Supreme Court, commencing with *Fletcher v. Peck* in 1810, relied upon "conflict preemption" until 1912.[6] In that year, the Court in *Southern Railway Company v. Reid* declared the supremacy of the *Interstate Commerce Act of 1887* over a conflicting North Carolina statute that required all railroad companies to carry freight "tendered at a regulation station," and removed from state legislatures the authority to enact any statute on the subject because "Congress has taken possession of the field of regulation."[7]

The Court until 1917 used the term "superseded" and not "preempted" when referring to the removal of regulatory powers from states. Justice Louis Brandeis in his 1917 dissent in *New York Central Railroad v. Winfield* wrote, "pre-empted the whole field," instead of "superseded," and the term "preemption" subsequently became a common federalism term.[8]

Preemption powers were not exercised often during the period commencing in 1835, described as one of dual federalism, yet Professor Woodrow Wilson of Princeton University in 1885 was concerned by the failure of the U.S. Supreme Court to check adequately the exercise of congressional powers by declaring certain statutes unconstitutional.[9] With the end of the era of dual federalism in 1937, the U.S. Supreme Court generally gave a broad reach to preemption statutes and seldom declared a section of such a statute unconstitutional as exceeding the powers of Congress until the last decade of the twentieth century.

It should be noted Congress may abrogate the Eleventh Amendment immunity of states from suit by exercising a delegated power narrowly addressing a violation of certain federal statutes. The *Individuals with Disabilities Education Act Amendments of 1997*, for example, contains the following provision: "A State shall not be immune under the Eleventh Amendment to the Constitution of the United States from suit in Federal court for a violation of this Act."[10]

This chapter (1) examines briefly the role of U.S. courts in ensuring citizens are protected against state and local government infringement of their rights as guaranteed by the U.S. Constitution, (2) concentrates on the criteria employed by the U.S. Supreme Court to determine the extent of congressional preemption powers and whether a congressional statute is preemptive in the absence of an explicit preemption clause, and (3) describes briefly the use of judicial forums by interest groups.

Constitutional Guarantees

All state and U.S. courts are reactors; they cannot initiate action. Once a suit is filed in a U.S. district court to resolve a controversy, the judge can exercise exceptional remedial powers, including judicial receivership of state and local governmental institutions. The U.S. Supreme Court, as explained in chapter 2, employed the guarantees of the First Amendment to the U.S. Constitution to invalidate sections of state corrupt-practices statutes that restricted campaign expenditures by candidates of their own funds and prohibited corporations from making expenditures to advertise their views on a referendum issue. These decisions have had a major impact on electoral and referenda campaigns.

Similarly, employees of state and local governments have First Amendment rights. The court in 1976 in *Elrod v. Burns* reversed the patronage dismissal of non-policymaking employees of the Cook County, Illinois, sheriff as violative of the guarantees of the First and Fourteenth Amendments by opining the dismissals restricted severely their right of association and their political beliefs.[11] The newly elected mayor of Cohoes, New York, dismissed a housing counselor, but the Appellate Division of the New York State Supreme Court cited *Elrod v. Burns* and ruled "Section 10 of the Cohoes City Charter can be applied constitutionally to all appointed officers in policy-making positions, but it can not be applied constitutionally to the petitioner since his position was in a non-policy making category."[12]

Assistant U.S. Attorney General William Bradford Reynolds in 1987 lambasted federal judges for infringing on the rights of states: "In order to 'remedy' constitutional violations, federal courts have abolished any pretense of state sovereignty by dictating such things as the temperature of the dish water in state hospitals, the appropriate wattage of lamps in state prison cells, and the specific location of a piano in a public school. Federal judges have even informed the local electorate that the court itself will raise taxes to finance its sweeping remedial schemes if the voters continue their churlish refusal to assume the additional fiscal burden voluntarily."[13]

Reynolds directed his criticism at federal court actions establishing constitutional judicial receiverships, which can last for a decade or more. U.S. District Court Judge Joseph Tauro, who placed seven Massachusetts institutions for the mentally retarded under protection of his court in 1978, directed Massachusetts officers in 1986 to establish an independent panel to monitor the schools because "the state government has to run this thing" and "I don't need to be around until every building is painted and every nail is nailed."[14]

Plaintiffs alleging infringement of their constitutional rights in a lawsuit do not always win. The U.S. Supreme Court in 1978 upheld a section of the *New York Executive Law* limiting the appointment of state police members to U.S. citizens. The court explained "it would be anomalous to conclude that citizens may be subjected to the broad discretionary powers of non-citizen police officers as it be to say that judicial officers and jurors with power to judge citizens can be aliens."[15] In 1990, the court rejected the argument that a Michigan state police–operated highway sobriety checkpoint program violates the Fourth Amendment's guarantee against seizure.[16]

A clash can occur between the constitutional rights of pupils in public schools and taxpayers if a U.S. district court levies a tax or increases the property tax rate to fund a public school integration program. U.S. District Court Judge Russell G. Clark in 1987 ordered an approximate doubling of the property tax levy in Kansas City, Missouri, and also levied an income tax surcharge upon persons employed within the city school district.[17] He justified the surtax on nonresidents on the theory many nonresidents had moved to suburban municipalities to avoid school integration. This decision was appealed. The U.S. Supreme Court in 1990 reversed the lower court decision as an "abuse of discretion" because of the court's failure to determine whether the integration goal could have been achieved by an alternative permissible action.[18]

Public School Desegregation

The direct operation of the Boston school system by U.S. District Court Judge W. Arthur Garrity, Jr., is perhaps the most controversial judicial receivership. Annoyed by the recalcitrance of the Boston School Committee to implement court orders to desegregate public schools, Garrity assumed complete control of the system in 1974 from the elected committee members and did not relinquish control to the committee until 1985.[19] He was severely criticized by members of the committee and elements of the media for his actions, which included issuance of approximately 240 court orders affecting the system's schools and determination of miniscule matters such as whether a ceiling in a particular school should be repaired.

In 1982, however, he relinquished day-to-day monitoring of court orders to the Massachusetts Board of Education on the condition it would issue to the court progress reports semiannually on desegregation in the system.[20] When he returned control of the system to the school committee, Judge Garrity issued final orders on: directing the assignments of pupils to schools on the basis of prescribed ratios reflective of the racial composition of the student body; the adopting of a school rehabilitation plan to enhance desegregation; and financing of the city-wide parents councils for at least three years.[21]

In 2003, Citizens for Preservation of Constitutional Rights filed a suit in the U.S. district court in Boston on behalf of ten white families. The suit alleged the rights of the children had been violated because they were not allowed to choose schools within walking distance of their homes in order to provide space in certain schools for "minority" pupils from other neighborhoods.[22] The Boston School Committee used race to assign students to schools under a policy initiated by Judge Garrity until 1999, when the committee adopted a plan reserving one-half of the places in each elementary and middle school for children residing within walking distance. Approximately 86 percent of the children in the public schools were classified as "minorities." Attorney Frances Cohen, representing the committee, told Judge Richard G. Stearns that the committee's assignment policy was race neutral, but his view was challenged by attorney Michael Williams, representing the citizens group, who maintained the assignment plan was based on racial balancing even though the plan contained no reference to race. Boston is among the twenty-two Massachusetts cities receiving commonwealth grants to ensure racial equity in public schools.

The U.S. Supreme Court in 2002 upheld the decision of the U.S. Court of Appeals for the Fourth Circuit that the Charlotte-Mecklenburg

School District in North Carolina had removed the last vestiges of racial segregation and that race-based student assignments would end at the beginning of the follow school year.[23] Fourteen years of litigation seeking to desegregate the Hartford, Connecticut, school ended with a negotiated settlement in early 2003.[24] The Connecticut Supreme Court in 1996 ruled the state has a constitutional obligation to provide students in public schools with substantially equal educational opportunity and the superior court in 1999 opined the state was in compliance with the Supreme Court's decision.[25] Litigation nevertheless continued until the settlement was reached.

Yonkers Housing and School Desegregation

Yonkers is the fourth largest city in New York State. The U.S. Department of Justice filed a suit accusing Yonkers of deliberately promoting public housing and public school segregation in violation of the equal protection of the laws clause of the Fourteenth Amendment to the U.S. Constitution.[26] The National Association for the Advancement of Colored People (NAACP) subsequently was accorded plaintiff-intervenor status in the suit. Approximately 19 percent of the city's residents were identified in 1980 as "minority."

The U.S. District Court for the Southern District of New York conducted a fourteen-month trial, involving thirty-eight depositions and thousands of exhibits, to determine whether the city and board of education were innocent or guilty of the charge. In 1985, the court found for the plaintiff by concluding the city intentionally promoted housing and school segregation by locating nearly all of its subsidized and public housing in one section of the city because of "constituent pressures to select or support only sites that would preserve existing patterns of racial segregation, and to reject or oppose sites that would threaten existing patterns of segregation."[27] Many nonminority residents were fearful the location of subsidized housing in their respective neighborhoods would create public safety problems and lower property values.[28] The decision was appealed and the U.S. Court of Appeals for the Second Circuit in 1987 upheld the lower court decision. It rejected the city's argument "elected officials may lawfully act with the purpose of achieving or preserving racial segregation in response to the urgings of their constituents so long as race is 'only' a significant, but not a dominant, factor in the constituents' motivation."[29]

The school district initiated actions to comply with the court ordered remedy, but the city council resisted the court-issued housing remedy order and informed the court on November 15, 1986, the city would not comply.[30] The court decided to enter into negotiations with the city, which agreed to appoint an advisor to identify potential sites for units of low-income housing and prepare a long-range plan. U.S. District Court Judge Leonard B. Sand on July 1, 1987, issued a warning that the city would be fined $100 the first day and that the fine would be doubled for each consecutive day if the city was found to be in contempt for failure to comply with the court order. The political situation was complicated by the 1987 city elections, which produced four councillors opposed to the order. The judge increased pressure on the city in November by issuing an order forbidding the city to promote commercial and/or residential development until there was compliance with the integration order. The U.S. Court of Appeals for the Second Circuit affirmed the remedial orders. The city became more cooperative and entered into a consent decree containing a schedule for construction of 200 low-income housing units and a pledge not to seek further review of the court-ordered housing remedy.

The city council later changed its mind and sought permission to delete its promise not to appeal the remedial order; the court rejected the request in March 1988.[31] The next month, the council announced it would not complete negotiations for the required housing and in June announced a moratorium on housing construction. Interestingly, a leader of the Tower Society, a black group opposed to integration, objected to "forced integration" and informed Judge Sand the court order would reduce black political power, including a "minority" ward produced by a court-ordered redistricting plan.[32]

The city council's rejection, by a 4 to 3 vote, of the housing integration plan on August 1, 1988, resulted in the court conducting a contempt hearing, holding the city and defiant council members in civil contempt, and imposing fines.[33] The U.S. Court of Appeals for the Second Circuit upheld the contempt ruling after reviewing the council members' procedural objections, charge of abuse of judicial discretion, assertion of the impossibility of complying with the order without violating state law, and claim of legislative immunity.[34] The court, however, ruled the doubling of fines "exceeds the bounds of the district court's discretion when the level of each day's fine exceeds $1 million."[35]

The U.S. Supreme Court in 1990, by a 5 to 4 vote, issued its opinion, which did not address the broad constitutional issues of whether the district court abridged the First Amendment rights of the petitioners and whether legislative immunity extends to city council members. The court ruled the district court's contempt sanctions were "an abuse of discretion under traditional equitable principles" and did not conform to the doctrine courts should exercise "the least possible power adequate to the end proposed."[36] The majority opinion explained the imposition of sanctions on individual council members "effects a much greater pervasion of the normal legislative process than does the imposition of sanctions on the city for the failure of these same legislators to enact an ordinance."[37] The majority suggested the threat of bankruptcy of the city would convince citizens to pressure council members to enact the ordinance. The court's decision did not impact the district court's finding that the city intentionally segregated public housing by race or the court's remedial orders. The housing units ordered by the court were constructed.

The U.S. Supreme Court in 1998 finally addressed directly the question of whether local government lawmakers possess absolute immunity from suit when it unanimously reversed the decision of the U.S. Court of Appeals for the First Circuit holding two officers of the City of Fall River, Massachusetts, guilty of violating the First Amendment rights of the administrator and sole employee of a city department by abolishing the department.[38] Judge Clarence Thomas delivered the court's opinion by noting Anglo-American law long has recognized the absolute immunity of legislators from suit for their legislative actions and emphasizing "rationales for according absolute immunity to federal, state, and regional legislators apply with equal force to local legislators."[39] The court specifically reversed the decision of the court of appeals that the actions were administrative rather than legislative by opining "the ordinance, in substance, bore all the hallmarks of traditional legislation."[40]

Litigation continued in Yonkers. In 1995, Judge Sand of the U.S. district court opined the State of New York, state board of regents, certain state education officers, and the state Urban Development Corporation were not liable for the conditions of unlawful *de jure* segregation in Yonkers, but did not decide the question of possible state liability under the *Equal Educational Opportunities Act of 1974*.[41] Later in the same year, Judge Sand allowed an amendment adding the state liability claim, mandating the state to participate in the remedial plan, and holding the state was not liable under Title VI of the act or its implementing regulations for the Yonkers Board of Education's discriminatory acts.[42] In 1998, Judge Sand ruled the city and the state were equally responsible for the failure to eliminate vestiges of segregation and must share the removal costs equally.[43] The U.S. Court of Appeals for the Second Circuit in 1999 reviewed Judge Sand's 1998 ruling and opined (1) evidence was lacking the school curriculum and teaching techniques were inadequately multicultural to the extent they represented a "vestige of segregation"; (2) the alleged low teacher expectations for black and Hispanic students had not been proved to be a vestige of prior school segregation; (3) regression analysis of racial disparities on standard achievement tests did not demonstrate the disparities were caused by prior segregation; (4) the sweeping remedial orders of the district court exceeded its powers; and (5) the district court did not exceed its powers in mandating the state to pay one-half of the costs of the previously ordered remedies.[44] The U.S. Supreme Court in 2000 dismissed the state's petition for the issuance of a writ of certiorari.[45]

In January 2002, a tentative settlement of the Yonkers school desegregation suit was reached by federal, state, city, school, and NAACP officers providing for the state to grant $300 million to the school district over five years for programs designed to improve the performance of black and Hispanic students and removal of the federal school monitor.[46] The New York state legislature appropriated the funds and Judge Sand in approving the settlement on March 26, 2002, described it as adequate and reasonable.[47]

How successful has court-ordered desegregation of Yonkers's public schools been? In 1995, President Kenneth W. Jenkins of the Yonkers branch of NAACP declared court-ordered busing of city's school children had "outlived its usefulness."[48] The following year, a report revealed black and Hispanic students, who were two grade levels below other students when the desegregation suit was filed, were still two grade levels below other students.[49]

Failure of Desegregation

Court-ordered public school desegregation, a type of judicial social engineering, has been a failure. The common court-prescribed remedy mandating busing of pupils to achieve the goal of "racial balance" in public schools of large cities is impossible to accomplish because of white flight, the sharp increase in the black and Latino population, and the great mobility of poor families. Busing black pupils, for example, from a neighborhood populated primarily by black students to a school in another neighborhood where the black percentage of the student body is slightly lower in the name of racial desegregation is not sound public policy. The relatively large cost—money and the time of pupils, administrators, and litigants—of attempting to achieve "racial balance" in public schools through busing raises a question of the cost-effectiveness of this approach, relative to other approaches, in constitutionally guaranteeing quality education for all pupils.

A 2003 national study revealed resegregation of public schools in large cities has occurred due to a number of factors, including the continuing movement of white families to suburban municipalities; the large increase in the number of Asian, black, and Latino students in the cities; segregated housing patterns; and termination of court-ordered public school desegregation in a relatively large number of cities where legal barriers to school integration have been removed.[50] Evidence suggests that as blacks, for example, gain control of a public school system, they will have less interest in U.S. district court intervention to promote school integration. On the other hand, they no doubt will use state courts to challenge the constitutionality of the state public school grant-in-aid system on the ground the state government is not providing sufficient funds to ensure that all large city public school students receive a quality education.[51]

Congressional Authority and Intent

Chapter 1 explained opponents of the proposed U.S. Constitution were fearful an all-powerful Congress would usurp the powers of the states and convert the United States into a unitary governmental system. They apparently were not concerned that the constitutionally established U.S. Supreme Court and other courts created by Congress might be a threat to states' rights. Alexander Hamilton, in "The Federalist Number 80," commented on "the proper extent of the federal judicature" by contending controversy should not extend to the types of cases that would be within their jurisdiction and added, relative to its judicial principles: "If some partial inconveniences should appear to be connected with the incorporation of any of them into the plan it ought to be recollected that the national legislature will have ample authority to make such exceptions and to prescribe such regulations as will be calculated to obviate or remove their inconveniences. The possibility of particular mischiefs can never be viewed, by a well-informed mind, as a solid objection to a general principle which is calculated to avoid general mischiefs and to obtain general advantages."[52]

The Articles of Confederation and Perpetual Union specifically stipulate: "Each state retains its sovereignty, freedom, and independence, and every power, jurisdiction, and right, which is not by this Confederation expressly delegated to the United States, in Congress assembled."[53] Hence, there were no incidental or implied powers. The absence of a similar "expressly delegated" limitation provision in the U.S. Constitution enabled Chief Justice John Marshall in *McCulloch v. Maryland* in 1819 to develop the doctrine of implied powers expanding tremendously the reach of the express or delegated powers of Congress.[54]

This doctrine is of great constitutional significance, yet the delegated power "to regulate commerce with foreign Nations, and among the several States, and with the Indian tribes" is considerably more important in terms of the expansion of the preemption powers of Congress.[55] The U.S. Supreme Court in 1824 for the first time gave a sweeping interpretation to this delegated power in *Gibbons v. Ogden* by formulating the doctrine of the "continuous journey."[56] The court interpreted the power to regulate commerce to encompass a steamship company operating solely within the boundaries of New York because some of the passengers and merchandise on the company's ships were in transit between states. The court in effect developed a "national-concern" doctrine bearing a striking similarity to the "state-concern" doctrine developed by Judge Benjamin N. Cardozo of the New York Court of Appeals in 1929 to justify state intervention into matters assigned exclusively to cities by the New York State Constitution.[57]

Justice Robert H. Jackson of the U.S. Supreme Court in 1949 highlighted the importance and the nature of the interstate commerce clause:

> The Commerce Clause is one of the most prolific sources of national power and an equally prolific source of conflict with legislation of the State. While the Constitution vests in Congress the power to regulate commerce among the States, it does not say what the States may or may not do in the absence of congressional action, nor how to draw the line between what is and what is not commerce among the States. Perhaps even more than by interpretation of its written word, this Court has advanced the solidarity and prosperity of this Nation by the meaning it has given to these great silences of the Constitution.[58]

The increased role played by Congress in the total governance system during the Great Depression and the immediate post–World War II period was of great concern to many Republican elected officers. President Dwight D. Eisenhower pledged during this 1952 election campaign that he would appoint a commission to study the federal system and offer recommendations for improvements. He appointed the Commission on Intergovernmental Relations in 1953, which issued a report in 1955 stressing: "And under present judicial interpretations of the Constitution, especially of the spending power and the commerce clause, the boundaries of possible national action are more and more subject to determination by legislative action. In brief, the policymaking authorities of the national government are for most purposes the arbiters of the federal system."[59]

Criticisms of judicial interpretations of the Constitution continued. U.S. Assistant Attorney General Reynolds, for example, was highly critical of federal courts in 1987:

> Perhaps the greatest irony of our day is that the judiciary was seen by the Founders as the "least dangerous" branch of all. Yet it is the judicial branch that has done the largest disservice to the Constitution, and the

bedrock principles on which it stands. The delicate balance struck in the Constitution's first three articles among legislative, executive, and judicial functions has long since been interpreted virtually out of existence by activist judges who through an overly expansive reading of the commerce and supremacy clauses have nationalized almost every social problem. The core principle of federalism enshrined in the Tenth Amendment—that reserves all powers to the states not constitutionally assigned to or reserved for the federal government—was recently removed almost in its entirety by the Supreme Court's pronouncement, in the case of *Garcia v. San Antonio Transit Authority*, that state sovereignty now exists only at the pleasure of Congress. According to *Garcia*, the States have no special status that is constitutionally immune to regulation by the national government.[60]

Justice William H. Rehnquist, a conservative member of the U.S. Supreme Court, held a different view in 1981:

> ...it would be a mistake to conclude that Congress' power to regulate pursuant to the commerce clause is unlimited. Some activities may be so private or local in nature that they simply may not be in commerce. Nor is it sufficient that the person or activity reached have some nexus with inter-state commerce. Our cases have consistently held that the regulated activity must have a substantial effect on interstate commerce....In short, unlike the reserved police powers of the States, which are plenary unless challenged as violating some specific provision of the Constitution, the connection with interstate commerce is itself a jurisdictional prerequisite for any substantive legislation by Congress under the commerce clause.[61]

Rehnquist's view of the scope of the interstate commerce clause became accepted by the Court, commencing in 1990, in several of its federalism decisions described below.

Preemption Criteria

The U.S. Supreme Court, in rendering decisions involving the question of preemption, acknowledged there are no precise criteria employable by the Court to determine whether Congress intended to preempt the regulatory authority of subnational governments absent an explicit statutory preemption statement. For a variety of political reasons, Congress often does not include a preemption statement (such as "this Act is intended to supersede any law of any State or political subdivision thereof inconsistent with its provisions") in a statute and the burden of determining congressional intent falls upon the courts.

It is difficult to disagree with attorney George B. Braden's explanation in 1942 that a rule stipulating a state law would remain in effect unless specifically prohibited by a congressional statute "would be intolerable. Congress could not be asked to anticipate all possible legislative conflicts, nor could it really solve the problem by blanket prohibition. In some instances a tag end proviso nullifying all statutes 'conflicting with this act' would only restate the problem. Some leeway must be left."[62]

The U.S. Supreme Court in 1941 emphasized that each challenge of a state law on the ground of inconsistency with federal law must be determined on the basis of the particular facts of the case.

> There is not—and from the very nature of the problem—there can not be any rigid formula or rule which can be used to determine the meaning and purpose of every act of Congress. This Court, in considering the validity of state laws in the light of treaties or federal laws touching on the same subject, has made use of the following expressions: Conflicting; contrary to; occupying the field; repugnance; difference; irreconcilability; violation; curtailment; and interference. But none of these expressions provides an infallible constitutional test or an exclusive constitutional yardstick. In the final analysis, there can be no one crystal clear distinctly marked formula. Our primary function is to determine whether, under the circumstances of this particular case, Pennsylvania's law stands as an obstacle to the accomplishment and execution of the full purposes and objectives of Congress.[63]

Five years later, the Court explicated two tests of congressional preemption: (1) "[T]he question in each case is what the purpose of Congress was," and (2) does the act of Congress involve "a field in which the federal interest is so dominant that the federal system will be assumed to preclude enforcement of state laws on the same subject?" In holding the *Noise Control Act of 1972* to be preemptive, the Court wrote: "Our prior cases on preemption are not precise guidelines in the present controversy, for each case turns on the peculiarities and special features of the federal regulatory scheme in question.... Control of noise is of course deep-seated in the police power of the States. Yet the pervasive control vested in EPA [Environmental Protection Agency] and FAA [Federal Aviation Administration] under the 1972 Act seems to us to leave no room for local curfews or other local controls."[64]

The Court in 1979 opined a statute granting the U.S. district court jurisdiction over allegations of violations of constitutional rights does not cover a suit based simply on the fact a state law conflicts with the federal Social Security Act.[65] Although the Court acknowledged the conflict between the laws violated the Constitution's supremacy of the law's clause, the Court ruled the violation is not the type of constitutional allegation conferring jurisdiction upon federal courts.

The reader should note the Court on occasion voids only the portion of a state or local law determined to be preempted. In 1978, a case reached the Court involving a three-section Washington state statute pertaining to Puget Sound. The statute required oil tankers to be guided by state-licensed pilots, specified oil tanker design standards, and excluded tankers over 125,000 deadweight tons.[66] The court rejected the field preemption claim, validated the first section, and ruled Congress had preempted the other two sections.[67]

The Court built upon its reasoning in *National League of Cities v. Usery*, described in chapter 4. In *Hodel v. Virginia Surface Mining and Reclamation Association*, it enunciated in 1981 three tests to determine whether the *Surface Mining Control and Reclamation Act of 1977* preempted state law on the same subject. "First, there must be a showing that the challenged statute regulates the 'States as States'...second, the federal regulation must address matters that are indisputably 'attributes of state sovereignty'.... And third, it must be apparent that the States' compliance with the federal law would directly impair their ability 'to structure integral operations in areas of traditional functions.'"[68]

Opining the plaintiffs had failed to demonstrate the federal law regulated the "States as States," the Court explained states are not required to enforce the law's standards because failure of a state to submit a proposed regulatory program consistent with federal standards to the secretary of the interior for approval results in the federal government becoming totally responsible for the regulatory burden.[69] The Court specifically rejected the argument "the Act commandeers the legislative processes of the States by directing compelling them to enact and enforce a federal regulatory program."[70]

Ultra Vires Laws

The U.S. Supreme Court on occasion limits the authority of Congress to preempt completely the regulatory authority of states. Congress in 1970 reduced the minimum voting age in all elections to eighteen, but the Court opined Congress lacks authority to establish such an age for state and local government elections.[71] Justice Hugo L. Black delivered the opinion of the Court and emphasized "the Equal Protection of the Laws Clause of the Fourteenth Amendment was never intended to destroy the States' power to govern themselves, making the Nineteenth and Twenty-Fourth Amendments superfluous."[72] He added the delegated powers of Congress to enforce the guarantees of this amendment and the Fifteenth Amendment were subject to at least three limitations: "First, Congress may not by legislation repeal other provisions of the Constitution. Second, the power granted to Congress was not intended to strip the States of their power to govern themselves or to convert our national government of enumerated powers into a central government of unrestrained authority over every inch of the whole Nation. Third, Congress may only 'enforce' the provisions of the amendments and may do so only by 'appropriate legislation.' "[73]

Six years later, the Court in *National League of Cities* struck down provisions of the *Fair Labor Standards Amendments of 1974* extending minimum wage and overtime-pay standards to nonsupervisory employees of subnational governments on the ground the extension violated the Tenth Amendment to the U.S. Constitution and threatened the "separate and independent existence" of these governments.[74] The Court in the same year rejected the argument a written examination for applicants for positions in a police department was unconstitutional because "a substantially disproportionate" burden is placed on blacks.[75] In 1977, the court opined school and housing desegregation can be ordered by the U.S. district court on a metropolitan-wide basis only if there is direct evidence actions were initiated deliberately by suburban governments to prevent housing and school integration in the past.[76]

The Court Forsakes *National League of Cities*

The 1976 U.S. Supreme Court's *National League of Cities* was viewed by subnational government officers as evidence the Court finally recognized states were sovereign relative to certain Tenth Amendment matters. The Court within four years, however, commenced to reduce the scope of its 1976 opinion by an expansive reading of the scope of congressional acts. In 1980, the Court in *Maine v. Thiboutot* and *Owen v. City of Independence* stripped state and local governments of immunity for actions of their employees by interpreting broadly section 1983 of the *Civil Rights Act of 1971*.[77] The section stipulates: "Every person who, under color of any statute, ordinance, regulation, custom, or usage, of any State or territory, subjects or causes to be subjected to, any citizen of the United States or other person within the jurisdiction thereof to the deprivation of any rights, privileges, or immunities secured by the Constitution and laws, shall be liable to the party injured in an action at law, suit in equity, or other proper proceeding for redress."

The Court interpreted the phrase "and laws" to provide a cause of action for deprivation of rights secured by any U.S. statute because Congress failed to provide explicitly for state and local governmental immunity. Until 1980, actions brought under the section had been limited to infringements of rights protected by the equal protection of the laws clause of the Fourteenth Amendment. The 1980s rulings mean state and local government officers can be held entirely responsible for violations even though officials of federal departments and agencies have equal administrative responsibility for the relevant programs. The Court in effect granted the judiciary unlimited authority to review actions of state and local government officers totally unrelated to civil rights, the subject matter of the 1971 act.

Justice Lewis Powell, Jr., dissented in *Thiboutot* and opined "no one can predict the extent to which litigation from today's decision will harass State and local officials; nor can one foresee the number of new findings in our already overburdened courts. But no one can doubt that these consequences will be substantial."[78] Included in his dissent is a list of numerous programs affected by the Court's decision.[79]

He also dissented in *Owen* and lamented that "[a]fter today's decision, municipalities will have gone in two short years from absolute immunity under §1983 to strict liability. As a policy matter, I believe that strict municipal liability unreasonably subjects local governments to damage judgments for actions that were reasonable when performed. It converts municipal governance into a hazardous station through constitutional obstacles that often are unknown and unknowable."[80]

The Court in 1982 opined the constitutional clause delegating to Congress the power to regulate commerce among sister states authorized enactment of a statute mandating state public utility commissions to consider Federal Energy Regulatory Commission's rate-making standards.[81] The Mississippi Public Service Commission sought a declaratory judgment in the U.S. District Court for the Southern District of Mississippi holding sections of the act mandating state actions to be unconstitutional under the interstate commerce clause and the Tenth Amendment. The court issued the declaratory judgment.[82] The U.S. Supreme Court reversed the lower court decision and explained it never sanctioned explicitly "a federal command to the States to promulgate and enforce laws and regulations," but noted "there are instances where the Court has upheld federal statutory structures that in effect directed state decision-makers to take or to refrain from taking certain actions." The Court added:

> We recognize, of course, that the choice put to the States—that of either abandoning regulation of the field altogether or considering the federal standards—may be a difficult one. And that is particularly true when Congress, as is the case here, has failed to provide an alternative regulatory mechanism to police the area in the event of state default. Yet in other contexts the Court has recognized that valid federal enactments may have an effect on state policy—and may, indeed, be designed to induce state action in areas that otherwise would be beyond Congress' regulatory authority.[83]

The Garcia Decision

Subnational governmental officers viewed the above decisions as major congressional encroachments upon state sovereignty, yet their reactions were relatively mild compared to their reactions to the U.S. Supreme Court's 1985 decision in *Garcia v. San Antonio Metropolitan Transit Authority* reversing the Court's opinion in *National League of Cities v. Usery.* The Court in *Garcia* declared: "Our examination of this 'function' standard applied in these and other cases over the last eight years now persuades us that the attempt to draw the boundaries of state regulatory immunity in terms of 'traditional governmental function' is not only unworkable but is inconsistent with established principles of federalism and, indeed, with those very federalism principles on which *National League of Cities* purported to rest. That case, accordingly, is overruled."[84]

The Court's rationale was similar to the one employed by a number of state supreme courts in stripping municipalities of their sovereign immunity from suits for torts while performing a governmental function, as opposed to a proprietary function where they possessed no immunity. These courts reached the conclusion the distinction between a governmental function and a proprietary function no longer was a rational one for determining whether a municipality could be sued.[85]

U.S. Assistant Attorney General Reynolds expressed anger at this decision and declared: "According to the *Garcia* majority, States apparently enjoy no special constitutional autonomy in relation to Congress. They are now held as nothing more sovereign than ordinary private entities when Congress seeks to flex the awesome muscle of its power to regulate commerce."[86] Chairman Robert B. Hawkins, Jr., of the U.S. Advisory Commission on Intergovernmental Relations, was equally upset by the decision:

> If one strips away all the verbiage in *Garcia*, the Court is saying that the Congress has the right to constrain the authority of state and local governments in any way it sees fit. Or the reverse, that the Congress has the authority to determine the scope of its own power. The principle is clear: What the sovereign giveth, the sovereign can take. Any restraint depends on the benevolence of the Congress and the Executive Branch, and the Court has no consitutional role to protect the rights of state and local governments. If such is true, then let's admit that we have not federalism, but centralized government.[87]

Professor R. Perry Sentell, Jr., of the University of Georgia Law School, emphasized the importance of the *Garcia* decision, expressed amazement at the Court's majority decision, and concluded "the

Constitution's historical commerce clause now emerges as one of the most potent regulatory weapons at Congress's disposal."[88]

Is there any limit to the scope of the regulatory power conferred on Congress by the interstate commerce clause? When reading the *Garcia* decision, the reader should refer to Justice William Rehnquist's caution in 1981 relative to the clause's reach.

> In sum, my difficulty with some of the recent commerce clause jurisprudence is that the Court often seems to forget that legislation enacted by Congress is subject to two different kinds of challenge, while that enacted by the States is subject to only one kind of challenge. Neither Congress nor the States may act in a manner prohibited by any provision of the Constitution. But Congress must bear an additional burden: If challenged as to its authority to act pursuant to the commerce clause, Congress must show that its regulatory activity has a substantial effect on interstate commerce.[89]

This caution became constitutional dictum commencing in the 1990s when Rehnquist was chief justice.

Post-Garcia Decisions

Also in 1985, the Court opined state or local governmental regulation of public health and safety matters is not presumed to be invalidated by the supremacy clause of the Constitution and that regulations of the federal Food and Drug Administration pertaining to blood plasma collection from paid blood donors do not preempt local ordinances on the same subject.[90]

In 1986, the Court rejected the argument of landlords that a Berkeley, California, ordinance imposing rent ceilings on residential real property violated the *Sherman Antitrust Act of 1890* and opined the ordinance lacked the concerted action required for per se violation of the act.[91] The Court in 1987 rendered several decisions, including four listed below, holding congressional statutes or administrative regulations did not preempt the concerned state laws and regulations.

In *California Coastal Commission v. Granite Rock Company*, the Court ruled imposition of permit requirements on the operation of an unpatented mining claim in a national forest was not preempted by the *Coastal Zone Management Act of 1972*, congressional land-use acts, or forest service rules and regulations.[92]

In another decision involving the commerce clause, the Court validated the constitutionality of a 1978 amendment of the *California Fair Employment and Housing Act* mandating employers to grant a leave of absence to and reinstate employees disabled by pregnancy on the ground the congressional *Pregnancy Discrimination Act of 1978* established only a floor and not a ceiling relative to guarantees.[93]

The Court reached a similar decision in a case involving the question of whether a Maine statute is preempted by the *Employee Retirement Income Security Act of 1974* and/or the *National Labor Relations Act of 1935*: "We hold that a Maine severance pay statute is not preempted by ERISA, since it does not 'relate to any employee benefit plan' under the statute, 29 U.S.C. §1144(a). We hold further that the law is not preempted by the NLRA since its establishment of a minimum labor standard does not impermissibly intrude upon the collective bargaining process."[94]

An Indiana statute designed to protect shareholders in corporate takeovers was determined in *CTS Corporation v. Dynamics Corporation of America* not to be preempted by the *Williams Act of 1968* because the conflict between the two laws did not frustrate achievement of the purposes of the *Williams Act*.[95]

South Carolina in 1988 invoked the Court's original jurisdiction by challenging, on Tenth Amendment and constitutional federalism grounds, a provision of the *Tax Equity and Fiscal Responsibility Act of 1982* removing federal income tax exemption for interest on long-term bearer municipal (state and local government) bonds.[96] The state, supported by the National Governors' Association, argued the removal of tax exemption compelled the state to issue only registered bonds. The Court, by a 7 to 1 vote, upheld the constitutionality of the act by declaring "*Garcia* holds that the limits are structural, not substantive—*i.e.*, that States must find their protection from congressional regulation through the national political process, not through judicially defined spheres of unregulable state activity."[97]

The Court in the same year, however, issued two decisions upholding federal preemption. In *City of New York v. Federal Communications Commission*, the Court rejected the city's contention the commission performed an *ultra vires* act in promulgating regulations preempting the city's technical standards for the quality of cable television signals.[98]

The second decision involved a challenge by the Mississippi attorney general and consumer groups of the Mississippi Public Service Commission's authorization for an electric utility company to increase its retail rates to recoup the cost of purchasing power from a nuclear power plant mandated by the Federal Energy Regulatory Commission. The Court ruled the latter commission's proceedings were reasonable and just, and preempted the state commission from conducting an inquiry into the

question of the prudence of managerial decisions resulting in the construction of the nuclear power plant.[99]

Two years later, the Court affirmed the authority of Oregon to
deny claimants unemployment compensation because of their religious
use of peyote (a hallucinogenic drug) and North Dakota laws regulating
alcoholic beverages sold to U.S. military bases located in the state.[100]

A notable change in the Court's federalism decisions commenced in
1991, when Missouri challenged the applicability of the 1982 amendments of the *Age Discrimination in Employment Act of 1967* (ADEA),
prohibiting superannuation of employees, to Missouri judges who were
required by the state constitution to retire at age seventy.[101] Justice
Sandra Day O'Connor delivered the Court's decision, observed "every
schoolchild learns our constitution established a system of dual sovereignty between the States and the Federal Government," and concluded,
"The people of Missouri have established a qualification for those who
would be their judges. It is their prerogative as citizens of a sovereign
state to do so. Neither the ADEA nor the Equal Protection Clause prohibits the choice they have made."[102]

In 1992, the Court invalidated a provision in the *Low-Level
Radioactive Waste Policy Amendments of 1985* requiring states to "take
title" to all low-level wastes within their respective jurisdiction if an
acceptable disposal site was not established by 1996.[103] The amendments
were designed to encourage states to form low-level radioactive waste
interstate compacts.[104] New York decided to challenge the "take title"
provision. The U.S. Supreme Court upheld various provisions of the
amendments, including financial incentives and authority of compact
commissions to refuse to accept wastes from nonmember states, but
struck down the "take-title" provision by declaring: "States are not mere
political subdivisions of the United States. State governments are neither
regional   offices   nor   administrative   agencies   of   the   Federal
Government.... [W]hatever the outer limits of that sovereignty [State]
may be, one thing is clear: The Federal Government may not compel the
States to enact or administer a federal regulatory program."[105]

The constitutionality of a provision of the *Gun-Free School Zones
Act of 1990* prohibiting the possession of a firearm within a school was
challenged on the ground of exceeding the constitutionally delegated
powers of Congress.[106] The Court in 1995 invalidated the provision and
explained: "The possession of a gun in a local school zone is in no sense
an economic activity that might, through repetition elsewhere, substantially affect any sort of interstate commerce. Respondent was a local student at a local school, there is no indication that he had recently moved
in interstate commerce, and there is no requirement that his possession
of the firearm have any concrete tie to interstate commerce."[107]

The Court in *Prinz v. United States* in 1997 examined the allegation a provision of the *Brady Handgun Violence Prevention Act of 1993* involved unconstitutional commandeering.[108] The act charged the chief law enforcement officer with responsibility for conducting a background check on any person seeking to purchase a handgun in a state that lacked a statute requiring an instant background check or a statute allowing a dealer to sell a handgun immediately if the intended purchaser possessed a state handgun permit issued after a background check.[109] The Court invalidated the mandate and opined: "We held in *New York* that Congress cannot compel the States to enact or enforce a federal regulatory program. Today we hold that Congress cannot circumvent that prohibition by conscripting the State's officers directly. The Federal Government may neither issue directives requiring the States to address particular problems, nor command the State's officers, or those of their political subdivisions, to administer or enforce a federal regulatory program."[110]

The Court addressed in *Seminole Tribe of Florida v. Florida* in 1996 another aspect of state sovereignty: immunity from private lawsuit.[111] The issue of such sovereignty was raised in a superfund case in 1989 involving the release of coal tar, produced by a gas company, from a storage area into a creek. The U.S. Environmental Protection Agency reimbursed the Commonwealth of Pennsylvania for the $720,000 expended to clean up the first superfund site and the United States sued the gas company on the ground it was liable for cleanup costs. In turn, the gas company sued the commonwealth, alleging it was responsible for part of the costs because one of its flood control projects contributed to the release of the coal tar. The Court in 1989 upheld the authority of Congress under the interstate commerce clause to abrogate the sovereign immunity of states and opined: "We thus hold the language of CERLA [*Comprehensive Environmental Response, Compensation, and Liability Act of 1980*] as amended by SARA [*Superfund Amendments and Reauthorization Act of 1986*] clearly evinces intent to hold States liable in damages in federal court."[112]

In the *Seminole Tribe* case, the court invalidated the section of the *Indian Gaming Regulatory Act of 1988* authorizing tribes to sue a state in the U.S. district court if the state did not negotiate in good faith a tribal-state compact regulating gambling.[113] The Court ruled: "The Eleventh Amendment prohibits Congress from making the State of Florida capable of being sued in federal court. The narrow exception to the Eleventh Amendment provided by *Ex Parte Young* doctrine cannot be used to enforce §2710(d)(3) because Congress enacted a remedial statute specifically designed for the enforcement of that right."[114]

In 2002, the U.S. Court of Appeals for the 1st Circuit held Rhode Island was protected by the Eleventh Amendment against a suit asserting whistleblower claims under the *Solid Waste Disposal Act*.[115] The U.S. Supreme Court in the same year issued two decisions involving the amendment. The court in *Federal Maritime Commission v. South Carolina State Ports Authority* opined state sovereign immunity forbids the commission to adjudicate a private party's suit against the state.[116] The Court in its second decision ruled a state waives its Eleventh Amendment immunity from suit when it removes a case to the U.S. district court under the *Removal of Causes Act of 1920*.[117]

The Court returned to the issue of the scope of the interstate commerce clause in 2000. The case involved the constitutionality of a provision of the *Civil Rights Remedies for Gender-Motivated Violence Act of 1994* that authorizes a federal civil remedy for a victim of gender-motivated violence.[118] The Court rejected "the argument that Congress may regulate noneconomic, violent criminal conduct based solely on that conduct's aggregate effect on interstate commerce. The Constitution requires a distinction between what is truly national and what is truly local.... The regulation and punishment of intrastate violence that is not directed at the instrumentalities, channels, or goods involved in interstate commerce has always been the province of the states."[119] Also rejected was the contention Congress possessed power under Section 5 of the Fourteenth Amendment to regulate such criminal behavior by explaining the amendment applies against states and does not extend the rights of one person against those of another person.[120]

The importance of the U.S. Supreme Court's preemption decisions cannot be underestimated, yet it should be noted the bulk of the preemption litigation in the federal judicial system occurs in the U.S. district courts and the U.S. courts of appeals. Our focus in the following section is the use of federal courts by interest groups.

Interest Groups and U.S. Courts

Interest groups, in order to achieve their goals, often encourage enactment of congressional preemption statutes and promulgation of implementing administrative rules and regulations by departments and agencies. Other groups challenge the constitutionality of such statutes and implementing. A sharp increase in judicial litigation is one product of Congress employing its preemption powers more frequently and in innovative ways commencing in 1965.

The great economic importance of congressional environmental preemption statutes has made them common subjects of litigation. Environmental protection groups in particular seek court orders mandating enforcement actions by federal and state administrators who derive their authority from minimum standards preemption acts, and industrial interest groups commonly use the courts in their attempts to nullify or weaken congressional preemption statutes and implementing administrative regulations. The complexity of the latter ensures opportunities for legal challenges and guarantees long delays in the rendering of decisions by courts.

Environmental or industrial groups challenge nearly every regulation promulgated by the U.S. EPA, thereby delaying implementation of the challenged regulations. The serious administrative problems created by such suits is illustrated by one filed against the EPA administrator by the Sierra Club, the decision of the U.S. District Court for the District of Columbia in 1972, and the upholding of the decision without an opinion by a split vote of the U.S. Supreme Court.[121] The trial court forbade states to permit significant deterioration of existing air quality without elaborating upon its ruling, and in consequence EPA was forced to execute a nondegradation policy without judicial guidelines.

To implement the district court's decision, EPA in 1974 promulgated final regulations for prevention of significant deterioration of existing air quality by establishing three classes of air zones.[122] New sulfur dioxide emissions and total suspended particulate matters would not be allowed in Class I areas; limited development would be allowed in Class II areas as such development would not cause "significant deterioration of air quality"; and deterioration of air quality up to secondary standards would be allowed in Class III areas.

Considerable litigation, initiated by the Sierra Club, revolved around these regulations and they were challenged in the U.S. Court of Appeals for the District of Columbia Circuit.[123] The court did not approve EPA's air quality regulations until 1976.[124] Congress was reviewing the air quality issue while the litigation was continuing and subsequently enacted the *Clean Air Act Amendments of 1977.*

Added to the *Clean Air Act* was a new Part C: "Prevention of Significant Deterioration of Air Quality," which contains provisions similar to the regulations promulgated by EPA. There is one major exception: Pollutants in Class III areas are limited to 50 percent of the amount allowed by the secondary standards.[125] The amendments also directed EPA to study four other pollutants—carbon monoxide, hydrocarbons, nitrogen oxides, and photochemical oxidants—and within two years to promulgate regulations designed to prevent significant deterioration of air quality by emission of these pollutants.[126]

Forum shopping is a particularly undesirable practice associated with certain congressional preemption statutes. It involves each litigant seeking the circuit of the U.S. court of appeals believed to be the most sympathetic to the claims of the litigant. Congress curtailed this practice relative to the *Clean Air Act, Noise Control Act, Safe Drinking Water Act,* and *Solid Waste Disposal Act* by assigning exclusive jurisdiction over review of the agency's nationally applicable regulations to a single circuit. Congress, however, did not curtail forum shopping relative to other acts until 1988.[127]

Forum shopping had been particularly common relative to administrative rules and regulations promulgated to implement the *Clean Water Act*. An industrial interest group which considered an agency regulation to be too stringent and an environmental interest group which considered the same regulation to be too lax on a number of occasions raced to what each group considered to be a friendly courthouse. Until 1988, the *United States Code* stipulated that in the event suits challenging the same regulation are filed in more than one circuit, the suits will be transferred to the circuit where a suit "was first instituted."[128] Although the recipient circuit can transfer the suits to another circuit "for the convenience of the parties in the interest of justice," the litigant first filing a challenging has an advantage.

The National Resources Defense Council in 1979 noted the importance of racing skills:

> The process of selecting a judicial review forum often resembles a circus. The time selected to commence a race ordinarily is tied to a physical action or event, such as signing a document, announcing regulations at a press conference, or logging-in a document at the Office of the Federal Register (OFR). In such circumstances, petitioners which have considerable resources have an unfair opportunity to win the race and select their favorite forum. For those who can afford it, the race will involve teams of many people using hand signals, open long-distance telephone lines or two-way radios, and even diversionary tactics.[129]

Presiding Administrative Law Judge Stephen L. Grossman of the Federal Energy Regulatory Commission in the same year described the technique employed by Tenneco to be the first litigant:

> Tenneco had in position a "human chain" extending from OPI [Office of Public Information] to a public telephone on the second floor of the Commission's Office. Each person in the five-person chain was in line-of-sight of the person behind and ahead. The chain began with counsel for Tenneco proximate to the Commission's Secretary and extended with a member in the open doorway from OPI to the first floor corridor, to a member at the bottom of the staircase to the second floor, to a member on the staircase, and ended with a member at the public telephone on the second floor. An open line to a representative of Tenneco at the Fifth Circuit Clerk's office had been established. Counsel, standing near the

Secretary, discerned that the time stamp machine advanced each minute at the time an electric wall clock in OPI indicated nine seconds after the minute. (The wall clock was not calibrated, nor was a calibration attempted, with any other time device.) He thus was prepared for the time stamp device to advance to its 3:02 P.M. EDT reading preceded, by from one to five seconds...the moment at which the Secretary cause Order No. 10-A to be time stamped.[130]

Congress and the courts generally have granted wide standing to citizens to bring environmental lawsuits. A 1987 U.S. Supreme Court decision, in a case initiated by an industrial firm, provides industrial firms with protection against citizen suits for violations corrected prior to the initiation of the suits. The Court in *Smithfield v. Chesapeake Bay Foundation* reversed the decision of the U.S. court of appeals allowing citizens to sue for civil penalties for violations of the *Clean Water Act* in the past.[131]

The accelerating pace of technological developments ensures congressional preemption statutes and implementing rules and regulations will be exceptionally complex and courts will be called upon more often in the future to interpret the extent and nature of preemption of the regulatory authority of state and local governments.

Summary

Suits are filed in the U.S. courts by citizens and interest groups seeking to (1) protect the constitutional guarantees of citizens alleged to be abridged by subnational governmental laws and regulations; (2) determine whether Congress intended to preempt these laws and regulations in the absence of an expressed intent to preempt; (3) set the boundaries of preempted state and local regulatory activities; and (4) review promulgated administrative rules and regulations. There have been numerous court challenges to the latter, producing long delays in their implementation.

Our review of major U.S. Supreme Court decisions reveals the Court has not developed precise criteria to be employed in determining whether state and local government laws are preempted by a congressional act and its decisions are made on a case-by-case basis.

Chapter 7 examines the arguments advanced in favor of and in opposition to congressional preemption; the Blackmun thesis positing the congressional political process offers states and their political subdivisions adequate protection against preemptive decisions of the courts; the political safeguards theory of federalism suggesting states should use the political process to protect themselves against unwanted congressional statutes; the responsibility problem associated with federal preemption, the fiscal implications of federal mandates; a typology of such mandates; mandate reimbursement; the *Unfunded Mandates Reform Act of 1995*; and cooperative federalism in the first decade of the twenty-first century. Chapter 7 concludes with a presentation of a more inclusive and dynamic non-equilibrium theory of U.S. federalism.

Chapter 7

METAMORPHIC FEDERALISM

The U.S. Constitution established an *imperium in imperio* by delegating significant powers to Congress, reserving other significant powers to the states, and authorizing several concurrent powers, including the power to tax. The fundamental document, however, contains no automatic overarching stabilizing mechanism designed to ensure a continuing balance between the powers of Congress and the powers of states; it instead assigns a referee role to the U.S. Supreme Court with respect to suits involving national-state relations. The Constitution's drafters did not intend the initial powers division to be permanent, as evidenced by inclusion of amendment procedures in Article V and the supremacy of the laws clause in Article VI. There is no evidence the drafters considered the possibility Congress might devolve a delegated power upon the states.

A twenty-first-century analysis reveals the 1789 system is still recognizable, but the complexity and fluidity of national-state relations—including the asymmetrical relations between the national government and individual states—no doubt would baffle the 1787 drafters. The initial systemic changes, other than congressional enactment of two complete preemption acts in 1790, are attributable primarily to judicial interpretation of several provisions of the Constitution and, commencing in the late nineteenth century, congressional enactment of statutes authorizing conditional grants-in-aid to states whose acceptance allows Congress to influence indirectly state government regulatory policies and service provision.

The grants-in-aid increased the complexity of the system, but pale in importance compared to the complicated changes flowing from congressional enactment of complete and partial preemption statutes during the last third of the twentieth century and the early years of the twenty-first century. Could any of the Constitution's drafters have envisioned a bill enacted by a state legislature and signed by the governor requiring prior to execution the approval of the U. S. attorney general or the U. S. District Court for the District of Columbia? Currently, the federal *Voting Rights Act of 1965* as amended contains such a requirement for covered states.[1]

Congress incorporated many mechanisms in numerous complete and partial preemption statutes structuring a wide variety of national-state relations that range from simple to complex. The only preemption statutes not adding to the complexity of such relations are complete ones with no provision for a limited turn-back of regulatory authority to the states. Chapter 4 explains how the *Voting Rights Act of 1965* and the *Transportation Safety Act of 1974* authorize issuance of a ruling by concerned federal administrators in response to a request for a determination whether a state or local government law or regulation is precluded by one of these statutes, thereby clarifying the authority of subnational governments.[2] The confusion produced by numerous preemption statutes, particularly ones lacking an explicit preemption clause, has resulted in plaintiffs seeking clarification of the scope of preemption in a federal or a state court, thereby adding to court congestion.

Caustic critics charge preemption statutes relating to areas of traditional state regulatory responsibility have led to the expansion of the powers of the national government and reduction of subnational governments to little more than administrative appendages of the federal government, have deprived states of many of their sovereign powers reserved by the Tenth Amendment, and have converted a polycentric governance system into a monocentric one. Critics often cite decisions of the U.S. Supreme Court validating congressional exercise of preemption powers as a major factor in the reduced governance role of the states and their political subdivisions. Chapter 1 refers to Herbert Wechsler's political safeguards theory of federalism, which posits states can employ the political process to defeat bills in Congress which would preempt one or more of the powers reserved to the states.[3] This chapter also refers to U.S. Supreme Court Justice Harry A. Blackmun's 1985 thesis, which posits states should seek relief from preemption statutes in Congress, the political branch of government, and not in the judicial branch.[4]

This chapter reviews our findings and draws conclusions relating to the (1) various types of congressional preemption devices utilized to restructure the federal system; (2) extent of the powers exercised by states subsequent to 1965 when Congress commenced to rely heavily upon its preemption powers to achieve national policy goals; (3) relative success of preemption statutes in achieving their declared goals; (4) responsiveness of Congress to the federalism concerns of the states and their political subdivisions; (5) success of the *Unfunded Mandates Reform Act of 1995*; (6) citizen understanding of the governance system; and (7) adequacy of the dual and cooperative theories of federalism in explaining the operation of the federal system in the opening decade of the twenty-first century.[5] In addition, postulates of a general theory of U.S. federalism are presented and recommendations are advanced to improve the functioning of the federal system in an era of congressional preemption.

Complete Congressional Preemption

Chapter 4 describes seventeen types of preemption statutes completely removing regulatory powers in a given field from states and their political subdivisions. The first type includes statutes administered successfully without subnational governmental assistance, as illustrated by ones providing there will be no federal or state economic regulation of the airline and bus industries, abolishing a mandatory retirement age for most employees, regulating bankruptcies, establishing a uniform time system, mandating health labeling on cigarette packages, and requiring poison-prevention packaging.

A complete preemption statute commonly raises more than one preemption issue, and the views of the states toward the various issues may differ. The *Poultry Products Inspection Act of 1968*, for example, preempts responsibility for inspection of interstate shipments of such products and states have registered no objection to this provision of the statute.[6] A number of states, however, object to the complete labeling preemption provision on the ground they should possess authority to require labels to indicate the state of origin. Several states also oppose the federal requirement the label must indicate the net weight at the time of introducing the poultry into the interstate commerce stream and prefer a label indicating the weight at the time of the retail sale because of the loss of weight during shipment.

Several statutory complete preemption types either need the assistance of subnational governments or authorize a very limited regulatory state and local government role. A chapter 4 case study reveals the Nuclear Regulatory Commission is dependent upon subnational governments for assistance in the event a radiation incident at a nuclear electric power plant necessitates evacuation of citizens residing within a given distance of the plant. However, the *Atomic Energy Act* as amended provides no role for these governments, and Congress apparently assumed these units will provide assistance in the event of a emergency at such a plant or an accident involving transportation of radioactive materials.[7]

The state activities exception to total preemption contained in the *National Traffic and Motor Vehicle Safety Act of 1966*, for motor vehicles operated by subnational governments, is unique.[8] Limited regulatory turn-backs authorized by several preemption statutes permit states to play a minor role in the regulatory activity. Although only eight states have assumed inspection and weighing functions under the *United States Grain Standards Act of 1968*, forty-four states have received a limited turn-back of regulatory authority from the Environmental Protection Agency under the *Resource Conservation and Recovery Act of 1976*, and thirty-one states participate in the federal railroad safety inspection program authorized by the *Federal Railroad Safety Act of 1970*.[9] The most successful program of this nature is the agreement states program of the Nuclear Regulatory Commission, authorized by the *Atomic Energy Act of 1959*.[10] All studies reveal the program is an excellent example of cooperative federalism.

The most undesirable types of a complete federal preemption statute, in the eyes of state and local government officers, are the *Voting Rights Act of 1965*, noted above, and ones mandating state legislatures to enact a specific statute law as illustrated by the *Equal Employment Opportunity Act of 1972*.[11] Experience reveals officers of the U.S. Department of Justice suggest to subnational government officers the changes to their proposed election systems that will have to be made before clearance is granted, thereby in effect mandating de facto changes.

The New York state legislature in 1972, following publication of the *1970 Census of Governments*, enacted a redistricting plan for its assembly and senate and submitted the plan to the Department of Justice for approval. Staff in its voting rights section informed legislative leaders the plan would not be approved unless specific changes were made, including the splitting in two of an assembly district in Brooklyn represented by a Hasidic Jew. Facing a deadline for preparation for 1972 congressional and state elections, the state legislature was called into special session on May 29, 1972, and redrew the district lines as directed.[12] The U.S. Supreme Court in 1977 upheld the constitutionality of the racial gerrymander.[13]

No consideration was given by the Department of Justice or the Court to alternative electoral systems, such as the single transferable vote system of proportional representation.[14] This system employs multimember electoral districts and is a preferential vote system ensuring each ethnic or racial group will elect a number of its members to office in direct proportion to the group's percentage of the total votes cast. This system has the additional advantage of making deliberate gerrymandering of district lines impossible. Two other multimember electoral district systems—cumulative voting and limited voting—have been employed subsequently by a number of local governments in southern states to resolve lawsuits alleging violation of the *Voting Rights Act of 1965* as amended.[15]

Evidence to date does not support the contention of the most critical subnational government officers that these types of statutes incrementally have destroyed the federal system by reducing states to the legal status of vassals of Congress, yet such statutes obviously hinder cooperative national-state relations. Should Congress decide it is essential that all state legislatures enact a uniform statute on a given subject, preference should be given to the use of conditional grants-in-aid, crossover sanctions, conditional tax credits, and other actions described below to prod state legislatures to enact the statute.

Partial Congressional Preemption

There are eleven distinctive types of congressional partial preemption statutes, which may be placed in two general categories. The first general category includes statutes occupying completely a segment of a regulatory field. This category typically has a relatively minor impact on states compared to the impact of statutes in the second category—minimum standards preemption, under which Congress and/or federal administrative departments and agencies establish minimum national regulatory standards. Each state may continue to regulate in the preempted field provided the state submits a plan to the concerned federal department or agency containing state standards at least as stringent as the national ones and information demonstrating the state has the necessary competent personnel and equipment essential for an effective regulatory program. If the plan is approved, the concerned federal department or agency delegates regulatory primacy to the state, which has sole responsibility for the regulatory function subject only to monitoring by the concerned federal department or agency.

Congressional minimum standards preemption statutes seek to form an administrative regulatory partnership between the national government and the states. To date, a majority of the states have applied for and received regulatory primacy under the various minimum standards preemption acts—*Clean Air Act, Clean Water Act, Resource Conservation and Recovery Act, Safe Drinking Water Act*, and *Surface Mining Control and Reclamation Act*. Congress provides funding to states granted regulatory primacy to assist them in achieving their objectives.

These statutes collectively produced a revolution in national-state relations and are evidence the cooperative federalism theory is not outdated, although it is in need of supplementation by a broader theory, as explained below. Minimum standards preemption also is examined in subsequent sections with respect to its success in achieving congressionally determined goals.

A number of partial preemption statutes devolve to state governors powers not granted to them by their respective state constitution or statutes. These devolved executive and administrative powers have attracted little public attention or scholarly examination. Such a devolution on occasion generates gubernatorial-legislative conflicts. The small number of such conflicts is attributable in part to voluminous congressional preemption statutes and implementing administrative rules and regulations beyond the ability of members of the typical state legislature to understand with respect to the significance of the devolutions.

Many objections directed against conditional federal grants-in-aid also are directed against partial preemption statutes. Critics are convinced such statutes and voluminous implementing administrative regulations reduce unnecessarily the discretionary authority of states and local governments; result in federal bureaucratic dominance and distortion of subnational governmental appropriations, contain no mechanism for ensuring adequate subnational governmental input into the enactment of preemption statutes and promulgation of implementing rules and regulations, burden states and local governments with inflexible programmatic requirements; and create an accountability problem. Critics often use polemical terms in their attacks on preemption statutes. Nevertheless, it is apparent a number of criticisms contain a degree of validity. The next section examines newer approaches to the use of Congress's supersession powers.

Innovative Statutes

Conservatives and subnational government officers often castigate Congress for enacting preemption statutes, yet many states supported enactment of particular preemption statutes, such as the *Abandoned Shipwreck Act of 1987*, the *Commercial Motor Vehicle Safety Act of 1986*, and various minimum standards preemption acts.[16] Congress in recent years has enacted several innovative preemption statutes respecting state sovereignty.

Congress possesses broad powers to regulate interstate commerce and in 1951 enacted the *Johnson Act*, which contains a section allowing a state to "opt-out" of a congressional provision. The act makes it unlawful for any person to transport a gambling device into a state. It includes a section authorizing a state legislature to enact a statute exempting the state from the provision and stipulating the provision does not "apply to any gambling device used or designed for use at or transported to licensed gambling establishments where betting is legal under applicable laws.[17]

The *Coastal Zone Management Act of 1972* and the *Nuclear Waste Policy Act of 1982* are partial preemption statutes containing a distinctive provision for a state suspensive veto of a decision by a federal department or agency subject to an override of the veto by the secretary of commerce and Congress, respectively.[18] In effect, these acts offer a degree of protection against federal government administrators by subjecting their decisions to a mandated review.

The former act is a particularly interesting one, stipulating that a state coastal-zone management program approved by the secretary of commerce prevents a federal department or agency from issuing a license or a permit to a private applicant to undertake an activity if the concerned state objects to the application. The act provides for a reverse type of preemption subject to an override by the secretary.

Congress in enacting the *Toxic Substances Control Act of 1976* accorded states a degree of regulatory flexibility by authorizing them to continue to regulate a chemical mixture and substance until the EPA administrator promulgates a rule applicable to the mixture or substances.[19] Furthermore, the administrator in promulgating a rule may exempt the concerned mixture or substance from the rule if state regulations do not place an undue burden on interstate commerce and offer a higher degree of public protection.

Another reverse preemption section is contained in the *Port and Tanker Safety Act of 1978*.[20] The requirement for federally licensed pilots on tankers engaged in foreign commerce in navigable waters is preempted when a state legislature enacts a statute mandating state-licensed pilots on such tankers and notifies the secretary of transportation.

The *Nuclear Waste Policy Act of 1982* empowers a state governor or a state legislature to veto a site for a high-level radioactive waste facility selected by the secretary of energy.[21] As explained in chapter 4, Congress in 1987 in effect nullified this innovative procedure by eliminating two of the three identified sites subject to further tests of the Yucca Mountain site in Nevada. In 2002, Congress overrode the veto of the Nevada site by the state's governor.[22]

Congress included in the *Coast Guard Authorization Act of 1984* a directive to the U.S. secretary of transportation to develop standards for determining whether a marine recreational vessel operator is intoxicated.[23] The Coast Guard, now a unit of the Department of Homeland Security, responded in 1987 by promulgating a rule stipulating a state blood alcohol content (BAC) standard, if one exists, is the national standard within the state. As a result, the national standard (currently 0.8 percent BAC) applies only in states lacking a BAC standard.

In 1986, Congress amended the *Atlantic Striped Bass Conservation Act* by including a contingent provision requiring states to comply with the management plan developed by the interstate-compact created Atlantic States Marine Fisheries Commission, which lacks enforcement powers, or be subject to a striped-bass fishing moratorium imposed by the U.S. Fish and Wildlife Service.[24]

The *Abandoned Shipwreck Act of 1987* is a complete preemption statute, but may be described as a state-friendly one.[25] Technological developments facilitate the location of numerous abandoned historic shipwrecks, but an important legal question had been raised with respect to the ownership of each located shipwreck. The statute solves this problem by asserting a federal government title to each such shipwreck and directing the transfer of the federal title to the state in whose waters the shipwreck is located.

In 1994, Congress enacted the *Riegle-Neal Interstate Banking and Branching Efficiency Act* containing an "opt out" section that authorizes a state legislature to enact a law prohibiting interstate branching within the state otherwise authorized by the act.[26] Furthermore, the act contains an "opt-in" section that allows a state legislature to permit interstate branching through *de novo* branches provided the state law "applies equally to all banks; and expressly permits all out-of-state banks to establish *de novo* branches" in the state.[27]

Congress in the same year revised, recodified, and added a new section to the transportation statutes stipulating, effective September 30, 1996, a state "may establish, maintain, or enforce a law or regulation that has a fuel use tax reporting requirement (including any tax reporting form) only if the requirement conforms with the International Fuel Tax Agreement."[28] The purpose of the section is to establish a uniform fuel use tax reporting system for trucking companies by encouraging states to adopt the international agreement. This section is respectful of state sovereignty because the agreement was developed and may be revised by states and Canadian provinces.[29]

The *Gramm-Leach-Bliley Financial Modernization Act of 1999* preempts state insurance statutes and regulations in thirteen regulatory areas and threatened to establish a national system of licensing insurance agents if twenty-six state legislatures did not enact by November 12, 2002, harmonius licensing statutes as determined by the National Association of Insurance Commissioners (NAIC).[30] On September 10, 2002, NAIC certified thirty-five states had enacted such statutes. Acting to forestall the enactment of additional congressional preemptive insurance statutes, the association in 2002 drafted an Interstate Insurance Product Regulation Compact providing for the creation of a commission with authority to promulgate uniform insurance rules and regulations applicable to disability income, individual and group annuity, life insurance, and long-term insurance policies. The compact contains a section allowing a member state to opt-out of a rule or regulation promulgated by the commission. Extensive state utilization of this section could result in nonharmonious insurance rules and regulations, thereby encouraging Congress to preempt additional state insurance regulatory laws and implementing rules and regulations.[31]

Congress enacted the *Electronic Signatures in Global and National Commerce Act of 2000*, which preempts completely forty-four state digital signatures laws with respect to interstate and foreign commerce. The act, however, exempts from preemption any state statute or rule constituting "an enactment or adoption of the Uniform Electronic Transaction Act as approved and recommended for enactment in all the States by the National Conference of Commissioners on Uniform State Laws."[32] This act is another example of Congress utilizing the threat of preemption to encourage state legislatures to enact harmonious regulatory statutes.

Note also should be made of two non-grant and non-preemptive federal statutes promoting uniform regulation by states. The *Hotel and Motel Fire Safety Act of* 1990 is designed to encourage states to adopt federal standards by stipulating federal government officers and employees may stay only in facilities meeting the safety standards specified by the *Federal Fire Prevention and Control Act of 1974*.[33] The governor of each state is authorized to provide the federal administrator of general services with a list of hotels and motels meeting the federal fire safety standards. In addition, federal conditional grants-in-aid to subnational governments may not be used to sponsor or to pay for a conference, convention, meeting, or training seminar in a hotel or motel failing to meet the national fire safety standards.

The Muhammad Ali Boxing Reform Act of 2000 seeks:

(1) to protect the rights and welfare of professional boxers on an interstate basis by preventing certain exploitive, oppressive, and unethical business practices;

(2) to assist State boxing commissioners in their efforts to provide more effective public oversight of the sport; and

(3) to promote honorable competition in professional boxing and enhance the overall integrity of the industry.[34]

The act stipulates the Association of Boxing Commissions, by a majority vote of its member state boxing commissions, must adopt "guidelines for objective and consistent written criteria for the ratings of professional boxers."[35] Instead of mandating state boxing commissions to follow the guidelines, the act provides simply it is "the sense of Congress" the guidelines should be followed.[36] Senator John McCain of Arizona, however, introduced S. 275—*Professional Boxing Amendments Act of 2003*—establishing a United States Boxing Administration with authority to establish minimum standards for boxing which must be followed by state boxing commissions, thereby superseding the 2000 act.

The Accountability-Responsibility Problem

The question of which plane of government has exclusive or concurrent jurisdiction over governmental regulatory functions automatically is associated with federalism, an abstract organizational principle for dividing political powers between the planes. The U.S. Constitution does not contain precise and permanent jurisdictional boundary lines between the various planes of governments. Congressional complete and partial preemption statutes, for political reasons, often are nondefinitive relative to the respective powers of the national and state planes of government, particularly the powers of the states at the peripheries of preempted regulatory areas.

The Constitution's drafters were aware conflicts would arise in the new federal system between states and between Congress and the states, and provided a neutral referee—the U.S. Supreme Court—to conduct a trial and render an authoritative decision for the first type of conflicts. The Constitution's supremacy of the laws clause specifically was included to resolve a conflict between a congressional regulatory statute, based upon a delegated power, and a state constitutional provision or law in favor of the former. This clause, of course, is inadequate today for determining the respective powers and responsibilities of the two planes as it is applicable only when the constitutionality of a state statute is challenged in court and Congress possesses the power to preempt completely or partially state regulatory powers in a given field in the absence of any state constitutional provision or statute.

The preamble to the Constitution declares the people established it "in order to form a more perfect union" of states capable of adapting

dynamically and effectively to changing conditions. The framers have
left us such a legacy, but it is inconceivable they could have envisioned
the current kaleidoscopic federal system with its extreme complexity and
interdependence of the three planes of government.

Informed citizens in a unitary nation or in a fully theoretical "dual"
federal system readily can hold a government responsible for failure to
solve a problem(s) or to provide adequate services. The theory of dual
federalism had considerable explanatory value until 1937, when the U.S.
Supreme Court reversed many of its previous state rights decisions. The
adequacy of the theory also was undermined, commencing in the 1960s,
by congressional enactment of numerous complete and partial preemption statutes of various types, precluding the electorate from readily
determining whether the states or the national government or both
should be held responsible for actions taken or not taken, or actions
taken incompetently.

Chapter 4 explains there are relatively few jurisdictional disputes
involving congressional preemption statutes that completely remove regulatory authority from states or contain a savings clause stipulating
Congress does not intend to occupy the entire regulatory field to the
exclusion of state regulation. There is, however, a jurisdictional morass
associated with expansively worded statutes lacking an explicit preemption statement and with certain partial preemption statutes whose scope
is unclear. The jurisdictional confusion is attributable in part to the
inclusions of many provisions in a single statute applicable to a variety of
situations or the *sub silentio* exercise of preemption powers by Congress
with respect to their reach. Congress ignores the 1967 advice of Senator
Howard H. Baker, Jr., of Tennessee: " . . . I respectfully suggest that we
ought to give very close attention to the language that we adopt so that
this question of preemption or nonpreemption or even personal legislative preemption is clearly spelled out, so that we do not hinder the
efforts of local authorities to respond to local circumstances."[37]

The basic premise of democratic theory is voter establishment of
government officers' responsibility to allow them to be held accountable
for malfeasance, misfeasance, nonfeasance, and/or failure to achieve
mandated goals. A federal system inherently is incapable of eliminating
all uncertainty relative to the responsibilities of each plane of government, but the national legislature is capable of reducing the uncertainties
when enacting preemption statutes.

Proposals are made periodically for a "swap" of specified functional
responsibilities between the national government and the states and
reflect dissatisfaction with the confused responsibility allocation. One
can predict with reasonable certainty a "swap" of responsibilities would

not eliminate all jurisdictional confusion and the passage of time would result in congressional enactment of preemption statutes and court decisions producing additional confusion.

Partial preemption statutes would lead to fewer disputes and confusion if they included a code of restrictions applicable to state and local activities in each of the partially preempted functional fields. While a code would not remove all statutory ambiguities, it would reduce interplane conflicts and the need for judicial forums, which act on a case-by-case basis, to resolve the conflicts.

A strong case also could be made for inclusion of such a code in complete preemption statutes, since state exercise of the police power may be reasonable under many circumstances and would not hinder the statutory goal achievements. Chapter 4 highlights the U.S. Supreme Court's interpretation of the preemption statute eliminating all economic regulation of airlines as depriving states of the power to investigate and punish airlines guilty of consumer fraud.

Acting upon its own authority, the U.S. Department of Transportation in effect has promulgated a code of restrictions with respect to administrative rules and regulations relating to the routing of motor carriers transporting radioactive materials. This code stipulates a state routing rule applicable to such carriers is preempted if

1. It prohibits transportation of highway route controlled quantity radioactive materials by highway between any two points without providing an alternative route for the duration of the prohibition; or
2. It does not meet all of the following criteria:
   (a) The rule is established by a State routing agency as defined in 171.8 of this subchapter;
   (b) The rule is based on a comparative radiological risk assessment process at least as sensitive as that outline in the "DOT Guidelines";
   (c) The rule is based on evaluation of radiological risk wherever it may occur, and on a solicitation and substantive consideration of views from each affected jurisdiction, including local jurisdictions and other States;
   (d) The rule ensures reasonable continuity of routes between jurisdictions.[38]

This code of restrictions also addresses local-routing rules and quantities of radioactive materials subject to mandatory placarding. Any other state or local government transportation rule is preempted if it:

A. Conflicts with physical security requirements which the Nuclear Regulatory Commission has established in 10 CFR Part 73 or requirements approved by the Department of Transportation under §173.22(c) of this subchapter;

B. Requires additional or special personnel, equipment, or escort;

C. Requires additional or different shipping paper entries, placards, or other hazard warning devices;

D. Requires filing route plans or other documents containing information that is specific to individual shipments;

E. Requires prenotification;

F. Requires accident or incident reporting other than as immediately necessary for emergency assistance; or

G. Unnecessarily delays transportation.[39]

Codes of restrictions will need updating periodically because fluidity will continue to characterize relations between the national and state planes of government as Congress enacts complete or partial preemption statutes and on rare occasions devolves a power to the states.

Preemption statutes are products of the politics of special interest groups, including state and local governments, in which opportunities for effective citizen participation typically are limited. The relative impotence of the citizenry has been increased by U.S. Supreme Court decisions—*Buckley v. Valeo* in 1976 and *First National Bank v. Bellotti* in 1978. These decisions invalidate provisions of state corrupt practices acts which respectively limit the amount of money a candidate may spend from his and her personal funds and prohibit corporations and labor unions to contribute funds to referendum campaigns.[40]

Participation in the public policy formation process by active and informed citizens is a key premise of democratic theory, but is ineffective when Congress makes preemption decisions. The process of enacting congressional statutes often includes public hearings, but such hearings are an ineffective process for citizens who lack funds and time to travel to Washington, D.C., and detailed technical information and staff support in comparison to resource-rich special interest groups.

The local government plane, with its relatively small scale, affords citizens the greatest opportunity to exert effective influence in the policymaking process. To the extent congressional preemption, directly or indirectly through the states, limits authority of general purpose local governments, participatory democracy will suffer. It has suffered, as reflected in public opinion polls that reveal the citizenry generally has the highest respect for general purpose local governments and the least respect for the national government.

Congressional Preemption and Goal Achievement

Congress enacted the first preemption statute in 1790, appeared to be reluctant to use its supersession powers in the late eighteenth and the nineteenth century, and did not enact a major statute based upon its power to regulate interstate commerce until 1887. Although the Articles of Confederation and Perpetual Union did not specifically authorize the unicameral Congress to make land grants to states, it enacted the Northwest Ordinance of 1785, reserving one square mile in each township for educational purposes in the geographical area covered by the ordinance[41] In 1862, Congress enacted the *Morrill Act*, providing land grants to states as an incentive for the establishment of state colleges of agriculture and mechanical arts.[42] The U.S. Supreme Court in 1866 opined the acceptance of a congressional grant with conditions by a state was a contract protected against infringement by the Constitution's contract clause.[43]

Congress in 1887 enacted the *Hatch Act*, establishing the first continuing grant-in-aid program, which encouraged states to establish agricultural experiment stations at state agricultural colleges.[44] In 1894, Congress for the first time attached a condition for the receipt of a grant-in-aid and with the passage of time gradually added conditions to new grants-in-aid.[45] Increased reliance was placed upon conditional grants-in-aid in the 1950s and the early 1960s as incentives for state and local governments to implement national policies.

A significant number of members of Congress by the mid-1960s questioned the effectiveness of conditional grants-in-aid and decided its powers of complete and partial preemption should be exercised more frequently to achieve national goals. Measuring preemption statutes' goal achievement is a difficult task for three reasons. First, Congress often employs grants-in-aid simultaneously with preemption statutes and disaggregation of the contribution of each to achieving national goals is a near impossibility.

Second, congressional enactment of a preemption statute to solve a particular problem may be desirable, but the standards established may be impossible to achieve with existing and perhaps future technology. Or the time frame mandated by Congress for goal achievement may be too short for a variety of reasons, as illustrated by the failure of the *Clean Air Act* and its amendments to achieve their stated objectives, thereby necessitating the grant by Congress of time extensions for states to achieve the mandated goals.

Third, preemption statutes may achieve their respective goal(s), but in the process create other public problems. The Atomic Energy Commission (now Nuclear Regulatory Commission) was established by the *Atomic Energy Act of 1946*, a preemption statute prospectively removing from states all powers to regulate ionizing radiation.[46] Amendments to the act in 1954 authorized the use of ionizing radiation for peaceful purposes, including the generation of electrical power.[47] The amendments encouraged construction and operation of a number of nuclear power plants, thereby raising concerns by subnational government officers and nearby residents with respect to the safety of such plants and the potential effectiveness of emergency plans for the evacuation of nearby residents.

Similar safety concerns are the product of congressional enactment of the *Surface Transportation Assistance Act of 1982*, which completely preempts state and local truck size and weight limits (see below).[48] There is no denying the act has facilitated the more efficient interstate transportation of goods and materials, thereby lowering their costs to consumers. Nevertheless, highway safety has been reduced by the permission granted to companies to operate large and oversize trucks and truck-trailer combinations on older highways not designed to accommodate safely such vehicles.

Congress may enact complete and partial statutes and federal agencies may promulgate implementing rules and regulations, but such actions do not guarantee their effective enforcement. The U.S. Advisory Commission on Intergovernmental Relations published a report examining the growth of intergovernmental regulation, its legal foundation, legislative origins, implementation, and impact of national intergovernmental regulation, and advanced recommendations to reform the intergovernmental regulation system.[49] The commission identified enforcement as "the weakest link" in intergovernmental regulation and concluded:

> As a general rule,...federal intergovernmental regulations have proven difficult to enforce, statutory deadlines have been repeatedly extended or ignored, and compliance—though probably better than one would anticipate, given the generally haphazard character of federal supervision—has fallen short of official expectations. Such shortcomings in performance account for the Doctor Jeckyll and Mr. Hyde reputation of the Office of Civil Rights (OCR) and many other federal regulatory agencies. OCR has been regarded as a hotbed of regulatory zealots by one set of critics and as a timid, lumbering bureaucracy by another. Both are correct—but each is looking at a different aspect of the process.[50]

The enforcement problems, according to the commission, were attributable to "administrative and technical problems, a lack of adequate resources, and political obstacles to the imposition of sanctions."[51] Although the report was published in 1984, it remains accurate in the first decade of the twenty-first century and probably will remain accurate during the foreseeable future. The national bureaucratic regulatory behemoth has major administrative and technical problems, and never has been granted adequate resources by Congress to execute in a most effective manner its many assigned duties, including supervision of the compliance of states granted regulatory primacy with the various minimum standards established by preemption statutes and implementing rules and regulations.

Furthermore, Congress is a political body responsive to strongly exerted pressure as reflected in the granting of extension of times to subnational governments to comply with statutory and administrative regulatory standards or in the granting of complete or partial exemption from regulatory standards for certain activities, such as runoff of water from agricultural lands and emissions from coal-burning electrical generating plants of sulfur dioxide, which produces acid rain and results in the death of marine life in lakes and ponds located in mountains. The following three sections briefly examine national air pollution abatement statutes, water pollution abatement statutes, and securities statutes in terms of goal achievement.

Air Pollution Abatement

Congressional regulation of air pollution dates to the enactment of the *Air Quality Act of 1967* (now *Clean Air Act*).[52] Immediately thereafter, Congress commenced to consider the enactment of more stringent standards. Director John Middleton of the National Center for Air Pollution of the U.S. Public Health Service in 1967 testified, before the U.S. Senate Subcommittee on Air and Water Pollution, "there are severe limitations on the technology now available for controlling many important sources of air pollution."[53] Ignoring these facts, Congress enacted the *Clean Air Act Amendments of 1970*, mandating national achievement of air quality goals by specified dates without taking into consideration the economic and/or technical feasibility of current abatement controls.[54] Commencing with 1975 models, automobiles were required to achieve a 90 percent reduction of emissions of carbon monoxide, hydrocarbons, and nitrogen oxide compared to the 1970 emission standards.

Chairman Edmund S. Muskie of the Senate Subcommittee on Air and Water Pollution provided the answer to the question why Congress ignored Middleton's advice: Muskie was convinced air quality could be improved only by the application of continuous strong congressional pressure on major air polluters and such pressure would foster technological developments facilitating the removal of pollutants from stationary and mobile sources.[55] This "command and control" approach, however, soon proved to be a failure.

The *Clean Air Act Amendments of 1977* reduced the effectiveness of the air pollution abatement program and the EPA administrator initiated other actions weakening the program.[56] In 1979, representative Barry Goldwater, Jr., of California highlighted the fact that the majority of air quality control regions did not meet ambient air quality standards as late as one year after the original deadline. Goldwater noted this failure should have resulted in questioning of the approach embodied in the 1970 amendments, and added: "The 1977 amendments...have revised the timetable again, but in talking with officials at the Environmental Protection Agency and with agency heads in California at the state and local level, I am convinced that this standard of procrastination has become par for the course. Let us fact it—we are bogged down in a cesspool of government rules which have already impacted on our economic growth and program to achieve energy self-sufficiency at a time when the economy and our energy situation are both very uncertain."[57]

EPA in 1979 extended the deadline for refiners to reduce the amount of lead in gasoline and relaxed pollution standards for individual electric power plants, including two operated by the Cleveland Electric Illuminating Company producing more air pollution than all consolidated Edison Company plants.[58] Although air quality had improved a decade later, the December 31, 1987, deadlines for achievement of air pollutant reduction goals were not met in most air quality regions of the country. The *Clean Air Act* as amended authorizes the EPA administrator to penalize areas not in compliance with the act and its implementing rules and regulations by prohibiting construction of new major sources of pollution or modifications of existing sources—electric-generating plants, industrial boilers, and petroleum refiners—and by reducing federal highway and Clean Air Act grants-in-aid. Congress responded late in 1987 to pressures from state and local government officers and extended the deadline for attainment of the act's goals.[59]

Congress readdressed the air pollution problem in the *Clean Air Act Amendments of 1990*, a massive statute containing 313 pages of fine print, with five extensive sections relating to nonattainment areas.[60] The amendments authorize the EPA administrator to require states to make "reasonable further progress" in reducing air pollution and to consider the "availability and feasibility of control measures" in determining the appropriate classification of nonattainment areas.[61] Furthermore, the amendments establish new extended deadlines for nonattainment areas to achieve attainment for various pollutants. Twenty years is allowed for ozone nonattainment areas classified as extreme to reach mandated air quality goals, but only five years is allowed for lead, nitrogen dioxide, and/or sulfur dioxide nonattainment areas to meet mandated goals.[62]

The one major innovation contained in the amendments is authorization for the trading of emission pollution allowances effective in

1995, an approach in sharp contrast to the previous command-and-control approach requiring pollution sources to install emission control equipment or construct replacement facilities emitting less air pollution. The amendments define an allowance as "a limited authorization to emit sulfur dioxide, a primary cause of acid rain, in accordance with provisions of this title."[63] The purpose of the authorized trading is to encourage electric-generating companies to construct coal-fired power plants emitting less sulfur dioxide or to install new pollution abatement equipment in existing plants. By lowering emissions of sulfur dioxide below the maximum allowable by the act, a company will gain allowances saleable to companies owning plants emitting more than the allowable amount of this pollutant pending the construction of new plants emitting less pollution.

Evidence reveals the trading program is effective in reducing overall emissions of sulfur dioxide; they have decreased from 9.40 million tons in 1980 to 4.35 million tons in 1999, according to EPA.[64] An independent study of sulfur dioxide emissions, subsequent to the 1990 amendments, reported "large reductions have occurred in Ohio, Indiana, West Virginia, Tennessee, Kentucky, Georgia, Missouri, and New York in the 1990s."[65] The study, however, concluded there had been little improvement in terms of emissions in Alabama, Florida, Illinois, North Carolina, and Pennsylvania.

Phase II commenced in 2000 and achieved in its second year a 5 percent reduction in sulfur dioxide emissions compared to 2000.[66] EPA projects the 1990 amendments will achieve their goal of reducing by 50 percent the 1980 sulfur dioxide emission level.[67] Congress and EPA commissioned the National Academy of Public Administration to review the New Source Review program requiring electric power–generating companies to install new pollution control devices when plants are expanded or upgraded. In its 2003 report, the academy concluded EPA's failure to enforce air pollution abatement standards permits older coal-fired power plants to continue to be major sources of emission of pollutants.[68]

Water Pollution Abatement

The *Water Quality Act of 1965* is the first national statute to regulate water pollution abatement and broke new ground in terms of the nature of congressional preemption by establishing minimum water quality standards throughout the nation.[69] The Council on Environmental Quality reported in 1978 "members of Congress expressed serious concern over the direction the grants program had taken—whether it had been used more to promote growth than to control pollution," but added "water quality is gradually improving" after thirteen years of partial congressional preemption.[70]

EPA administrator Douglas M. Costle in 1979 reported "no substantial change in the concentration of conventional pollutants in our water for the nation as a whole between 1974 and 1978," but responded to the expressed congressional concern as follows: "We've made mistakes in the water program, no doubt about it. We've learned to analyze grant applications to make sure that they address genuine community needs rather than subsidizing community growth."[71]

EPA reported 80 percent of the industrial discharge sources met the congressionally mandated July 1, 1977, deadline for water pollution abatement, but approximately 60 percent of the 17,000 municipal sewerage plants failed to meet the deadline even though municipalities had received grants totaling approximately $28 billion to improve existing plants and construct new ones.

Industrial firms complained the removal of all nontoxic discharges into waterways would cost more than they already had expended to remove up to 98 percent of such discharges. EPA reacted to the complaints in 1979 by relaxing water quality standards for sixty-four subcategories of discharges on the ground the *Clean Water Act of 1977* requires the nontoxic standards to be "reasonably" economic.[72]

Initially, municipalities were required to meet secondary treatment standards by 1977, but Congress extended the deadline to 1983 and subsequently to March 31, 1989.[73] Nevertheless, approximately 1,500 major sewage treatment plants and approximately 1,000 minor treatment facilities were not in compliance with the standards in 1988.[74]

Municipalities complained the reduction in achieving the secondary treatment standards in part was due to a reduction in federal grants-in-aid for sewerage treatment facilities and EPA's decision to seek court fines for municipalities failing to meet the standards. Such fines were particularly burdensome for the most common offenders—economically depressed municipalities.[75]

In 2003, the EPA's inspector general issued a report detailing the failure of the agency's water pollution abatement program by noting the computer system is obsolete, contains inaccurate data, and omits thousands of the more than 64,000 sources of water pollution.[76] The report specifically warns the national system of water discharge permits is mismanaged as thousands of permits expire each year and are not renewed, and the system has failed to ensure waterways are suitable for fishing, swimming, and other activities. Shortly thereafter, EPA released a second report revealing approximately 25 percent of the largest industrial plants and water treatment facilities violate water quality standards, but only a few have been subjected to enforcement action.[77]

John B. Stephenson, EPA's director of natural resources and environment, testified before a U.S. House of Representatives subcommittee on June 19, 2003, "states rely heavily on EPA-developed 'criteria documents'" relating to various types of pollutants to identify and clean up polluted waters, and added there are no such criteria for "approximately 50 percent of water quality impairments nationwide."[78] EPA's failure to develop criteria for sedimentation and nutrients, such as phosphorus and nitrogen, compounds the problem of abating water pollution.

The safe drinking water program has been plagued by similar problems. EPA in 1989 had only 43 enforcement officers who took action on only 800 of approximately 80,000 complaints. Nevertheless, a 2003 EPA report maintained 94 percent of citizens consumed drinking water meeting national health standards, compared to 79 percent in 1993.[79] Five days after EPA issued the report, the agency's inspector general launched an investigation to determine whether EPA deliberately misled the public by not considering its audits that revealed state underestimation of violations of the act.[80]

Critics of time extensions for the achievement of air and water quality standards maintain the compliance burden is shifted from older facilities to new facilities required to meet the standards immediately.[81] Furthermore, states and municipalities causing problems for their neighbors escape some of the economic burdens carried by good neighbor states and municipalities conscientiously initiating actions over the years to prevent or to reduce environmental pollution.

Regulation of the Securities Industry

State regulation of the securities industry in the form of "Blue Sky" laws dates to a 1911 Kansas statute.[82] Today, all states have such laws and a dual regulatory system exists for the securities industry in common with the banking industry.[83] Congress enacted ten statutes regulating areas of the former industry beyond the jurisdiction of individual states: *Securities Act of 1933, Securities Exchange Act of 1934, Public Utility Holding Company Act of 1935, Trust Indenture Act of 1939, Investment Company Act of 1940, Investment Advisers Act of 1940, Private Securities Litigation Reform Act of 1995, National Securities Markets Improvement Act of 1996, Securities Litigation Uniform Standards Act of 1998,* and *Sabanes-Oxley Act of 2002.*[84] The above acts have been amended over the years; the *Securities Act of 1933* has twenty-two amendments. The 1996 act, for example, preempted existing state authority to mandate pre-sale registration disclosures and the *Sabanes-Oxley Act of 2002* created the Public Company Accounting Oversight Board, with authority to exercise powers conferred upon it "without regard to any qualification, licensing, or other provision of law in effect in such State (or a political subdivision thereof)."[85]

It would be reasonable to assume these statutes grant the U.S. Securities and Exchange Commission (SEC) adequate authority to protect the interests of investors in securities. New York State Attorney General Eliot Spitzer, however, proved the inadequacy of federal regulation when he revived the dormant 1921 Martin Act, a state statute, and brought successful suits against Merrill Lynch and other Wall Street brokerage firms for fraud.[86] The suits alleged security salespersons urged clients to purchase certain stocks knowing they were a poor investment because the firms were seeking the lucrative investment banking business and associated fees of the companies planning to issue stocks. Subsequently, SEC Chairman Harvey L. Pitt announced the commission would conduct a joint investigation with Spitzer and regulators in other states.[87] In 2003, the ten largest brokerage firms agreed to pay $1.4 billion in fines and to make changes in their practices in order to settle the suits.[88] States will receive $437 million in the settlement and SEC will deposit its settlement proceeds in a fund to reimburse investors.[89]

Massachusetts Secretary of the Commonwealth William F. Galvin and Spitzer announced in 2003 a joint investigation into the mutual fund sales practices of Morgan Stanley, focusing upon allegations the firm offered its brokers incentives to sell proprietary (in house) funds which may not have been in the best interests of the purchasers.[90] Continuing investigations of the securities industry by state investigators have increased state-SEC tensions.

Investment banks wield considerable power in Congress and responded to Spitzer's investigations by persuading Republican Representative Richard H. Baker of Louisiana to introduce a bill—*Securities Fraud Deterrence and Investor Restitution Act of 2003*—preempting state statutes and regulations differing from regulations promulgated by the Securities and Exchange Commission or self-regulating bodies such as the New York and other stock exchanges.[91] This bill bears a striking similarity to a 2002 proposed amendment, according to congressional staffers, supported by Morgan Stanley, which stipulated "no law, rule, regulation, order, administrative action, judgment, consent order, or settlement agreement shall be imposed by any state or people subject to SEC rules."[92] State attorneys general will be deprived of their state authority to investigate security fraud should the bill become law.

Congressional Responsiveness

Reference has been made above to the partial response of Congress to the regulatory concerns of municipalities and industries. This section has two primary foci. The first is the Wechsler political safeguards theory of U.S. federalism, which is examined briefly in terms of the responsiveness of Congress to state complaints relating to preemption statutes. The second focus is Justice Harry A. Blackmun's advice to states to seek relief from preemptive judicial opinions by employing the built-in provisions of the U.S. Constitution to apply pressure upon Congress to obtain relief from regulatory decisions of the Supreme Court.[93] Chapter 6 examines the preemption role of the courts and places emphasis upon the fact many judicial decisions clearly intrude significantly upon the reserved powers of the states although they nevertheless retain significant powers.

The Political Safeguards Thesis

The Wechsler thesis posits the U.S. Constitution contains provisions allowing states to employ them to prevent the enactment of statutes and to receive relief from burdensome statutes. We examine the validity of the thesis in terms of five brief case studies.

Nuclear Power Plant Evacuation Plans. Chapter 4 contains a case study relating to the expressed serious concerns of state and local government officers' with respect to the adequacy of emergency response plans in the event of an incident at nuclear electric power–generation plants. The officers presented solid evidence the plans of the Nuclear Regulatory Commission (NRC) for the safe evacuation of all residents within a ten-mile radius of a nuclear electric power–generating plant in the event of the discharge of radioactive materials were inadequate. Congress nevertheless has not responded to these concerns by authorizing states to play a major formal role in developing such plans, perhaps because such plants are not located in all states.

New York City Air Pollution Abatement Plan. Chapter 5 explains the *Clean Air Act Amendments of 1970* were a dramatic change from the earlier air pollution abatement approach.[94] The amendments provide for considerably more stringent air quality standards to protect the health of citizens and set precise dates for state adoption and implementation of abatement plans without consideration of the economic and technical feasibility of air pollution abatement systems. The failure of stationary source controls, combined with motor vehicle emission controls, to achieve the attainment of statutory ambient air quality standards within an air quality control region automatically mandates adoption of transportation controls, which will force significant changes in the lifestyles of the region's residents.

Governor Nelson A. Rockefeller in 1973 transmitted to the EPA administrator a plan developed in cooperation with Mayor John V. Lindsay of New York City. The administrator approved the plan, providing for imposition of transportation controls, including mandatory vehicle emission inspection, placement of tolls on East River and Harlem River bridges in the city, staggering of work hours, a sharp reduction in the number of midtown Manhattan parking spaces, improved street traffic management, designation of exclusive bus lanes, and a selective ban on taxicab cruising in midtown Manhattan. Friends of the Earth challenged the plan in the U.S. District Court; the court's decision was appealed to the U.S. Court of Appeals for the Second Circuit, which upheld the validity of the plan in 1974.[95]

In 1975, newly elected Mayor Abraham Beame of New York City sought to have the required tolling of the bridges and vehicle emission inspection eliminated from the transportation control plan. He successfully mobilized the New York State congressional delegation, which succeeded in inserting an amendment in the *Clean Air Act Amendments of 1977* directing the EPA administrator to delete from a transportation control plan the required bridge tolling upon application of the governor of the state.[96] Governor Hugh L. Carey of New York in 1977 so notified the administrator and the requirement was deleted from the plan.[97]

Highway Safety. Congress also considered seriously subnational governmental complaints alleging the *Surface Transportation Assistance Act of 1982*, by preempting completely state maximum truck size and weight limits, created serious safety problems. It allowed large trucks, including tandem and triple trailer trucks to operate on numbered interstate highways, constructed prior to the *National Interstate and Defense Highways Act of 1956*, and access roads (to and from terminals) which were not designed to accommodate such vehicles.[98] Congress enacted two statutes addressing the concerns of subnational government officers.

The *Tandem Truck Safety Act of 1984* establishes a procedure by which the governor of a state may determine a section of the interstate highway system cannot accommodate safely large trucks and notify the secretary of transportation of the need for a restriction on such trucks operating on the section.[99] This act specifically stipulates it does not prevent a state or a local government "from imposing any reasonable restriction, based on safety considerations, on truck tractor-semi-trailer combinations."[100]

The *Motor Carrier Safety Act of 1984* directed the secretary of transportation to complete within eighteen months a study and promulgate
minimum commercial vehicle safety standard and to establish a safety
advisory panel. Further, it authorizes states to enforce one of its commercial vehicle safety laws or regulations unless the secretary determines
the law or regulation in question would provide no safety benefit or
place an undue burden on interstate commerce.[101]

The *National Highway System Designation Act of 1995* repealed
two so-called mandates: States no longer are required to enforce the
national highway speed limit or the wearing of helmets by motorcy-
clists.[102] These mandates were conditions attached to federal highway
grants-in-aid to states. Offsetting this relief was an indirect mandate
establishing as a condition of such funding a requirement that state legislatures enact statutes making it illegal for a driver under twenty-one
years of age to operate a motor vehicle with a blood alcohol level of 0.08
percent or higher.[103]

Congressional failure to respond to complaints relating to incident
response plans at a nuclear electric power–generating plant stands in contrast to the congressional sympathetic response to large truck highway
safety concerns. This response difference appears to be a reflection of
political reality: not all states have a nuclear power plant and such plants
are not located throughout a state, in contrast to the national highways
system which covers all states. Not surprisingly, all members of Congress
have a personal interest in highway safety, whereas most members do not
have a nuclear power plant in their respective district or state.

Superannuation. Congress also responded positively to state and local
government complaints directed at the 1982 amendment of the *Age
Discrimination in Employment Act of 1967* that abolish superannuation
requirements, thereby allowing employees to work as long as they
wish.[104] Subnational governments objected to the application of the
amendment to firefighters and law enforcement officers. The *Age
Discrimination in Employment Amendments of 1986* addresses these
complaints by stipulating it is not illegal for a state or a local government
to refuse to hire or discharge such an individual provided the action is
taken "pursuant to a *bonafide* hiring or retirement plan that is not a sub-
terfuge to evade the purposes of this Act."[105]

Unfunded Mandate Relief. Federal mandates and restraints imposed on
states by Congress and courts have been the principal irritants in
national-state relations since 1964, as Congress increasingly employed its
preemption powers. The term "federal mandate" must be distinguished
from conditions attached to grants-in-aid and a federal restraint. A man-

date requires a subnational government to initiate a specific action and a restraint forbids such a government to take a specified action.

A typology of mandates will promote rational analysis of the question whether Congress should reimburse in full or in part all such mandates. Listed below are nine types of mandates.

1. Civil Rights. These mandates are designed to ensure state and local governments do not engage in discriminatory practices. Court orders relating to school busing to promote racial integration and hiring of minority persons by police and fire departments contain many mandates.

2. Good Neighbor. These seek to prevent individual state or local governments from spilling problems, such as air and water pollution, and resulting costs over their boundary lines to neighboring jurisdictions.

3. Personnel. Such mandates relate to equal employment opportunities and fair labor standards, including working conditions and pay.

4. Public Health. These requirements are designed to ensure grains, meat, and poultry are safe for human consumption and drinking water is potable.

5. Public Safety. These mandates seek to ensure states initiate action to ensure the public is properly protected.

6. Service Level. Such mandates require state and/or local governments to provide specified services meeting minimum national standards. The *Safe Drinking Water Act*, for example, applies to all suppliers of drinking water to the general public.

7. Tax. These mandates are designed to ensure protection of federal tax resources. The *Tax Equity and Fiscal Responsibility Act of 1982*, for example, requires subnational governments making income tax refunds to their taxpayers to report the refunds to the Internal Revenue Service.

8. Worker Safety. The purpose of these mandates is to protect workers from injuries and the deleterious effects of materials they employ in their productive activities. The Occupational Safety and Health Administration's mandates, EPA's banning of asbestos, and mine safety and health standards are examples of worker safety mandates.

9. Voting Rights. These mandates specifically protect the electoral privileges of blacks and specified foreign language minority individuals.

The fiscal impact of mandates upon state and local governments is difficult to measure, due in part to problems of determining the precise total or marginal cost of each mandate. A single mandate may not add significantly to expenditures of a state or a local government, yet a series of mandates may have a burdensome cumulative effect. Mandates imposing major costs upon subnational governments reduce their discretionary authority and make them less responsive to the needs of their citizenry unless the costs are offset by federal government financial assistance.

The November 5, 1994, election of a Congress controlled by Republicans, effective in January 1995, produced an almost immediate change in national-state relations as Congress enacted the *Unfunded Mandates Reform Act of 1995* and President William J. Clinton signed the bill into law on March 22, 1995.[106] This act is prospective in nature and does not apply to existing intergovernmental sector or private sector unfunded mandates, or to a bill, joint resolution, or a provision in a proposed or final federal regulation that "enforces constitutional rights of individuals, prohibits discrimination, provides emergency assistance, involves national security or implementation of the obligations of a treaty with a foreign nation, or relates to the old-age, survivors, and disability insurance program."[107]

Each committee reporting to the floor a bill or joint resolution must provide a copy to the director of the Congressional Budget Office and include in its report identification of new federal mandates and estimated state and local government implementation costs.[108] Each committee report also must "contain, if relevant to the bill or joint resolution, an explicit statement on the extent to which the bill or joint resolution is intended to preempt any state, local, or tribal law, and, if so, an explanation of the effect of such preemption."[109] Numerous congressional statutes have been held to be preemptive by courts in the absence of a clear statement of intent to preempt.

The director of the Congressional Budget Office is directed, upon finding intergovernmental mandates will exceed $50 million in the first year of imposition, to prepare estimates of the total costs and an explanation of how the estimates were made.[110]

The act establishes a new procedure for each house by allowing a member to raise a point of order if a committee report fails to contain the information required or does not include "an authorization for appropriations in an amount equal to or exceeding the direct costs of such mandate."[111] If a senator makes a point of order and it is sustained by the chair, the mandate automatically is removed from the bill or resolution and may not be offered as a floor amendment. If a representative raises a point of order, the member and an opponent each may debate the "point of order" for ten minutes and the house decides the matter.

The U.S. Advisory Commission on Intergovernmental Relations (ACIR) was directed by the act to conduct a comprehensive study of the impact of federal mandates on intergovernmental relations.[112] The commission's preliminary draft report pertained to fourteen mandates and immediately generated considerable controversy.[113] Congress took no action on the report and ACIR's budget, which had been cut annually by Congress for several years, received no new appropriations for fiscal year 1997. The commission officially terminated its operations on September 30, 1996. Congress subsequently extended the life of the commission to allow it to complete a contractual study for the National Gambling Impact Study Commission with the stipulation ACIR "shall terminate on the date of the completion of such contract."[114]

Is the act a toothless tiger, as critics allege, since a house point of order objection can be overridden by a simple majority vote? The National Governors' Association, the principal proponent of the act, reported "unfunded mandates are now questioned on a regular basis in Congress, and only two new regulatory mandates have been issued since the law went into effect" up to June 1996.[115]

Daniel H. Cole and Carol S. Comer reviewed the act in 1997 and were convinced the new procedural requirements were helpful. They concluded the requirements "change the way administrative agencies do business."[116] Elizabeth Garrett in 1997, however, wrote the act "may have little real impact on much legislation that implicates federalism, but it can serve as an accessible exemplar to shed light into the black box of Congress."[117]

Reviewing the act in 2002, John C. Eastman concluded it "appears to have been very effective in imposing some much-needed discipline on Congress, but the exemptions...hamper its ability to achieve the kind of far-reaching reform that was its motivating purpose."[118] He was particularly critical of the fact each federal department and agency determines whether a proposed mandate exceeds the statutory threshold and lack of judicial review of the assessment of the regulatory impact.

In contrast to the federal act, fifteen states amended their constitutions to (1) prohibit the imposition of specified or all types of state mandates without the permission of the concerned local governments; (2) require reimbursement of all or part of the costs associated with mandates; (3) delay the effective date of a mandate; (4) authorize local governments to ignore an unfunded mandate; (5) require a two-thirds vote of each house of the state legislature to impose a mandate; (6) authorize the governor to suspend a mandate; or (7) provide for a delay in the effective date of a mandate until the following year.[119] In addition, six-teen state legislatures enacted statutory mandate relief statutes.

Congress to date has not reimbursed state and local governments for mandated costs, and it is improbable Congress will appropriate reimbursement funds in the foreseeable future. However, Congress has provided grants-in-aid to state and local governments in the mandated regulatory fields, thereby reducing the direct implementation costs of these units. Furthermore, many mandates, particularly environmental ones, have proved to be beneficial to the citizens of state and local governments and one can argue these governments should bear at least part of the mandated costs. Should Congress decide to reimburse subnational governments for such costs, a unit will have to be created to determine whether submitted mandate cost claims are eligible for reimbursement and a decision will have to be made whether to reimburse on the basis of submitted expenses for each subnational government or on the basis of the average cost for implementing each mandate based upon population.

The Blackmun Thesis

Is the Blackmun congressional responsiveness thesis supported by evidence? Case studies in Chapter 6 provide mixed support for the thesis. We examine briefly three U.S. Supreme Court decisions and the responsiveness of Congress to the pressure from subnational governments to override the decisions.

Regulation of Insurance. The business of insurance was a minor one at the time the U.S. Constitution became effective, Congress did not employ its interstate commerce power to regulate the business, which historically was regulated by state legislatures. The U.S. Supreme Court in *Paul v. Virginia* in 1869 affirmed the constitutional validity of such regulation by opining the business of insurance was not interstate commerce and hence Congress lacked a delegated power to regulate the business.[120]

The Court in 1944, however, reversed this decision.[121] Responding to pressures from the states, Congress enacted the *McCarran-Ferguson Act of 1945*, devolving power to the states to regulate the business of insurance.[122] Continuation of nonharmonious state regulation of the insurance industry, however, led to enactment of the *Gramm-Leach-Bliley Financial Modernization Act of 1999*. This act preempts completely thirteen specific areas of state regulation of the business of insurance and threatened to establish a federal system of licensing insurance agents if twenty-six states did not establish a uniform licensing system by November 12, 2002.[123] Thirty-five states have been certified as having such a system.

Municipal Antitrust Immunity. The U.S. Supreme Court in *Parker v. Brown* in 1945 opined Congress, in accordance with basic federalism principles, did not intend to apply its antitrust statutes to a state if it made a deliberate decision to exclude competition by private firms (in this case a California sponsored raisin cartel) in the conduct of state economic affairs.[124] Congress possesses the constitutional authority to overturn this Court decision, took no action to do so, and the presumption was made the immunity of states from federal antitrust laws extended to their political subdivisions.

The U.S. Supreme Court in 1978 and in 1982 issued decisions clarifying the extension of immunity to municipal corporations was not automatic. The first decision announced the Court's intent to examine carefully whether the antitrust laws apply to such corporations.[125]

The second decision—*Community Communications Corporation v. City of Boulder*—upset municipal officers throughout the nation. The Court opined a municipality's anticompetitive conduct, based upon a home rule power, was subject to the federal antitrust statutes.[126] The Court specifically refused to accept the contention that a general state "home rule" authorization automatically provided a "state action" exemption from the antitrust laws and held there must be a clearly expressed state policy to displace competition with municipal monopolization or regulation if the exemption is to apply to the municipality. The Court added a state policy allowing its municipalities "to do as they please can hardly be said to have 'contemplated' the specific anticompetitive actions for which municipal liability is sought. Nor can those actions be truly described as 'comprehensive within the powers grants' since the term, 'granted,' necessarily implies an affirmative addressing of the subject by the State."[127]

The congressional response to local government officers' pleas for relief came in the form of the *Local Government Antitrust Act of 1984*, which stipulates damages, interest on damages, and plaintiffs' legal fees may not be recovered from municipal defendants in the damage phase of a *Clayton Antitrust Act* lawsuit, but plaintiffs can be awarded legal fees for costs incurred in their efforts to obtain issuance of a writ of injunction.[128] The act also exempts from liability municipal officers and their employees acting in an "official capacity" and private parties acting in accordance with directions of municipal officers. The act does not apply retroactively, but the U.S. District Court possesses discretionary authority to exempt municipal defendants from damages if they prove damages should not be assessed. The section of the act stipulating plaintiffs may not collect the costs of their legal fees from municipal government was designed to discourage the filing of frivolous lawsuits.

Surprisingly, several state officers urged Congress not to grant municipal governments complete immunity from the antitrust laws because such action would be a congressional intrusion upon the constitutionally reserved powers of states to control their political subdivisions.[129]

Fair Labor Standards. The U.S. Supreme Court in *National League of Cities v. Usery* in 1976 opined Congress had exceeded its delegated powers in applying federal labor standards to subnational governments, but reversed itself in *Garcia v. San Antonio Metropolitan Transit Authority* in 1985 (see chapter 6).[130] The Congressional Budget Office in the same year estimated the latter decision would impose upon subnational governments "initial annual compliance costs totaling between $0.5 billion and $1.5 billion nationwide."[131] The bulk of the compliance costs is attributable to the requirement employees be paid for overtime work instead of receiving compensatory time off.

Congress, responding to pressure from subnational governments, enacted the *Fair Labor Standards Amendments of 1985.* The amendments allow these governments to offer employees compensatory time off at a rate of one and one-half hours for each hour of overtime work in lieu of overtime compensation, specify the labor standards are not applicable to volunteers, and grant subnational governmental legislative employees the identical exemptions from the standards as those for congressional employees.[132]

Preemption and the Federal System

As recently as 1961, M. J. C. Vile, an English observer, wrote "the day-to-day relations between Federal and state governments became the object of congressional attention not as a legislature intent upon curbing state power, but as a legislative body composed of local politicians concerned to defend state power unless a great national problem converts Congress temporarily into a legislature of national statesmen."[133] It is apparent the statement lacks validity today because the sharp increase in the number of congressional preemption statutes abrogating states' regulatory powers completely or partially since the mid-1960s has had a greater impact than grants-in-aid on the nature of the federal system.

The very limited available evidence reveals numerous state and local governments often do not comply completely or in a timely manner with mandate and restraint requirements contained in congressional preemption statutes. Elazar's three political cultures—individualistic, moralistic, and traditionalistic—and his classification of each state by political culture help to explain state cooperation or resistance to congressional mandates and restraints.[134]

There is relatively little academic interest in preemption, and Congress has not reviewed the various types of complete and partial preemption statutes comprehensively to determine which ones have the most beneficial effects and the most harmful systemic effects.

Senator James M. Jeffords of Vermont, Chairman of the Senate Committee on Environment and Public Works, requested the U.S. General Accounting Office in 2001 to examine regulatory programs where the federal government and the states share regulatory responsibilities. The General Accounting Office identified five regulatory and standard-setting mechanisms: (1) complete preemption, (2) minimum standards preemption, (3) conditional grants-in-aid, (4) cooperative programs with voluntary standards drafted by federal and state officers, and (5) state adoption of voluntary standards developed by quasi-official organizations.[135] Each approach has specific advantages and limitations with respect to uniformity, capacity, and accountability. The General Accounting Office selected two or more regulatory programs involving use of each of the above mechanisms for study.

The General Accounting Office concluded several minimum standards programs preserve "in part the leadership role that states had performed before the federal government stepped in" and cited as an example state "standards for hazards, such as ergonomic injury, for which no federal standard has yet been established."[136] The General Accounting Office also identified two programs—food safety and highway safety—where standards were developed by federal and state officers jointly.[137] A table in the report compares the five mechanisms in terms of uniformity, flexibility, capacity, and accountability.

The report suggests circumstances under which direct federal regulatory administration might be appropriate, but adds such administration was not examined in depth and "experience certainly suggests that this option has its own set of challenges and limitations."[138] The General Accounting Office also raised the question of whether sole state responsibility for a regulatory function would be preferable in view of the possibility of their limited capacity to assume such responsibility.

This report clearly outlined five policy alternatives for Congress to examine prior to enacting a statute to solve a national problem. To date, there is no evidence that Congress has paid heed to this report and preemption bills have been introduced on a variety of subjects including boxing, motor vehicle operator licenses, mortgages, and telemedicine.[139]

Federalism Theory

Seeds for the development of the theories of dual and cooperative federalism are contained in the original U.S. Constitution's division of exercisable political powers between Congress and the states (reinforced by the Tenth Amendment), and incorporation of provisions promoting cooperative national state relations: state conduct of elections of federal officers, state legislatures' consideration of constitutional amendments proposed by Congress, and state militia training in accordance with nationally prescribed discipline.[140] Furthermore, the Fourteenth Amendment, ratified in 1868, recognizes dual sovereignty with the declaration "all persons born or naturalized in the United States, and subject to the jurisdiction thereof, are citizens of the United States and of the State wherein they reside." The U.S. Supreme Court in *Chisholm v. Georgia* in 1793 emphasized dual federalism by opining "the United States are sovereign as to all the powers actually surrendered: each State in the Union is sovereign as to all the powers reserved."[141]

Based upon the evidence presented in this volume, how adequate are the theories of dual and cooperative federalism in explaining national-state relations today? The theory of dual federalism is a simple one which retains a degree of explanatory value since the national government and individual states each possess partial sovereignty; there are limits to the scope of Congress's preemption powers, and Congress lacks the power to provide services, except the postal service, within states other than on federal properties. The theory, however, suggests there are fixed exclusive spheres of national and state powers, and fails to explain national-state cooperation, coercive use of congressional powers, or congressional devolution of a power to states.

The cooperative federalism theory also is a relatively simple one and, in common with the dual federalism theory, accepts a division of national and state powers. The former theory, however, has greater explanatory value as many national-state relations, including ones structured by preemption statutes, are cooperative in nature and the theory more accurately describes the day-to-day functioning of the federal system in terms of a mutuality model. Daniel J. Elazar's 1959 Ph.D. dissertation at the University of Chicago was a groundbreaking theoretical one demonstrating relations between the national government and the states had been cooperative from the early decades of the nineteenth century to 1913.[142] This theory nevertheless does not explain the structuring of national-state relations by the coercive use of plenary and partial preemption statutes (including mandates and restraints), crossover sanctions, and tax sanctions, or occasional congressional devolution of legislative powers to states.

A need exists for a more general theory of U.S. federalism that explains the continuous readjustment of the respective regulatory competences of Congress and the states, and encompasses dual, cooperative, coercive, and devolution postulates explaining the ever-changing nature of the system. Chapter 1 notes the framers of the U.S. Constitution produced a lithe and flexible document capable of responding to dramatically different conditions as they arise in the future without the need for constitutional amendments under most circumstances. Procrustean discrete division of powers was avoided by the constitutional grant of powers, including the necessary and proper clause, in general terms reinforced by the supremacy of the laws clause, allowing Congress at any time to remove completely or partially regulatory powers from states and their political subdivisions. The fact Congress used its latent powers of complete and partial preemption on a limited basis until the mid-1960s should not blind the reader to the fact these powers potentially were exercisable during an earlier period. Politically, Congress probably would have been unable to exercise its powers of complete supersession of state laws in certain regulatory fields if external conditions had been otherwise. The Cold War facilitated and almost mandated Congress's complete preemption of the power to regulate ionizing radiation.

Changing national-state relations can be explained primarily in terms of the three roles played by Congress: facilitator, inhibitor, and initiator. The first and third roles may be played simultaneously. Congress is a facilitator when it provides to states and their political subdivisions direct and indirect financial assistance—exemption of municipal bond interest from national income taxation, grants-in-aid, insurance, loans and loan guarantees, tax deductions, and tax credits—and technical assistance and training to promote subnational governmental regulation and service provision in accordance with national standards.

Congress plays an inhibiting role when it (1) enacts complete preemption statutes nullifying state regulatory laws and implementing administrative rules, and prohibiting future enactment of such laws and state promulgation of such rules, and (2) forbids subnational governments to initiate a specified action, such as dumping sewage sludge in an ocean. Similarly, Congress inhibits state freedom to act by enacting partial preemption statutes either removing all state regulatory authority over a segment of a regulatory field or by establishing minimum national regulatory standards.

Congress's initiator role is a leadership one and involves enactment (1) of minimum national regulatory standards to provide a framework for new regulatory programs involving a partnership between the national and state governments, and (2) conditional grants-in-aid and

crossover sanction statutes to persuade states to adopt national regulatory policies and/or to provide services meeting national standards.
Critics charge the minimum standards approach involves commandeering of the states' resources by Congress, but such charges are overly sim-
plistic as states often wish to initiate action but fear stringent regulation
of industrial polluters, for example, will give the state an antibusiness
image hindering industrial recruitment efforts and also drive firms from
the state. National minimum standards prevent polluters from escaping
from regulation while allowing individual states to determine the need
for higher standards.

The emphasis placed by Congress on each of these roles at any
one time affects the reliance we can place on the theory of cooperative federalism as an adequate explanation of the functioning of the
federal system.

The widespread and increasing use by Congress of its preemption
powers during the past four decades has led to a paradox; that is, total
power exercised by states has increased due primarily to congressional
statutes establishing minimum regulatory standards and authorizing federal departments and agencies to delegate regulatory primacy to states in
various fields provided the concerned states submit a plan with standards
meeting or exceeding the national ones and adequate enforcement equipment and personnel. Regulatory primacy may be viewed as an alternative to federal regulation in several fields. Crossover and tax sanctions
also have encouraged states to enact statutes. In effect, states have lost
their right not to exercise certain reserved powers.

The federal system has evolved from one exhibiting primarily dual
federalism features, when contacts between the national government and
states were limited and generally symbiotic in nature, to a system
exhibiting a number of characteristics of a unitary system. Congress currently acts as a central legislative body exercising nearly plenary powers
in several traditional areas of state regulatory responsibility. The era of
cooperative federalism was a transitional phase between an essentially
dual federalism phase and the current more coercive phase which retains
cooperative features. Congress's facilitating role comports with Elazar's
conception of cooperative federalism, as do minimum standards preemption statutes and a few complete preemption statutes. The coercive use of
congressional regulatory powers is at odds with the theory of cooperative federalism. Elazar wrote to the author in 1992 that "[y]our addition
of federal mandates and preemption to the older theories of dual and
cooperative federalism is quite helpful."[143]

A general theory of U.S. federalism of necessity incorporates a relatively large number of postulates, listed below, to have full explanatory

value, compared to the small number of postulates incorporated into each of the other two theories:

1. Congress possesses enumerated powers supplemented by implied powers, and states possess residual powers.
2. Congress occasionally devolves one of its legislative powers to states.
3. Relations between Congress and individual states are asymmetrical.
4. Congress uses conditional grants-in-aid and national technical assistance to obtain subnational governmental cooperation.
5. Regulatory tension exists between states and Congress, which encourages them to enact uniform laws and interstate compacts in a wide variety of regulatory areas.
6. Congress at its will removes state regulatory powers completely or partially in various fields.
7. Subnational governments employ the political process in efforts to defeat preemption bills, except requested ones, and to reverse rulings of United States courts holding a congressional statute lacking an explicit preemption statement to be preemptive.
8. Congress enacts minimum standards preemption statutes and encourages states to assume regulatory primacy and to employ regulatory powers more fully.
9. Congress imposes mandates and restraints on subnational governments and on occasion responds affirmatively to subnational governmental requests for relief from burdensome mandates and restraints.

These postulates are in need of further testing to determine whether they are universally valid, but nevertheless can serve as the basis of a more general non-equilibrium theory of federalism. This theory reflects the fluid economic and societal changes that generate pressures of varying intensities for readjustment of the respective regulatory competences of the three planes of government with the result the system is in a perpetual state of locomotion describable as kaleidoscopic rather than linear in nature. With respect to the first postulate, the asymmetrical national-state relationship is affected by many factors, including the amount of nationally owned land, presence of Indian reservations and large national government facilities, wealth of the state, political influence of a state's congressional delegation, extent of discretionary authority of regional offices of national regulatory departments and agencies, willingness of individual states to apply for and accept regulatory primacy, return of regulatory primacy to a national department, and other factors.

It should be noted a still broader theory of U.S. federalism would include competitive, cooperative, and conflictive postulates relating to interstate relations.

Concluding Comments

The evidence presented in this volume reveals a major transformation of a fundamental nature has occurred in the federal system, yet does not support the critics' conclusion the system is being converted into a unitary one. The system approximates a mutuality model emphasizing interplane interdependence, with the federal government and states each relying on the other for the performance of certain functions such as standard setting, enforcement, financial assistance, and technical assistance. Minimum standards preemption, in particular, helps to retain the diffusion of political power to a large extent, thereby preventing over-centralization of political power flowing from complete congressional preemption of state regulatory powers.

No attempt was made to evaluate fully each type of preemption statute. The evidence presented, however, reveals certain types are more respectful of federalist principles by preserving basic state regulatory responsibilities. We do not know whether states have lost part of their ability to respond in innovative ways to solve problems in completely and partially preempted areas, but there is abundant evidence states continue to innovate and the federal government is a follower. For example, the *Do-Not-Call Implementation Act of* 2003, based upon earlier state do-not-call telephone registries, authorizes the Federal Trade Commission to establish and enforce a similar registry.[144] Subsequently, the New York state legislature enacted a statute merging its do-not-call registry with the federal one.[145]

The growing power of a number of economic special interest groups is reflected in the enactment of preemption statutes removing regulatory decision-making authority completely or partially from state capitols to the national arena in Washington, D.C. Chapters 4 and 5 document the variety and complexity of congressional preemption statutes and their effect in reducing citizen understanding of the overall governance system and ability to control congressional policymaking, thereby raising questions relative to the effectiveness of electoral control, which is a basic tenet of democratic theory. It is apparent the average citizen today is unable to determine which plane of government is responsible for many regulatory functions or whether the federal government and the state government share such responsibility. In particular, does the price paid for congressional preemption statutes include a partial loss of governmental accountability and responsibility in most regulatory fields to the voters? There is no national initiative, protest referendum, or recall, in contrast to twenty-four states with the initiative, twenty-four states with the protest referendum, and eighteen states with the recall.[146]

One of the most interesting features of the increased use of Congress's preemption powers is the nearly simultaneous occurrence of the nearly complete deregulation of the banking, communications, and transportation industries since 1978 and increasing regulation of subnational governments as polities.

The Constitution's drafters sought "a more perfect union" of states by authorizing unifying actions as conditions changed and a consensus developed in Congress for an enlarged national governance role, thereby producing such a union. The national government currently administers directly few programs it did not administer prior to the mid-1960s, but plays an enlarged role in state-administered programs primarily designed to reduce negative externalities.

Congress tends to enact restructuring policies in a conceptual vacuum as ad hoc responses to individual problems and the policies collectively have resulted in a comprehensive and unplanned restructuring of national-state relations. Henry M. Hart, Jr., concluded in 1954, with respect to national-state relations, "the opportunity for long-range and systematic thinking lies with the courts and the legal profession, with such help as political science can muster."[147] Congress's failure to understand the impact of preemption statutes on state and local governments is due in part to the fact that an increasing number of its members lack previous state and/or local government experience and to the growing influence of interest groups which contribute funds to congressional election campaigns. This failure is illustrated by the comments of Mayor Edward I. Koch of New York City:

> As a member of Congress I voted for many of the laws,...and did so with every confidence that we were enacting sensible permanent solutions to critical problems. It took a plunge into the Mayor's job to drive home how misguided my congressional outlook had been. The bills I voted for in Washington came to the floor in a form that compelled approval. After all, who can vote against clean air and water, or better access and education for the handicapped. But as I look back it is hard to believe I could have been taken in by the simplicity of what the Congress was doing and by the flimsy empirical support—often no more than a carefully orchestrated hearing record of a single consultant's

report—offered to persuade the members that the proposed solution could work throughout the country.[148]

Prior to enacting a preemption bill, Congress should examine the broader federalism implications of the bill to ensure it achieves national goals without unnecessarily removing powers from states and their political subdivisions. To the extent practicable, preference should be given to innovative statutes capable of solving national problems while preserving to the maximum extent the regulatory authority of states, thereby allowing them to respond to local conditions and to serve as laboratories of democracy. In particular, Congress should (1) offer incentives to state legislatures to enact harmonious parallel regulatory statutes, including ones drafted by the National Conference of Commissioners on Uniform State Laws, and to enter into interstate regulatory compacts; (2) enact regulatory statutes containing a provision for a state legislature to opt-out of the statutes where feasible; and (3) rely more heavily upon minimum standards preemption statutes.[149]

The above congressional actions will help to reinvigorate the federal system, prevent additional centralization of regulatory powers in Washington, D.C., and enable citizens to play a fuller role in the development and monitoring of regulatory policies. Congress should note Article I-9 of the draft constitution for the European Union includes subsidiarity as a fundamental principle, holding "in areas which do not fall within its exclusive competence the Union shall act only if and insofar as the objectives of the intended action cannot be sufficiently achieved by the Member States, either at central level or at regional and local level, but can rather, by reason of the scale or effects of the proposed action, be better achieved at Union level."

In sum, several original features of the federal system remain in place with states, as residuary sovereigns, playing key roles in an extremely complex and changing governance system as Congress displaces completely or partially states' regulatory powers. Congress has become a unitary government in regulatory fields where it has exercised its power of complete supersession of state authority and finances its policies in several other fields in part by imposing burdensome mandates and restraints on subnational governments. Abundant evidence—in the form of technological developments, increasing globalization of the economy, international trade treaties, and interest group lobbying—indicates Congress will play an increasingly dominant role in domestic governance by enactment of preemption statutes in the fields of banking, communications, financial services, and taxation.

Notes

Preface

1. Joseph F. Zimmerman, *Federal Preemption: The Silent Revolution* (Ames: Iowa State University Press, 1991).

1. Congressional Preemption

1. *McCulloch v. Maryland*, 17 U.S. 316 at 421, 4 Wheat. 316 at 421 (1819).

2. 1 Stat. 54 (1789).

3. *Shipping Statute of 1983*, 97 Stat. 553, 46 U.S.C. §8501.

4. *McCarran-Ferguson Act of 1945*, 59 Stat. 33, 15 U.S.C. §1011. See also *United States v. South-Eastern Underwriters Association*, 322 U.S. 533, 64 S.Ct. 1162 (1944).

5. *Gramm-Leach-Bliley Financial Modernization Act of 1999*, 113 Stat. 1423, 15 U.S.C. §6751.

6. *Interstate Horseracing Act of 1978*, 92 Stat. 1813, 15 U.S.C. §3004.

7. *Kentucky Division, Horsemen's Benevolent & Protective Association, Incorporated v. Turfway Park Racing Association*, 832 F.Supp. 1097 (E.D.Ky 1993).

8. *Kentucky Division, Horsemen's Benevolent & Protective Association, Incorporated v. Turfway Park Racing Association*, 20 F.3d 1406 at 1416–17 (6th Cir. 1994).

9. Mr. Gerry's letter of October 18, 1787, was published in the *New Hampshire Spy*, November 6, 1787, and is quoted in Charles E. Clark, "New Hampshire's First Look at the Anti-ratification Arguments," *Keene (NH) Sentinel*, November 18, 1987, p. 5.

10. *Copyright Act of 1790*, 1 Stat. 124, 17 U.S.C. §101, and *Patent Act of 1790*, 1 Stat. 109, 35 U.S.C. §1.

11. *An Act to Regulate Commerce of 1887*, 24 Stat. 379, 49 U.S.C. §1.

12. *Interstate Commerce Commission Termination Act of 1995*, 109 Stat. 803, 49 U.S.C. §101.

13. Joseph F. Zimmerman and Sharon Lawrence, *Federal Statutory Preemption of State and Local Authority: History, Inventory, and Issues* (Washington, DC: U.S. Advisory Commission on Intergovernmental Relations, 1992), p. 45.

14. *State v. Reese*, 91 U.S. 214, 2 Otto 214 (1875).

15. Luther Gulick, "Reorganization of the State," *Civil Engineering* 3, August 1933, p. 421.

16. Harold J. Laski, "The Obsolescence of Federalism," *New Republic* 98, May 3, 1939, p. 362, and Harold J. Laski, *The American Democracy: A Commentary and an Interpretation* (New York: Viking Press, 1948), p. 139.

17. Felix Morley, *Freedom and Federalism* (Chicago: Henry Regnery Company, 1959), p. 209, quoting Alexander Hamilton in *The Federalist Papers*, ed. Rossiter (New York: New American Library, 1961), p. 119.

18. Morley, *Freedom and Federalism*, p. 209.

19. Dennis W. Brogan, *Politics in America* (Garden City, NY: Anchor Books, 1960), p. 228.

20. Zimmerman and Lawrence, *Federal Statutory Preemption of State and Local Authority*.

21. Joseph F. Zimmerman, *Contemporary American Federalism:* The Growth of National Power (Leicester: Leicester University Press, 1992).

22. *Bankruptcy Reform Act of 1994*, 108 Stat. 4106, 11 U.S.C. §101; *Federal Trademark Dilution Act of 1995*, 109 Stat. 985, 15 U.S.C. §1051; *Riegle-Neal Amendments Act of 1997*, 111 Stat. 238, 12 U.S.C. §1811; and *Internet Tax Nondiscrimination Act of 2001*, 115 Stat. 703, 47 U.S.C. §151.

23. Joseph F. Zimmerman, *Federally Induced Costs Affecting State and Local Governments* (Washington, DC: U.S. Advisory Commission on Intergovernmental Relations, 1994).

24. *Unfunded Mandates Reform Act of 1995*, 109 Stat. 48, 2 U.S.C. §1501.

25. *Safe Drinking Water Act Amendments of 1996*, 110 Stat. 1613, 42 U.S.C. §300f, and *Safe Drinking Water Act Amendments of 1986*, 100 Stat. 651, 42 U.S.C. §300.

26. *Telecommunications Act of 1996*, 110 Stat. 61, 47 U.S.C. §609.

27. Ibid., 110 Stat. 61 at 124–25, 47 U.S.C. §541(b)(3)(A).

28. *Internet Tax Nondiscrimination Act of 2001*, 115 Stat. 703, 47 U.S.C. §§151 and 609.

29. *Commercial Motor Vehicle Safety Act of 1986*, 100 Stat. 3207, 49 U.S.C. §2701.

30. *Commission on Intergovernmental Relations; A Report to the President for Transmittal to the Congress* (Washington, DC: U.S. Government Printing Office, 1955), pp. 63–64.

31. Ibid., p. 70.

32. *Atomic Energy Act of 1959*, 73 Stat. 688, 42 U.S.C. §2021.

33. *Regulatory Federalism: Policy, Process, Impact, and Reform*. (Washington, DC: U.S. Advisory Commission on Intergovernmental Relations, 1984, p. 259.

34. Ronald Reagan, "Federalism: Executive Order 12612, October 26, 1987," *Weekly Compilation of Presidential Documents*, November 2, 1987, p. 1231.

35. Richard S. Williamson, "The Self-Government Balancing Act: A View from the White House," *National Civic Review* 71, January 1982, p. 19.

36. Joseph F. Zimmerman, "Federal Preemption Under Reagan's New Federalism," *Publius* 21, Winter 1991, pp. 7–28.

37. *Atomic Energy Act of 1946*, 60 Stat. 755, 42 U.S.C. §2011.

38. *Voting Rights Act of 1965*, 79 Stat. 438, 42 U.S.C. §1973. See also Joseph F. Zimmerman, "The Federal Voting Rights Act and Alternative Election Systems," *William and Mary Law Review* 19, Summer 1978, pp. 621-60.

39. *Gramm-Leach-Bliley Financial Modernization Act of 1999*, 113 Stat. 1422, 15 U.S.C. §6751.

40. "Members Certify GLBA Reciprocity Requirement Met," a news release issued by the National Association of Insurance Commissioners, Kansas City, Mo., September 10, 2002.

41. *Garcia v. San Antonio Metropolitan Transit Authority*, 469 U.S. 556, 105 S.Ct. 1005 (1985).

42. Paul L. Posner, *Regulatory Programs: Balancing Federal and State Responsibilities for Standard Setting and Implementation* (Washington, DC: U.S. General Accounting Office, 2002), p. 36.

43. *Morales v. Trans World Airlines Incorporated*, 504 U.S. 374, 112 S.Ct. 2031 (1992). See also the *Airline Deregulation Act of 1978*, 92 Stat. 1708, 49 U.S.C. §1305.

44. Richard Perz-Pena and Patrick McGeehan, "Assault on Wall St. Misdeeds Raises Spitzer's U.S. Profile," *New York Times*, November 4, 2002, pp. 1 and B6.

45. Jackson Pemberton, "A New Message: On Amendment XVII," *The Freeman* 26, November 1976, p. 657.

46. *Gibbons v. Ogden*, 9 Wheat. 1 at 197, 22 U.S. 1 at 197 (1824).

47. Herbert Wechsler, "The Political Safeguards of Federalism: The Role of the States in the Composition and Selection of the National Government," *Columbia Law Review* 54, 1953, pp. 543–60.

48. *Garcia v. San Antonio Metropolitan Transit Authority*, 469 U.S. 528 at 556, 105 S.Ct. 1005 at 1020 (1985).

49. Consult Joseph F. Zimmerman, *State-Local Relations: A Partnership Approach*, 2nd ed. (Westport, CT: Praeger Publishers, 1995), pp. 85–118.

50. *Unfunded Mandates Reform Act of 1995*, 109 Stat. 49, 2 U.S.C. §1501.

51. William H. Stewart, *Concepts of Federalism* (Lanham, MD: University Press of America, 1984), p. 4.

52. Daniel J. Elazar, *Exploring Federalism* (Tuscaloosa: University of Alabama Press, 1987), p. 225.

2. Establishment of a Federation

1. *Water Quality Act of 1965*, 79 Stat. 903, 33 U.S.C. §1151.

2. William F. Swindler, "Our First Constitution: The Articles of Confederation," *American Bar Association Journal* 69, February 1981, pp. 166–69.

3. Thomas A. Bailey, *The American Pageant: A History of the Republic*, 3rd ed. (Boston: D. C. Heath, 1967), p. 136.

4. Ibid., p. 137.

5. Richard Hofstadter, William Miller, and Daniel Aaron, *The American Republic* (Englewood Cliffs, NJ: Prentice-Hall, Inc., 1959), p. 223.

6. *Virginia v. Tennessee*, 148 U.S. 503, 13 S.Ct. 728 (1893).

7. *Michelin Tire Corporation v. Wages*, 423 U.S. 276 at 286, 96 S.Ct. 535 at 541 (1975).

8. *R. J. Reynolds Tobacco Company v. Durham County*, 479 U.S. 130, 107 S.Ct. 499 (1986).

9. *Constitution of the United States*, Art. VII. For the views of the anti-federalists, consult Ralph Ketcham, ed., *The Anti-Federalist Papers and the Constitutional Convention Debates* (New York: New American Library, 1986) and Herbert J. Storing, *What the Anti-Federalists Were For* (Chicago: University of Chicago Press, 1981).

10. *The Federalist Papers* (New York: New American Library, 1961).

11. Ibid., p. 119.

12. Ibid., pp. 201–04.

13. Ibid., p. 202.

14. Ibid., pp. 284–85.

15. Ibid., p. 285.

16. Ibid., pp. 292 and 296.

17. Robert H. Walker, ed. *The Reform Spirit in America: A Documentation of Reform in the American Republic* (New York: G. P. Putnam, 1976), pp. 25–26.

18. Ibid., pp. 26–27.

19. Alan V. Briceland, "Virginia's Ratification of the U.S. Constitution," *Newsletter* (Institute of Government, University of Virginia) 61, October 1984, p. 2.

20. Paul L. Ford, ed. *The Writings of Thomas Jefferson*, vol. 9 (New York: G. P. Putnam, 1898), p. 452.

21. *An Act to Regulate Commerce of 1887*, 24 Stat. 379, 49 U.S.C. §1 and *An Act to Establish a Uniform System of Bankruptcy of 1898*, 30 Stat. 544, 11 U.S.C. §1.

22. Joseph F. Zimmerman and Sharon Lawrence, *Federal Statutory Preemption of State and Local Authority: History, Inventory, and Issues* (Washington, DC: U.S. Advisory Commission on Intergovernmental Relations, 1992), p. 45.

23. *Atomic Energy Act of 1946*, 60 Stat. 755, 42 U.S.C. §2011 and *Atomic Energy Act of 1959*, 73 Stat. 688, 42 U.S.C. §2021.

24. *Uniform Time Act of 1966*, 80 Stat. 107, 15 U.S.C. §260.

25. *Water Quality Act of 1965*, 79 Stat. 903, 33 U.S.C. §1151 and *Air Quality Act of 1967*, 81 Stat. 485, 42 U.S.C. §1857.

26. *Federal Water Pollution Control Act Amendments of 1972*, 86 Stat. 498, 33 U.S.C. §1151.

27. *McCulloch v. Maryland*, 17 U.S. 316, 4 Wheat. 316 (1819) and *Gibbons v. Ogden*, 22 U.S. 1, 9 Wheat. 1 (1824).

28. Woodrow Wilson, *Congressional Government* (Boston: Houghton Mifflin, 1925), pp. 36–37.

29. *Buckley v. Valeo*, 424 U.S. 1, 96 S.Ct. 612 (1976).

30. Ibid., 424 U.S. 1 at 52, 96 S.Ct. 612 at 651.

31. Ibid., 424 U.S. 1 at 52–53, 96 S.Ct. at 651.

32. *First National Bank of Boston v. Bellotti*, 435 U.S. 765, 98 S.Ct. 1407 (1978).

33. Joseph F. Zimmerman, *The Referendum: The People Decide Public Policy* (Westport, CT: Praeger Publishers, 2001).

34. Edwin Meese III, "The Attorney General's View of the Supreme Court: Toward a Jurisprudence of Original Intention," *Public Administration Review* 45, November 1985, p. 704.

35. William J. Brennan, Jr., "The Constitution of the United States. Contemporary Ratification." A paper presented at a text and teaching symposium, Georgetown University, Washington, D.C., October 12, 1985, p. 4.

36. Robert H. Bork, "The Constitution, Original Intent, and Economic Rights." An address presented at the University of San Diego Law School, November 18, 1985, p. 8.

37. H. Jefferson Powell, "The Original Understanding of Original Intent," *Harvard Law Review* 98, March 1985, p. 948.

3. Spending Power Preemption

1. "An Ordinance for Ascertaining the Mode of Disposing of Lands in the Western Territory," *Journal of the American Congress, from 1774 to 1788* (Washington, DC: 1823), pp. 395–400. See in particular p. 398.

2. V.O. Key, Jr., *The Administration of Federal Grants to States* (Chicago: Public Administration Service, 1937), p. 6.

3. 9 Stat. 519 (1850) and *Morrill Act of 1862*, 12 Stat. 503, 7 U.S.C. § 301.

4. *Hatch Act of 1887*, 24 Stat. 440, 7 U.S.C. §362.

5. *Morrill Act of 1890*, 26 Stat. 417, 7 U.S.C. §321.

6. *Smith-Lever Act of 1914*, 38 Stat. 372, 7 U.S.C. §341.

7. *Weeks Act of 1911*, 36 Stat. 961, 16 U.S.C. §480, and Key, *The Administration of Federal Grants to States*, p. 10.

8. *Federal Road Aid Act of 1916*, 39 Stat. 355. See also Paul H. Douglas, "The Development of a System of Federal Grants-in-Aid I," *Political Science Quarterly* 35, June 1920, 255–71 and Paul H. Douglas, "The Development of a System of Federal Grants-in-Aid II," *Political Science Quarterly* 35, December 1920, pp. 522–44.

9. *Federal Road Aid Act of 1921*, 42 Stat. 212.

10. *National Interstate and Defense Highways Act of 1956*, 70 Stat. 374, 23 U.S.C. §101.

11. *Smith-Hughes Act of 1917*, 39 Stat. 929, 20 U.S.C. §11.

12. *Vocational Rehabilitation Act of 1920*, 41 Stat. 735, 29 U.S.C. §31.

13. Key, *The Administration of Federal Grants to States*, pp. 15–21. See also the *Chamberlain-Kahn Act of 1918*, 40 Stat. 886.

14. Key, *The Administration of Federal Grants to States*, pp. 178–205.

15. Ibid., p. 179.

16. Ibid., pp. 378–83.

17. *McGee v. Mathias*, 71 U.S. 314, 4 Wall. 143 (1877).

18. *Massachusetts v. Mellon*, 262 U.S. 447, 43 S.Ct. 597 (1923). See the *Sheppard-Towner Act*, 42 Stat. 224 (1921).

19. 2 Stat. 490 (1808).

20. *Hatch Act of 1887*, 24 Stat. 440, 7 U.S.C. §362.

21. *Morrill Act of 1890*, 26 Stat. 417, 7 U.S.C. §321.

22. *Weeks Act of 1911*, 36 Stat. 961, 16 U.S.C. §552.

23. *Carey Act of 1894*, 28 Stat. 422, 43 U.S.C. §641.

24. *Federal Road Aid Act of 1916*, 39 Stat. 355.

25. *Federal Road Aid Act of 1921*, 42 Stat. 212.

26. *Social Security Act of 1935*, 49 Stat. 620, 42 U.S.C. §301. For details of a case involving Florida, consult *The Federal Influence on State and Local Roles in the Federal System* (Washington, DC: U.S. Advisory Commission on Intergovernmental Relations, 1981), p. 43.

27. *Hayden-Cartwright Act of 1934*, 49 Stat. 993, 23 U.S.C. §101.

28. *Social Security Act of 1935*, 49 Stat. 620, 42 U.S.C. §301.

29. *Hatch Act of 1939*, 53 Stat. 1147, 5 U.S.C. §118i and *Hatch Act of 1940*, 54 Stat. 767, 5 U.S.C. §118i.

30. *United States Housing Act of 1937*, 50 Stat. 888, 12 U.S.C. §1701.

31. Joseph F. Harris, "The Future of Federal Grants-in-Aid," in "Intergovernmental Relations in the United States," ed. W. Brooke Graves, *Annals of the American Academy of Political and Social Science* 207, January 1940, p. 14.

32. *Fiscal Balance in the American Federal System* (Washington, DC: U.S. Advisory Commission on Intergovernmental Relations, 1967), pp. 139, 145.

33. *Federal Aid to States Fiscal Year 1980* (Washington, DC: U.S. Department of the Treasury, 1981), p. 1.

34. *Fiscal Balance in the American Federal System*, p. 145.

35. *National Interstate and Defense Highways Act of 1956*, 70 Stat. 374, 23 U.S.C. §101.

36. Carl W. Stenberg, "Federal-Local Relations in a Cutback Environment: Issues and Future Directions." A paper presented at the Annual Conference of the American Politics Group of the United Kingdom Political Studies Association, Manchester, England, January 4, 1980, p. 5.

37. U.S. Census Bureau, "Federal Aid to State and Local Governments, Fiscal Year 2000," http://www.census.gov/govs/faads/022sumus.htm.

38. *Hatch Act of 1939*, 53 Stat. 1147, 5 U.S.C. §118i.

39. *Emergency Highway Energy Conservation Act of 1974*, 87 Stat. 1046, 23 U.S.C. §154.

40. *Energy Policy and Conservation Act of 1975*, 89 Stat. 933, 42 U.S.C. §6201.

41. *National Minimum Drinking Age Amendments of 1984*, 98 Stat. 437, 23 U.S.C. §158.

42. *South Dakota v. Dole*, 483 U.S. 203, 107 S.Ct. 2793 (1987).

43. *Transportation Equity Act for the 21st Century of 1998*, 112 Stat. 240, 12 U.S.C. §163.

44. Elizabeth Benjamin, "Tougher DWI Limit Finally Sails Through," *Times Union (Albany, NY)*, December 18, 2002, pp.1, A8.

45. Nick Madigan, "In a City of Few Limits, One Just Got Lower," *New York Times*, September 24, 2003, p. A18.

46. *State Comprehensive Mental Health Services Plan Act of 1986*, 100 Stat. 3494, 42 U.S.C. §201.

47. *Department of Transportation and Related Agencies Appropriations Act of 1991*, 104 Stat. 2185, 23 U.S.C. §104.

48. *Department of Transportation and Related Agencies Appropriations Act of 1992*, 105 Stat. 944, 23 U.S.C. §159.

49. *Transportation Equity Act for the 21st Century of 1998*, 112 Stat. 126, 23 U.S.C. §159.

50. Harris, "Future of Federal Grants-in-Aid," p. 17.

51. The Commission on Intergovernmental Relations, *A Report to the President for Transmittal to the Congress* (Washington, DC: U.S. Government Printing Office, 1955), p. 59.

52. Harris, "Future of Federal Grants-in-Aid," p. 17.

53. See David B. Walker, *Toward a Functioning Federalism* (Cambridge, MA: Winthrop Publishers, 1981), and David B. Walker, *The Rebirth of Federalism:* (New York: Chatham House Publishers, 2000).

54. *Categorical Grants: Their Role and Design* (Washington, DC: U.S. Advisory Commission on Intergovernmental Relations, 1978), p. 42.

55. Ibid., pp. 52–53.

56. Deil S. Wright, *Understanding Intergovernmental Relations*, 3rd ed. (Pacific Grove, CA: Brooks/Cole Publishing Co. 1988).

57. Charles L. Schultze, "Federal Spending: Past, Present, and Future." In *Setting National Priorities: The Next Ten Years*, ed. Henry Owen and Charles L. Schultze (Washington, DC: Brookings Institution, 1976), p. 367.

58. James L. Buckley, "The Trouble with Federalism: It Isn't Being Tried," *Commonsense* 1, Summer 1978, p. 13.

59. Ibid., p. 14.

60. *Categorical Grants*, p. 281.

61. *MacManus v. Love*, 499 P.2d 609 (1972) and *Sego v. Kirkpatrick*, 524 P.2d 975 (1974).

62. *Anderson v. Regan*, 53 N.Y.2d 356 at 366 (1981). See also *Anderson v. Regan*, 197 Misc.2d 335 (1981).

63. *Wheeler v. Barrera*, 417 U.S. 402 at 416-19, 416-19, 94 S.Ct. 2274 at 2283–284 (1972).

64. *Shapp v. Casey*, 439 U.S. 1043, 99 S.Ct. 717 (1979) and *Shapp v. Sloan*, 391 A.2d 595 (1978).

65. G. Homer Durham, "Politics and Administration in Intergovernmental Relations," *Annals of the American Academy of Political and Social Science* 207, January 1940, p. 5.

66. *Proposed Changes in Federal Matching and Maintenance of Effort Requirements for State and Local Governments* (Washington, DC: U.S. General Accounting Office, 1980), p. 61.

67. V.O. Key, Jr., "State Legislation Facilitative of Federal Action," *Annals of the American Academy of Political and Social Science* 207, January 1940, p. 24.

68. *Fiscal Balance*, p. 153.

69. *Florida Department of Health and Rehabilitative Services v. Califano*, 490 F. Supp. 274, 585 F.2d 150 (5th Cir.), cert. denied, 441 U.S. 931, 99 S.Ct. 2051 (1979).

70. *South Dakota v. Dole*, 483 U.S. 203, 107 S.Ct. 2793 (1987).

71. Stenberg, "Federal-Local Relations," p. 13.

72. *United States Housing Act of 1937*, 50 Stat. 888, 12 U.S.C. §1701.

73. Carl W. Stenberg, *State Involvement in Federal-Local Grant Programs: A Case Study of the "Buying In" Approach* (Washington, DC: U.S. Advisory Commission on Intergovernmental Relations, 1970), p. 2.

74. Ibid., p. 67.

75. *Intergovernmental Cooperation Act of 1968*, 82 Stat. 1098, 42 U.S.C. §§531–35, 4201.

76. *Federal Financial Assistance Management Improvement Act of 1999*, 113 Stat. 1489, 31 U.S.C. §6101 note.

77. Paul L. Posner, *Federal Assistance: Grant System Continues to Be Highly Fragmented* (Washington, DC: U.S. General Accounting Office, 2003), p. 3.

78. *Revenue Act of 1926*, 44 Stat. 9, 48 U.S.C. §845.

79. *Social Security Act of 1935*, 49 Stat. 620, 42 U.S.C. §301.

80. *Economic Recovery Tax Act of 1981*, 95 Stat. 399, 26 U.S.C. §103.

81. *Tax Equity and Fiscal Responsibility Act of 1982*, 96 Stat. 324, 26 U.S.C. §1.

82. *South Carolina v. Baker*, 485 U.S. 505, 108 S.Ct. 1355 (1988).

83. *Tax Reform Act of 1986*, 100 Stat. 2085, 26 U.S.C. §1.

84. The Commission on the Organization of the Executive Branch of the Federal Government, *Overseas Administration, Federal-State Relations, Federal Research* (Washington, DC: U.S. Government Printing Office, 1949), p. 36.

85. *Comprehensive Health Planning and Public Health Services Amendments of 1966*, 80 Stat. 1180, 42 U.S.C. §§243, 246.

86. *The Partnership for Health Act: Lessons from a Pioneering Block Grant* (Washington, DC: U.S. Advisory Commission on Intergovernmental Relations, 1977), pp. 4–5.

87. Michael D. Reagan and John G. Sanzone, *The New Federalism*, 2nd ed. (New York: Oxford University Press, 1981), pp. 129–30.

88. *Housing and Community Development Act of 1974*, 88 Stat. 633, 42 U.S.C. §5301.

89. Richard S. Williamson, "Block Grants—A Federalist Tool," *State Government* 54, no. 4, 1981, p. 115.

90. *Maternal and Child Health Block Grant: Program Changes Emerging under State Administration* (Washington, DC: U.S. General Accounting Office,

1984), p. 37; *States Use Added Flexibility Offered by the Preventive Health and Health Services Block Grant* (Washington, DC: U.S. General Accounting Office, 1984); and *Education Block Grant Alters State Role and Provides Greater Local Discretion* (Washington, DC: U.S. General Accounting Office, 1984).

91. Michael M. Knapp and Craig H. Blakely, *The Education Block Grant at the Local Level: The Implementation of Chapter 2 of the Education Consolidation and Improvement Act in Districts and Schools* (Menlo Park, CA: SRI International, 1986), p. iii.

92. *State and Local Fiscal Assistance Act of 1972*, 86 Stat. 919, 33 U.S.C. §1221.

93. Richard P. Nathan, "The New Federalism Versus the Emerging New Structuralism," *Publius* 5, Summer 1975, p. 112.

94. "Text of Reagan's Speech Accepting the Republican Nomination," *New York Times*, July 18, 1980, p. A8.

95. Charles A. Bowsher, "Federal Cutbacks Strengthen State Role," *State Government News* 29, February 1986, p. 19.

96. *Single Audit Act of 1984*, 98 Stat. 2327, 31 U.S.C. §7501. See also *Circular A-128* (Washington, DC: U.S. Office of Management and Budget, 1985), and *Single Audit* (Washington, DC: Arthur Andersen and Company, 1985).

97. "The Reagan Record," *Urban Institute Policy and Research Report* 14, August 1984, p. 11.

98. Ronald Reagan, "America's Agenda for the Future," *Congressional Record*, February 6, 1986, p. S1142.

99. *Ocean Dumping Ban Act of 1988*, 102 Stat. 4138, 33 U.S.C. §1401A.

4. Complete Field Preemption

1. W. Brooke Graves, ed., "Intergovernmental Relations in the United States," *Annals of the American Academy of Political and Social Science* 207, January 1940, pp. 1–218.

2. Richard H. Leach, ed., "Intergovernmental Relations in America Today," *Annals of the American Academy of Political and Social Science* 416, November 1974. See in particular, Deil S. Wright, "Intergovernmental Relations: An Analytical Overview," pp. 1–16; Brevard Crihfield and H. Clyde Reeves, "Intergovernmental Relations: A View from the States," pp. 99–107; and Joseph F. Zimmerman, "The Metropolitan Area Problem," pp. 137–47.

3. John Kincaid, ed., "American Federalism: The Third Century," *Annals of the American Academy of Political and Social Science* 509, May 1990, pp. 1–152. See Joseph F. Zimmerman, "Regulating Intergovernmental Relations in the 1990s," pp. 48–59; Eugene W. Hickok, Jr., "Federalism's Future Before the

U.S. Supreme Court," pp. 73–82; and John Kincaid, "From Cooperative to Coercive Federalism," pp. 139–52.

4. *Policy Positions: 1980–81* (Washington, DC: National Governors' Association, 1980).

5. *Surface Transportation Assistance Act of 1982*, 96 Stat. 2097, 23 U.S.C. §101, and *Motor Vehicle Width Regulations of 1983*, 97 Stat. 59, 49 U.S.C. §2316.

6. *Goals for State-Federal Action, 1984–1986* (Washington, DC: National Conference of State Legislatures, n.d.), p. 48.

7. *Uruguay Round Agreements Act of 1994*, 108 Stat. 4817, 19 U.S.C. §3512.

8. *Rural Telephone Cooperative Associations ERISA Amendments Act of 1991*, 105 Stat. 446, 29 U.S.C. §1001 note. See also *Employee Retirement Income Security Act of 1974*, 88 Stat. 829, 29 U.S.C. §1002(40).

9. *An Act to Amend Title I of the Employee Retirement Income Security Act of 1974*, 114 Stat. 499, 29 U.S.C. §1144a.

10. Ibid., 114 Stat. 500, 29 U.S.C. §1144a(d).

11. *Department of Transportation and Related Agencies Appropriations Act of 1992*, 105 Stat. 959, 49 U.S.C. app. §2727.

12. Ibid., 105 Stat. 960, 49 U.S.C. app. §2717(e).

13. *Petroleum Marketing Practices Act Amendments of 1994*, 108 Stat. 3485, 15 U.S.C. §2806(a)(2).

14. *Flammable Fabrics Act of 1967*, 81 Stat. 574, 15 U.S.C. §1191.

15. *Telephone Operator Consumer Services Improvement Act of 1990*, 104 Stat. 989, 47 U.S.C. §226.

16. *Radiation Control for Health and Safety Act of 1968*, 82 Stat. 1173, 42 U.S.C. §263b.

17. *United States Grain Standards Act of 1968*, 82 Stat. 769, 7 U.S.C. §71.

18. *Gun Control Act of 1968*, 82 Stat. 1226, 18 U.S.C. §921.

19. *Drug Abuse Control Amendments of 1965*, 79 Stat. 235, 21 U.S.C. §321.

20. *Children's Bicycle Helmet Safety Act of 1994*, 108 Stat. 726, 15 U.S.C. §6001.

21. *Civil Rights Act of 1991*, 105 Stat. 1071, 42 U.S.C. §1981, and *Ward Cove Packing Company v. Atonio*, 490 U.S. 642, 109 S.Ct. 2115 (1989).

22. *Civil Rights Act of 1964*, 78 Stat. 253, 42 U.S.C. §2000e.

23. *Gibbons v. Ogden*, 22 U.S 1 at 197, 9 Wheat. 1 at 197 (1824).

24. Herbert Wechsler, "The Political Safeguards of Federalism: The Role of the States in the Composition and Selection of the National Government," *Columbia Law Review* 54, 1953, pp. 543–60.

25. *Garcia v. San Antonio Metropolitan Transit Authority*, 469 U.S. 528 at 556, 105 S.Ct. 1005 at 1020 (1985).

26. *Copyright Act of 1790*, 1 Stat. 124, 17 U.S.C. §101, and *Patent Act of 1790*, 1 Stat. 109, 35 U.S.C. §1.

27. *Sonny Bono Copyright Term Extension Act of 1998*, 112 Stat. 2827, 17 U.S.C. §101, and *Digital Millennium Copyright Act of 1998*, 112 Stat. 2860, 17 U.S.C. §101.

28. *Sonny Bono Copyright Term Extension Act of 1998*, 112 Stat. 2827, 17 U.S.C. §§301(c), 302(a-b), 302(c)(A)B), 302(e)(A)(B).

29. Max Heuer, "Supreme Court Hears Debate over Copyright Changes," *Union Leader (Manchester, NH)*, October 10, 2002, p. 1.

30. *Eldred et al. v. Ashcroft*, 537 U.S. 186, 123 S.Ct. 769 (2003).

31. "The Coming of Copyright Perpetuity," *New York Times*, January 16, 2003, p. A28.

32. *Zacchini v. Scripps-Howard Broadcasting Company*, 433 U.S. 562, 97 S.Ct. 2849 (1977).

33. Ibid., 433 U.S. 562 at 579, 97 S.Ct. 2849 at 2859.

34. *An Act to Establish a Uniform System of Bankruptcy of 1898*, 30 Stat. 544, 11 U.S.C. §1.

35. *Bankruptcy Act of 1933*, 47 Stat. 1467, 11 U.S.C. §101.

36. *In Re World Auxiliary Power Company v. Silicon Valley Bank*, 244 B.R.149 (1999).

37. *In Re World Auxiliary Power Company*, 303 F.3d 1120 (9th Cir. 2002).

38. Ibid., 303F. 3d at 1128.

39. *Air Quality Act of 1967*, 81 Stat. 485, 42 U.S.C. §1857.

40. *Clean Air Act Amendments of 1970*, 84 Stat. 1676, 42 U.S.C. §1857 and 49 U.S.C. §§1421, 1430.

41. *Religious Freedom Restoration Act of 1993*, 107 Stat. 1488, 42 U.S.C. §2000bb-1.

42. *City of Boerne v. Flores*, 521 U.S. 507, 117 S.Ct. 2157 (1997).

43. *Limitation on State Income Taxation of Certain Pension Income Act of 1996*, 109 Stat. 979, 4 U.S.C. §114(a-b), and *Internet Tax Nondiscrimination Act of 2001*, 115 Stat. 703, 47 U.S.C. §151.

44. *Needlestick Safety and Prevention Act of 2000*, 114 Stat. 1903.

45. *Airline Deregulation Act of 1978*, 92 Stat. 1708, 49 U.S.C. §1305.

46. *Motor Carrier Act of 1980*, 94 Stat. 793, 49 U.S.C. §1101, and *Bus Regulatory Reform Act of 1982*, 96 Stat. 1104, 49 U.S.C. §10521.

47. *Miller-Tydings Act of 1937*, 50 Stat. 693, 15 U.S.C. §1. See also *The Act of July 2, 1890*, 26 Stat. 209, 15 U.S.C. §1.

48. *An Act to Amend the Sherman Antitrust Act to Provide Lower Prices for Consumers of 1975*, 89 Stat. 801.

49. *Age Discrimination in Employment Act of 1967*, 81 Stat. 381, 29 U.S.C. §623.

50. *Tax Equity and Fiscal Responsibility Act of 1982*, 96 Stat. 324, 26 U.S.C. §1.

51. *Age Discrimination in Employment Amendments of 1986*, 100 Stat. 3342, 29 U.S.C. §623.

52. "Emergency Plans," 10 CFR §50.47 (1986).

53. *Commercial Motor Vehicle Safety Act of 1986*, 100 Stat. 3207, 49 U.S.C. §2701.

54. *Motor Carrier Safety Improvement Act of 1999*, 113 Stat. 1760-763, 49 U.S.C. §31311(a-c).

55. *Safe Drinking Water Act Amendments of 1986*, 100 Stat. 651, 42 U.S.C. §300g.

56. *National Traffic and Motor Vehicle Safety Act of 1966*, 80 Stat. 719, 15 U.S.C. §1392d.

57. *Professional and Amateur Sports Protection Act of 1992*, 106 Stat. 4228, 28 U.S.C. §3702.

58. Ibid., 106 Stat. 4228, 28 U.S.C. §3704.

59. Telephone interview with Neil Porter, Compliance Division, Grain Inspection and Packers and Stockyard Administration, United States Department of Agriculture, April 21, 2003. See also *Official Agency Directory* (Washington, DC: Grain Inspection, Packers and Stockyards Administration, Federal Grain Inspection Service, U.S. Department of Agriculture, 2003), p. 1.

60. *Resource Conservation and Recovery Act of 1976*, 90 Stat. 2809, 42 U.S.C. §6926.

61. *Hazardous and Solid Waste Amendments of 1984*, 98 Stat. 3256, 42 U.S.C. §§6297–6928.

62. *Federal Railroad Safety Act of 1970*, 84 Stat. 971, 45 U.S.C. §431.

63. E-mail message to author from Mike Calhoun of the Federal Railroad Administration, August 5, 2003.

64. *Safe Drinking Water Act Amendments of 1986*, 100 Stat. 651, 42 U.S.C. §330g.

65. *Atomic Energy Act of 1959*, 73 Stat. 688, 42 U.S.C. §2021.

66. Letter to author from Deputy Director Josephine M. Piccone of the Nuclear Regulatory Commission's Office of State and Tribal Programs dated November 6, 2002.

67. Committee on Energy and Environment, *The Agreement State Program: A State Perspective* (Washington, DC: National Governors' Association, 1983), p. 3.

68. Memorandum dated March 19, 1986, to New Mexico Governor Toney Anaya from Director Denise Fort of the Environmental Improvement Division, pp. 4–5. See also *Uranium Mill Tailings Radiation Control Act of 1978*, 92 Stat. 3021, 42 U.S.C. §2014.

69. *Equal Employment Opportunity Act of 1972*, 86 Stat. 104, 42 U.S.C. §2000(e)(5).

70. *Fair Labor Standards Amendments of 1974*, 88 Stat. 55, 29 U.S.C. §203(d).

71. *National League of Cities v. Usery*, 426 U.S. 833, 96 S.Ct. 2465 (1976).

72. *Garcia v. San Antonio Metropolitan Transit Authority*, 469 U.S. 528, 105 S.Ct. 1005 (1985).

73. *Armored Car Industry Reciprocity Act of 1993*, 107 Stat. 276, 15 U.S.C. §5901.

74. *National Child Protection Act of 1993*, 107 Stat. 2490, 42 U.S.C. §5101.

75. *Full Faith and Credit for Child Support Orders Act of 1994*, 108 Stat. 4063, 28 U.S.C. §1.

76. *Violence Against Women Act of 2000*, 114 Stat. 1493, 42 U.S.C.§3796hh-1(b)(B)(a)(1).

77. *Campus Sex Crimes Prevention Act of 2000*, 114 Stat. 1537, 20 U.S.C. §10001(j).

78. *Help America Vote Act of 2002*, 116 Stat. 1704, 42 U.S.C. §15481 and 116 Stat. 1728, 42 U.S.C. §1973gg-6(b)(2)(A-B). See also the *National Voter Registration Act of 1993*, 107 Stat. 77, 42 U.S.C. §1973gg.

79. *Ocean Dumping Ban Act of 1988*, 102 Stat. 4139, 33 U.S.C. §1401A.

80. *Driver's Privacy Protection Act of 1994*, 108 Stat. 2099, 18 U.S.C. §2721.

81. Ibid., 108 Stat. 2101, 18 U.S.C. §2723.

82. *Low-level Radioactive Waste Policy Act of 1980*, 94 Stat. 3347, 42 U.S.C. §2021d.

83. Consult Joseph F. Zimmerman, *Interstate Cooperation: Compacts and Administrative Agreements* (Westport, CT: Praeger Publishers, 2002).

84. *Texas Low-Level Radioactive Waste Disposal Compact*, 112 Stat. 2542.

85. *Low-Level Radioactive Wastes: States Are Not Developing Disposal Facilities* (Washington, DC: U.S. General Accounting Office, 1999), pp. 26, 29, 15.

86. *A Joint Resolution Making Further Continuing Appropriations for the Fiscal Year 1986, and for Other Purposes*, 90 Stat. 1288.

87. *Nuclear Waste Policy Act of 1982*, 96 Stat. 2217, 42 U.S.C. §10125.

88. *Omnibus Budget Reconciliation Act of 1988*, 98 Stat. 437, 23 U.S.C. §158.

89. *Yucca Mountain High Level Radioactive Waste Site Act of 2002*, 116 Stat. 735, 42 U.S.C. §10135.

90. *Voting Rights Act of 1965*, 79 Stat. 437, 42 U.S.C. §1973. For details on the act, consult Joseph F. Zimmerman, "The Federal Voting Rights Act and Alternative Election Systems," *William and Mary Law Review* 19, Summer 1978, pp. 621–60.

91. *Voting Rights Language Assistance Act of 1992*, 106 Stat. 921, 42 U.S.C. §1071.

92. *Prescription Drug Amendments of 1992*, 106 Stat. 941, 221 U.S.C. §301.

93. *Atlantic Striped Bass Conservation Act Amendments of 1986*, 100 Stat. 989, 16 U.S.C. §1851.

94. *Abandoned Shipwreck Act of 1987*, 102 Stat. 432, 43 U.S.C. §2101.

95. *Age Discrimination in Employment Amendments of 1986*, 100 Stat. 3342, 29 U.S.C. §623.

96. *Oil Pollution Act of 1990*, 104 Stat. 506, 33 U.S.C. §2719.

97. *Anti Car Theft Act of 1992*, 106 Stat. 3390, 3394, 15 U.S.C. §§2022, 2042.

98. Ibid., 106 Stat. 3384, 18 U.S.C. §2119.

99. *Telemarketing and Consumer Fraud and Abuse Prevention Act of 1994*, 108 Stat. 1548, 15 U.S.C. §6103.

100. *Consumer Credit Reporting Reform Act of 1996*, 110 Stat. 3009-451 to 3009-453, 15 U.S.C. §1681s(2)(b-c). Consult also *Consumer Reporting Employment Clarification Act of 1998*, 112 Stat. 3208, 15 U.S.C. §1601.

101. *Antiterrorism and Effective Death Penalty Act of 1996*, 110 Stat. 1276, 8 U.S.C. §1252c.

102. *Children's Online Privacy Protection Act of 1998*, 112 Stat. 2681-733, 15 U.S.C. §6504.

103. *State and Local Enforcement of Federal Communications Commission Regulations on Use of Citizens Band Radio Equipment Act of 2000*, 114 Stat. 2438, 47 U.S.C. §302a(f)(1).

104. *Telephone Disclosure and Dispute Resolution Act of 1992*, 106 Stat. 4190, 15 U.S.C. §5712.

105. *Electronic Signatures in Global and National Commerce Act of 2000*, 114 Stat. 467, 15 U.S.C. §7002.

106. Ibid.

107. *Food Quality Protection Act of 1996*, 110 Stat. 1493, 7 U.S.C. §136w-5. See also *Federal Insecticide, Fungicide, and Rodenticide Act of 1975*, 89 Stat. 751, 7 U.S.C. §136.

108. *Congressional Record*, May 25, 1983, pp. S7556–557.

109. Letter from Governor Mario M. Cuomo of New York to U.S. Secretary of Energy John S. Herrington dated March 28, 1985. *Public Papers of Governor Mario M. Cuomo.* Albany: Executive Chamber, 1989, pp. 928–29.

110. Brad Pokorny and Ray Richard, "Seabrook Tests Evacuation Plans," *Boston Globe*, February 27, 1986, p. 23.

111. Richard March, "Seabrook Drill Called a Failure," *Keene (NH) Sentinel*, March 1, 1986, pp. 1–2.

112. "Full Participation in Seabrook Drill Is Critical to Plan, Critics Assert," *Keene (NH) Sentinel*, March 3, 1986, p. 6.

113. "Massachusetts Governor Seeks to Stop Nuclear Plant Opening," *New York Times*, September 21, 1986, p. 24.

114. "Public Service Argues for 2-Mile Safety Zone," *Keene (NH) Sentinel*, September 27, 1986, p. 3.

115. *Federal Register*, August 8, 1980, p. 55409, 10 C.F.R. §50.47, and "Nuclear Regulatory Commissioners Vote to Seek Public Comment on Proposed Rule Change in Emergency Planning Rule," *United States Nuclear Regulatory Commission News Releases*, March 3, 1987, p. 1.

116. "Licensing of Nuclear Power Plants Where State and/or Local Governments Decline to Cooperate in Offsite emergency Planning," *United States Nuclear Regulatory Commission News Releases*, March 10, 1987, p. 2.

117. Ben A. Franklin, "Nuclear Panel Denies Waiver on New Hampshire Reactor," *New York Times*, April 23, 1987, p. A24.

118. *Federal Register*, November 3, 1987, pp. 42078–087, 10 C.F.R. Part 50.

119. Larry Tye, "NRC Approves Licensing of Seabrook," *Boston Globe*, March 2, 1990, pp. 1, 12, and James L. Franklin, "Court Denies License Delay at Seabrook," *Boston Globe*, March 15, 1990, pp. 1, 22.

120. Randal C. Archibold, "Disaster Plan for Indian Point Is Called Inadequate," *New York Times*, January 11, 2003, pp. 1, B4.

121. Randal C. Archibold, "3 Counties Maneuver in Bid to Close Down Indian Point," *New York Times*, January 16, 2003, p. B5, Randal C. Archibold, "Albany Says It Can't Certify Indian Pt. Plan," *New York Times*, January 31, 2003, pp. B1, B5; and Winnie Hu, "Indian Point Battle Lines Are Redrawn," *New York Times*, February 1, 2003, p. B5.

122. Lisa W. Foderaro, "Study Sees a Longer Time for Evacuating Indian Pt.," *New York Times*, July 3, 2003, p. B5.

123. Randal C. Archibold, "FEMA Says It Can't Approve Emergency Plan for Indian Pt," *New York Times*, February 22, 2003, pp. B1, B8, and Randal C. Archibold and Matthew L. Wald, "U.S. Approves Evacuation Plan for Indian Point Nuclear Plant," *New York Times*, July 26, 2003, pp. 1, B4.

124. Lydia Polgreen, "Indian Point Is Said to Pass U.S. Test in Mock Attack," *New York Times*, August 12, 2003, pp. B5.

125. Matthew L. Wald, "Safety Problem at Nuclear Plants Is Cited," *New York Times*, September 8, 2003, p. A14.

126. "Brattleboro Board Questions Evacuation Plan," *Keene (NH) Sentinel*, June 25, 2003, p. 3.

127. "Hinsdale Not Satisfied with Disaster Plan," *Union Leader (Manchester, NH)*, June 11, 2003, p. B1.

128. *Surface Transportation Assistance Act of 1982*, 96 Stat. 2097, 23 U.S.C. §101.

129. Ibid., 96 Stat. 2159, 49 U.S.C. §2311.

130. Ibid., 96 Stat. 2124, 23 U.S.C. §101.

131. *Implementing Nationally Uniform Truck Laws* (Albany: New York State Legislative Commission on Critical Transportation Choices, August 1983), p. 8.

132. Ibid., p. 9.

133. *Federal Register*, May 3, 1983, pp. 22028-029.

134. *Motor Vehicle Width Regulations*, 97 Stat. 59, 49 U.S.C. §2316.

135. Ernest Holsendolph, "Double-Trailer Plan Stirs Outcry in Some Unexpected Quarters," *New York Times*, April 11, 1983, p. A14.

136. Ernest Holsendolph, "State Officials Gather to Plan Resistance to Big Truck Rules," *New York Times*, April 15, 1983, p. B10.

137. *Tandem Truck Safety Act of 1984*, 98 Stat. 1829–830, 49 U.S.C. app. §2301, and *Motor Carrier Safety Act of 1984*, 98 Stat. 2832, 49 U.S.C. §1509.

138. *Tandem Truck Safety Act of 1984*, 98 Stat. 2829, 42 U.S.C. §2301–302.

139. Ibid., 98 Stat. 2832, 49 U.S.C. §2312.

140. *Motor Carrier Safety Act of 1984*, 98 Stat. 2834, 49 U.S.C. §2502.

141. Ibid., 98 Stat. 2837, 49 U.S.C. §2508.

142. Ibid.

143. Ibid.

5. *Imperium in Imperio* and Limited Preemption

1. *Connecticut General Statutes Annotated*, §§19-523, 19-524 (1967 Supp.); *New Jersey Statutes Annotated*, §§32-29-1 to 3239-39 (1968); and *New York Public Health Law*, §1299-m (1967 Supp.). Consult also "Air Pollution: Message from the President of the United States," *Congressional Record*, January 30, 1967, p. H737. For detailed information on interstate compacts, see Joseph F. Zimmerman, *Interstate Cooperation: Compacts and Administrative Agreements* (Westport, CT: Praeger Publishers, 2002).

2. Joseph F. Zimmerman, "The Interstate Insurance Product Regulation Compact," a paper presented at a meeting of the National Conference of State Legislatures Executive Committee's Task Force to Streamline and Simplify Insurance Regulation, New York, N.Y., March 22, 2003.

3. *The Federalist Papers* (New York: New American Library, 1961), p. 198.

4. *H. P. Hood & Sons, Incorporated v. DuMond*, 336 U.S. 525 at 534-35, 69 S.Ct. 657 at 663 (1949).

5. *Voting Rights Act of 1870*, 16 Stat. 140.

6. *Voting Rights Act Amendments of 1871*, 16 Stat. 433.

7. *United States v. Reese*, 92 U.S. 214, 2 Otto 214 (1875).

8. *Wages v. Michelin Tire Corporation*, 233 Ga. 712, 214 S.E.2d 349 (1975).

9. *Michelin Tire Corporation v. Wages*, 423 U.S. 276 at 302, 96 S.Ct. 535 at 548 (1975).

10. *Trailer Train Company v. State Board of Equalization*, 538 F. Supp. 509 at 599 (N.D. 1981).

11. *Virginia v. Tennessee*, 148 U.S. 503, 13 S.Ct. 728 (1893). Consult Zimmerman, *Interstate Cooperation.*

12. 37 Stat. 25 (1911).

13. *Civil Rights Act of 1964*, 78 Stat. 241, 28 U.S.C. §1442 and 42 U.S.C. §1971.

14. *Drug Abuse Control Amendments of 1965*, 79 Stat. 235, 21 U.S.C. §321.

15. *Gun Control Act of 1968*, 82 Stat. 1226, 18 U.S.C. §921.

16. *Truth in Lending Act of 1968*, 82 Stat. 151, 12 U.S.C. §1818.

17. *Federal Election Campaign Act Amendments of 1974*, 88 Stat. 1277, 2 U.S.C. §431.

18. *Federal Railroad Safety Act of 1970*, 84 Stat. 971, 45 U.S.C. §431.

19. *Occupational Safety and Health Act of 1970*, 84 Stat. 1608, 5 U.S.C. §5108.

20. *Federal Election Campaign Act of 1971*, 86 Stat. 20, 42 U.S.C. §2701.

21. *Truth in Savings Act of 1991*, 105 Stat. 2342, 12 U.S.C. §4312.

22. *Telephone Disclosure and Dispute Resolution Act of 1992*, 106 Stat. 4192, 15 U.S.C. §5722.

23. *Interstate Commerce Commission Termination Act of 1995*, 109 Stat. 900, 902, 49 U.S.C. §§14502, 14504.

24. *National Securities Markets Improvement Act of 1996*, 110 Stat. 3435, 15 U.S.C. §80b-18a.

25. *Health Insurance Portability and Accountability Act of 1996*, 110 Stat. 1046, 29 U.S.C. §1184; 110 Stat. 1971, 42 U.S.C. §300gg-23.

26. Ibid., 110 Stat. 1984, 42 U.S.C. §300gg-44; 110 Stat. 2030, 42 U.S.C. 1320d-6.

27. *Intercountry Adoption Act of 2000*, 114 Stat. 843, 42 U.S.C. §14953.

28. *Mobile Telecommunications Sourcing Act of 2000*, 114 Stat. 627, 4 U.S.C. §116.

29. Ibid.

30. 1 Stat. 54 (1789).

31. *Shipping Statute of 1983*, 97 Stat. 553, 46 U.S.C. §8501.

32. Ibid., 46 U.S.C. §8502(c).

33. *Coast Guard Authorization Act of 1984*, 98 Stat. 2862, 46 U.S.C. §2302(c).

34. *Port and Tanker Safety Act of 1978*, 92 Stat. 1471, 33 U.S.C. §1226.

35. *Voting Rights Act of 1965*, 79 Stat. 437, 42 U.S.C. §1973.

36. *Voting Rights Act Amendments of 1975*, 89 Stat. 438, 42 U.S.C. §§1973a, 1973d, 1973l.

37. *Voting Rights Act of 1965*, 79 Stat. 437, 42 U.S.C. §1973c. For the impact of the act on covered local governments, consult Joseph F. Zimmerman, "Local Representation: Designing a Fair System," *National Civic Review* 69, June 1980, pp. 307–12.

38. *Hazardous Materials Transportation Act of 1974*, 88 Stat. 2156, 49 U.S.C. App. §1801. See also 49 C.F.R. §§170–79.

39. Department of Transportation, "Hazardous Materials: Inconsistency Rulings IR-7 through IR-15," *Federal Register*, November 27, 1984, p. 46633.

40. Ibid., p. 46646.

41. *USA Patriot Act of 2001*, 115 Stat. 396, 49 U.S.C. §5103a(a)(1).

42. *Removal of Causes Act of 1920*, 41 Stat. 554, 28 U.S.C. §1441.

43. *Private Securities Litigation Reform Act of 1995*, 109 Stat. 737, 15 U.S.C. §78a note.

44. *Securities Litigation Uniform Standards Act of 1998*, 112 Stat. 3227, 15 U.S.C. §78a note.

45. Ibid., 112 Stat. 3231, 15 U.S.C. §77v(a).

46. *Department of Transportation and Related Agencies Appropriations Act of 1997*, 110 Stat. 2974, 49 U.S.C. §24902(m).

47. *Paul v. Virginia*, 75 U.S. 168, 8 Wall. 168 (1868).

48. *United States v. South-Eastern Underwriters Association*, 322 U.S. 533, 64 S.Ct. 533 (1944).

49. *McCarran-Ferguson Act of 1945*, 59 Stat. 33, 15 U.S.C. §1011.

50. *Gramm-Leach-Bliley Financial Modernization Act of 1999*, 113 Stat. 1353, 11422, 15 U.S.C. §§6701(d)(2)(A), 6751.

51. *Terrorism Risk Insurance Act of 2002*, 116 Stat. 2322, 15 U.S.C. §6701.

52. Ibid., 116 Stat. 2334, 15 U.S.C. 6701(b).

53. *Kentucky Revised Statutes Annotated*, §304. *Employee Retirement Income Security Act of 1974*, 88 Stat. 829, 29 U.S.C. §1001.

54. *Kentucky Association of Health Plans, Incorporated et al. v. Miller*, 538 U.S. 329, 123 S.Ct. 1471 (2003).

55. Ibid. 538 U.S. 329 at 341, 123 S.Ct. 1471 at 1479.

56. Interview with Richard Wiebe, a former assistant program secretary to Governor Nelson A. Rockefeller of New York, Albany, New York, February 26, 1982. Hereinafter referred to as Wiebe interview.

57. *Water Quality Act of 1965*, 79 Stat. 903, 33 U.S.C. §1151.

58. *Federal Water Pollution Control Act Amendments of 1972*, 86 Stat. 816, 33 U.S.C. §1151.

59. *Federal Register*, September 14, 1973, pp. 25681 *et seq.*

60. Wiebe interview.

61. *Clean Water Act of 1977*, 91 Stat. 1567, 33 U.S.C. §1251.

62. Patricia M. Crotty, "The New Federalism Game: Options for the States." A paper presented at the annual meeting of the Northeastern Political Science Association, Philadelphia, November 14–16, 1985.

63. *Clean Water Act of 1977*, 91 Stat. 1577, 33 U.S.C. §1342l.

64. *Air Quality Act of 1967*, 81 Stat. 485, 42 U.S.C. §18570.

65. *Clean Air Act Amendments of 1970*, 84 Stat. 1676, 42 U.S.C. §1857.

66. *Fri v. Sierra Club*, 412 U.S. 541, 93 S.Ct. 2770 (1973). See also *Sierra Club v. Ruckelshaus*, 344 F. Supp. 253 (D.D.C. 1972).

67. For an excellent description and analysis of EPA's compliance with the court order, consult Albert C. Hyde, "The Politics of Environmental Decision Making: The Non-Decision Issue" (unpublished Ph. D. dissertation, State University of New York at Albany, 1980). See also R. Shep Melnick, *Regulation and the Courts: The Case of the Clean Air Act* (Washington, DC: Brookings Institution, 1983).

68. "Prevention of Significant Deterioration (PSD) of Air Quality: Supplemental Delegation of Authority to North Carolina," *Federal Register*, September 21, 1984, p. 37064. Consult also 40 C.F.R. §52.

69. Crotty, "The New Federalism Game," p. 13. See also Joseph F. Zimmerman, "The Role of the State Legislature in Air Pollution Abatement," *Suffolk University Law Review* 5, Spring 1971, pp. 850–77.

70. *Clean Air Act Amendments of 1990*, 104 Stat. 2399, 42 U.S.C. §7407(d).

71. Ibid., 104 Stat. 2419, 42 U.S.C. §7506a.

72. Zimmerman, *Interstate Cooperation*, pp. 176–177 and 218.

73. *Clean Air Act Amendments of 1990*, 104 Stat. 2529, 42 U.S.C. §7507.

74. Ibid., 104 Stat. 2589, 42 U.S.C. §7651b.

75. *EPA's Acid Rain Program: Results of Phase I, Outlook for Phase II* (Washington, DC: U.S. Environmental Protection Agency, 2001), p. 2.

76. *Economic Report of the President* (Washington, DC: U.S. Government Printing Office, 2002), p. 235.

77. *Clean Air Act Amendments of 1990*, 104 Stat. 2643, 42 U.S.C. §7661d.

78. *Restrictions on the Stringency of State and Local Air Quality Programs* (Washington, DC: State and Territorial Air Pollution Program Administrators and the Association of Local Air Pollution Control Officials, 2002), p. 1.

79. *Safe Drinking Water Act of 1974*, 88 Stat. 1665, 42 U.S.C. §201.

80. *Safe Drinking Water Act Amendments of 1986*, 100 Stat. 642, 42 U.S.C. §300g-1.

81. Ibid., 100 Stat. 643, 42 U.S.C. §300g-1.

82. *Safe Drinking Water Act Amendments of 1996*, 110 Stat. 1613, 42 U.S.C. §201 note.

83. Ibid., 100 Stat. 647, 42 U.S.C. §300g-3.

84. Telephone interview with Bridget O'Grady of the Association of State Drinking Water Administrators, Washington, D.C., March 4, 2003, and letter to author from Charlene E. Shaw of the Office of Ground Water and Drinking Water, United States Environmental Protection Agency dated February 5, 2003.

85. U.S. Environmental Protection Agency, "Responsibility for the UIC Program (Delegation Status,") http://www.epa.gov/safewater/uic/primary2html.

86. *Public Health Security and Bioterrorism Preparedness and Response Act of 2002*, 116 Stat. 682, 42 U.S.C. §300i-2.

87. *Surface Mining Control and Reclamation Act of 1977*, 91 Stat. 445, 30 U.S.C. §1201.

88. *Hodel v. Virginia Surface Mining and Reclamation Association*, 452 U.S. 264 at 288, 101 S.Ct. 2352 at 2366.

89. Letter to author from Chief Annello L. Cheek of the Division of Permit and Environmental Analysis of the U.S. Department of the Interior dated February 13, 1987, and letter to author from Acting Assistant Director for Program Support Richard G. Bryson of the Office of Surface Mining dated February 13, 2003.

90. *Occupational Safety and Health Act of 1970*, 84 Stat. 1590, 5 U.S.C. §5108.

91. Ibid., 84 Stat. 1608, 29 U.S.C. §667.

92. Ibid.

93. Letter to author from Bruce Hillenbrand, Director of Federal-State Operations of the Occupational Safety and Health Administration dated August 5, 1988. See also *State Programs: Background* (Washington, DC: Occupational Safety and Health Administration, 1985), p. 1.

94. Letter to author from Director Paula O. White of Cooperative and State Programs of the United States Department of Labor dated February 12, 2003.

95. *Ohio Manufacturers' Association v. City of Akron*, 801 F.2d 824 at 831 (6th Cir. 1986).

96. *Federal Register*, July 12, 1985, pp. 28530 *et seq.* Consult also the *Toxic Substance Control Act*, 90 Stat. 2003, 15 U.S.C. §2601.

97. *Riegle-Neal Interstate Banking and Branching Efficiency Act of 1994*, 108 Stat. 2338, 12 U.S.C. §1811.

98. Ibid., 108 Stat. 2352, 12 U.S.C. §215.

99. Ibid., 108 Stat. 2343, 12 U.S.C. §1831u.

100. Philip E. Strahan, "The Real Effects of U.S. Banking Deregulation," *Federal Reserve Bank of St. Louis Review* 85, July/August 2003, p. 113.

101. Ibid., p. 126.

102. *Wholesome Meat Act of 1967*, 81 Stat. 595, 21 U.S.C. §71.

103. *Poultry Products Inspection Act of 1968*, 82 Stat. 791, 21 U.S.C. §451.

104. *Newborns' and Mothers' Health Protection Act of 1996*, 110 Stat. 2937, 29 U.S.C. §1185.

105. *Toxic Substances Control Act of 1976*, 90 Stat. 2038, 15 U.S.C. §2617.

106. Ibid, 90 Stat. 2039, 15 U.S.C. §2617.

107. *Needlestick Safety and Prevention Act of 2000*, 114 Stat. 1903.

108. *Port and Tanker Safety Act of 1978*, 92 Stat. 1475, 33 U.S.C. §1225. Part of this act subsequently was repealed by Congress. See 46 U.S.C. §7101.

109. *Natural Gas Policy Act of 1978*, 92 Stat. 3409, 15 U.S.C. §3431.

110. *Telephone Consumer Protection Act of 1991*, 105 Stat. 2400, 47 U.S.C. §227(e).

111. Ibid., 105 Stat. 2400, 47 U.S.C. §227(f).

112. *Gramm-Leach-Bliley Financial Modernization Act of 1999*, 113 Stat. 1442, 15 U.S.C. §6807.

113. *Federal Environmental Pesticide Control Act of 1972*, 86 Stat. 996–97, 7 U.S.C. §§136u-136v.

114. *Federal Railroad Safety Act of 1970*, 84 Stat. 971, 45 U.S.C. §431.

115. *Federal Environmental Pesticide Control Act of 1972*, 86 Stat. 996–97, 7 U.S.C. §§136u-136v.

116. *Federal Insecticide, Fungicide, and Rodenticide Act of 1947*, 61 Stat. 163, 7 U.S.C. §136.

117. *Cable Communications Policy Act of 1984*, 98 Stat. 2792, 47 U.S.C. §546.

118. Ibid., 98 Stat. 2800, 47 U.S.C. §555.

119. *Telecommunications Act of 1996*, 110 Stat. 124, 47 U.S.C. §541(b)(3)(A)(i).

120. Ibid., 110 Stat. 144–45, 47 U.S.C. §152.

121. *Coastal Zone Management Act of 1972*, 86 Stat. 1280, 16 U.S.C. §1451.

122. Ibid., 86 Stat, 1282, 16 U.S.C. §1454.

123. Ibid., 86 Stat. 1286, 16 U.S.C. §1456(d).

124. *Coast Guard Authorization Act of 1998*, 112 Stat. 3450, 16 U.S.C. §1451 note.

125. *National Voter Registration Act of 1993*, 107 Stat. 78–79, 42 U.S.C. §§1973gg-3, 1973gg-4.

126. *Federal Environmental Pesticide Control Act of 1972*, 86 Stat. 983, 7 U.S.C. §136b(2). Consult also the *Emergency Energy Conservation Act of 1979*, 93 Stat. 759, 42 U.S.C. §8512.

127. *Clean Air Act Amendments of 1977*, 91 Stat. 722, 42 U.S.C. §7424.

128. *Federal Water Pollution Control Act Amendments of 1972*, 86 Stat. 841, 33 U.S.C. §1151.

129. *Emergency Highway Energy Conservation Act of 1974*, 87 Stat. 1046, 23 U.S.C. §154. See also 23 C.F.R. §658.6.

130. *Surface Transportation and Uniform Relocation Assistance Act of 1987*, 101 Stat. 135, 23 U.S.C. §101 note. See also R. W. Apple, Jr., "Senate Rejects Reagan Plan and Votes 67-33 to Override His Veto of Highway Funds," *New York Times*, April 3, 1987, pp. 1, A25.

131. *Safe Drinking Water Act of 1974*, 88 Stat. 1676, 42 U.S.C. §300h.

132. *Federal Metal and Nonmetallic Mine Safety Act of 1966*, 80 Stat. 783, 42 U. S. C. §2011. This act has been replaced by the *Federal Mine Safety and Health Act of 1977*, 91 Stat. 1290, 30 U.S.C. §801.

133. *Wholesome Meat Act of 1967*, 81 Stat. 596, 21 U.S.C. §71, and *Poultry Products Inspection Act of 1968*, 82 Stat. 797, 21 U.S.C. §451.

134. *National Health Planning and Resources Development Act of 1974*, 88 Stat. 2242, 42 U.S.C. §300m.

135. *Federal Water Pollution Control Act Amendments of 1972*, 86 Stat. 840, 842, 33 U.S.C. §1151.

136. *Clean Air Act Amendments of 1977*, 91 Stat. 749, 42 U.S.C. §7504. Consult also the *Federal Environmental Pesticide Control Act of 1972*, 86 Stat. 983, 7 U.S.C. §136b(2).

137. *Surface Transportation Assistance Act of 1978*, 92 Stat. 2724, 23 U.S.C. §134.

138. *National Health Planning and Resources Development Act of 1974*, 88 Stat. 2247, 42 U.S.C. §300m-3.

139. *Highway Safety Act of 1966*, 80 Stat. 731, 23 U.S.C. §402(b)(1).

140. "State of New York Executive Order No. 75," *Public Papers of Nelson A. Rockefeller: Fifty-Third Governor of the State of New York, 1973* (Albany: State of New York, n.d.), pp. 811–12.

141. "Executive Order 12140 of May 29, 1979," *Federal Register*, May 3, 1979, p. 31159. This delegation of authority is based upon the power vested in the president by the *Emergency Petroleum Allocation Act of 1973* [87 Stat. 627, 15 U.S.C. §751] and his inherent powers.

142. *Tandem Truck Safety Act of 1984*, 98 Stat. 2384, 42 U.S.C. §2312.

143. *Sierra Club v. Ruckelshaus*, 344 F. Supp. 253 (D.D.C. 1972), and *Fri v. Sierra Club*, 412 U.S. 541, 93 S.Ct. 2770 (1973).

144. *Federal Register*, December 5, 1977, p. 61543. Consult also *New York State Air Quality Implementation Plan: The Moynihan/Holtzman Amendment Submission: Transit Improvements in the New York City Metropolitan Area* (Albany: New York State Department of Environmental Conservation and State Department of Transportation, 1979).

145. *Clean Air Act Amendments of 1977*, 91 Stat. 731, 42 U.S.C. §7470.

146. Ibid., 91 Stat. 734, 42 U.S.C. §7474.

147. *Clean Air Act Amendments of 1990*, 104 Stat. 2400, 42 U.S.C. 7407(d)(1)(B)(iii).

148. Ibid., 104 Stat. 2403, 42 U.S.C. §7407(d).

149. *Clean Air Act Amendments of 1977*, 91 Stat. 733, 42 U.S.C. §7473.

150. Ibid., 91 Stat. 737, 42 U.S.C. §7475.

151. Ibid., 91 Stat. 695, 42 U.S.C. §7410.

152. *Federal Register*, December 5, 1977, p. 61543. Consult also the *New York State Air Quality Implementation Plan: The Moynihan/Holtzman Amendment Submission: Transit Improvements in the New York City Metropolitan Area* (Albany, NY: New York State Department of Environmental Conservation and State Department of Transportation, 1979).

153. *Clean Air Act Amendments of 1977*, 91 Stat. 723, 42 U.S.C. §7425.

154. *Clean Air Act Amendments of 1990*, 104 Stat. 2419, 42 U.S.C. §7506a.

6. Judicially Determined Preemption

1. *Judiciary Act of 1789*, 1 Stat. at 80–81.

2. *Removal of Causes Act of 1920*, 41 Stat. 554, 28 U.S.C. §1441. See also 28 U.S.C. §1331.

3. Mark R. Kravitz, "Removal Remands," *National Law Journal* 23, June 25, 2001, p. A10.

4. *Removal of Causes Act*, 41 Stat. 554, 28 U.S.C. §1441(b). See also *Merrell Dow Pharmaceuticals Incorporated v. Thompson*, 478 U.S. 804, 106 S.Ct. 3229 (1986).

5. *McCulloch v. Maryland*, 17 U.S. 316 at 421, 4 Wheat. 316 at 421 (1819).

6. *Fletcher v. Peck*, 10 U.S. 87, 6 Cranch 87 (1810).

7. *Southern Railway Company v. Reid*, 222 U.S. 424 at 442, 32 S.Ct. 140 at 144 (1912).

8. *New York Central Railroad v. Winfield*, 244 U.S. 147 at 169, 37 S.Ct. 546 at 555 (1917).

9. Woodrow Wilson, *Congressional Government* (Boston: Houghton Mifflin, 1925), pp. 36–37.

10. *Individuals with Disabilities Education Act Amendments of 1997*, 111 Stat. 47, 20 U.S.C. §1403.

11. *Elrod v. Burns*, 427 U.S. 347, 96 S.Ct. 2673 (1976). The court in 1990 opined promotions, recalls, and transfers of state employees based on political affiliation or support infringe upon public employees' First Amendment rights (*Rutan et al. v. Republican Party of Illinois*, 497 U.S. 62, 110 S.Ct. 2729 [1990]).

12. *Corbell v. Canestrari*, 47 A.D.2d 153 (1977). Section 10 of the Cohoes charter stipulates that "where the term of an appointive officer is not specifically fixed by statute, it shall be deemed to continue only during the pleasure of the officer, officers, board, or body authorized to make the appointment."

13. William Bradford Reynolds, "The Bicentennial: A Constitutional Restoration," a paper presented at the University of Texas, Austin, Texas, February 19, 1987, p. 8.

14. "Federal Judge Orders a Panel to Monitor State Schools for Retarded," *Boston Globe*, March 15, 1986, p. 16.

15. *Foley v. Connelie*, 435 U.S. 291 at 299-300, 98 S.Ct. 1072-073 (1978).

16. *Michigan Department of State Police v. Sitz*, 496 U.S. 444, 110 S.Ct. 2481 (1990).

17. *Jenkins v. Missouri*, 672 F. Supp. 400 (W.D.Mo. 1987). See also Lynn Bycznski, "Judge Raises Taxes to Pay for School Bias Remedy," *National Law Journal* 10, October 5, 1987, p. 25.

18. *Missouri v. Jenkins*, 495 U.S. 33, 110 S.Ct. 1651 (1990).

19. *Morgan v. Hennigan*, 379 F.Supp. 410 (D. Mass. 1974). Affirmed *Morgan v. Kerrigan*, 509 F.2d. 580 (1st Cir. 1974). Denial of issuance of a writ of certiorari, *Kerrigan v. Morgan*, 421 U.S. 963, 95 S.Ct. 1950 (1975).

20. Peggy Hernandez, "Garrity Expected to Yield Control of Schools Today," *The Boston Globe*, September 3, 1985, p. 15.

21. *Memorandum Regarding Final Orders: Civil Action No. 72-911-G* (Boston: U.S. District Court, November 1, 1985). See also *Viewpoints and Guidelines on Court Appointed Citizens Monitoring Commissions in School Desegregation* (Washington, DC: U.S. Department of Justice, 1978). For a critical review of this judicial receivership, see Elizabeth A. Marek, "Education by Decree," *New Perspectives* 17, Summer 1985, pp. 36–41. Letters expressing objections to Marek's views and her reply appear in "Busing in Boston," *New Perspectives* 17, Fall 1985, pp. 36-37.

22. Anand Vaishnav, "City Defends Assignment Plan: US Court Hears School Lawsuit," *Boston Globe*, February 11, 2003, p. B2.

23. *Capacchione v. Belk*, 535 U.S. 986, 122 S.Ct. 1538 (2002). See also *Belk v. Capacchione*, 269 F.3d 305 (C.A. 4th cir. 2001).

24. Robert A. Frahm, "SETTLEMENT: A Four-Year Effort Begins to Help Undo Hartford's School Segregation," *Hartford Courant*, January 24, 2003, p. 1.

25. *Sheff v. O'Neill*, 678 A.2d 1267 (Conn. 1996) and *Sheff v. O'Neill*, 733 A.2d 925 (Conn. 1999).

26. *Civil Rights Act of 1968*, 82 Stat. 73, 42 U.S.C. §3601-1619. For an extended analysis of this case, consult Joseph F. Zimmerman, "Federal Judicial Remedial Power: The Yonkers Case," *Publius* 20, Summer 1990, pp. 45–61.

27. *United States v. Yonkers Board of Education*, 624 F. Supp. 1276 at 1373 (S.D. NY 1985).

28. "Yonkers Residents Fight Low Income Housing," *Times Union (Albany, NY)*, June 6, 1988, p. 1.

29. *United States v. Yonkers*, 827 F.2d 1181 at 1223 (2d Cir. 1987).

30. *Housing Remedial Order*, 635 F. Supp. 1577 (1986) and *Modification Order* dated July 8, 1986 (unreported).

31. James Feron, "Yonkers Seeks to End Pact on Housing Ruling," *New York Times*, March 3, 1988, p. B2.

32. James Feron, "Judge Tells Yonkers Crowd 'Chapter Is Closed' in Case," *New York Times*, June 17, 1988, p. B2.

33. James Feron, "Yonkers Council, in a 4 to 3 vote, Defies Judge on Integration Plan," *New York Times*, August 2, 1988, p. 1.

34. *United States v. Yonkers*, 856 F.2d 444 (2d Cir. 1988).

35. Ibid. at 460.

36. *Spallone v. United States*, 493 U.S. 265 at 275, 110 S.Ct. 625 at 632 (1990) quoting *Anderson v. Dunn*, 19 U.S. 204 at 231, 6 Wheat. 204 at 231 (1821).

37. *Spallone v. United States* 493 U.S. 265 at 278–79, 110 S.Ct. 625 at 634 (1990).

38. *Bogan and Roderick v. Scott-Harris*, 523 U.S. 44, 118 S.Ct. 966 (1998). See also Linda Greenhouse, "Local Lawmakers Immune From Suits Too, Court Says," *New York Times*, March 4, 1998, p. A14.

39. *Bogan and Roderick v. Scott-Harris*, 523 U.S. 44 at 49 at 52 and 118 S.Ct. 966 at 970–71.

40. Ibid, 523 U.S. 44 at 56, 118 S.Ct. 966 at 973.

41. *United States v. Yonkers*, 880 F.Supp. 212 at 236 (S.D.N.Y. 1995).

42. *United States v. City of Yonkers*, 888 F.Supp. 591 (S.D.N.Y. 1995).

43. *United States v. Yonkers Board of Education*, 7 F.Supp. 396 (S.D.N.Y. 1998).

44. *United States v. City of Yonkers*, 197 F.3d 41 (2d cir. 1999).

45. *New York v. Yonkers Board of Education*, 529 U.S. 1130, 120 S.Ct. 2005 (2000).

46. Winnie Hu, "Accord Is Reached in School Bias Suit Involving Yonkers," *New York Times,* January 9, 2002, pp. 1, B4.

47. Winnie Hu, "Judge Approves Settlement in Yonkers Desegregation Suit," *New York Times,* March 27, 2002, p. B6.

48. Raymond Hernandez, "N.A.A.C.P. Suspends Yonkers Head," *New York Times,* November 1, 1995, p. B1, B4.

49. Raymond Hernandez, "Neither Separate Nor Equal," *New York Times,* December 20, 1996, p. B1.

50. Greg Winter, "Schools Resegregate, Study Finds," *New York Times,* January 21, 2003, p. A14.

51. Brian J. Nickerson, "Interest Group Involvement in New York State Public School Aid: Litigation and Lobbying" (Unpublished Ph.D. dissertation, State University of New York at Albany, 2002).

52. Alexander Hamilton, "The Federalist Number 80," in *The Federalist Papers,* ed. Rossiter (New York: New American Library, 1961), p. 481.

53. *Articles of Confederation and Perpetual Union,* Art. II.

54. *McCulloch v. Maryland,* 17 U.S. 316, 4 Wheat. 316 (1819).

55. *U.S. Constitution,* Art. I, §8.

56. *Gibbons v. Ogden,* 22 U.S. 1, 9 Wheat. 1 (1824).

57. *Adler v. Deegan,* 251 N.Y. 467 at 491, 167 N.E. 705 at 714 (1929).

58. *H.P. Hood & Sons v. DuMond,* 336 U.S. 525 at 534–35, 69 S.Ct. 657 at 664–65.

59. Commission on Intergovernmental Relations, *A Report to the President for Transmittal to the Congress* (Washington, DC: U.S. Government Printing Office, 1955), p. 59.

60. "Address of William Bradford Reynolds, Assistant Attorney General, Civil Rights Division, Counselor to the Attorney General, United States Department of Justice before the Conservative Law Students—A Federalist Society Chapter, Washington University, St. Louis, Missouri, October 28, 1987," p. 5.

61. *Hodel v. Virginia Surface Mining and Reclamation Association,* 452 U.S. 264 at 310–11, 101 S.Ct. 2352 at 2391 (1981).

62. George B. Braden, "Umpire to the Federal System," *University of Chicago Law Review* 10, October 1942, p. 45.

63. *Hines v. Davidowitz,* 312 U.S. 52 at 67, 61 S.Ct. 399 at 404 (1941).

64. *City of Burbank v. Lockheed Air Terminal*, 411 U.S. 624–632, 93 S.Ct. 1854–1859 (1973).

65. *Chapman v. Houston Welfare Rights Organization*, 441 U.S. 600, 99 S.Ct. 1905 (1979).

66. *Washington Revised Code*, §§88.1670–88.1690 (1975 Supp.).

67. *Ray v. Atlantic Richfield Company*, 435 U.S. 151, 98 S.Ct. 988 (1978).

68. *Hodel v. Virginia Surface Mining and Reclamation Association*, 452 U.S. 264 at 287, 101 S.Ct. 2352 at 2366 (1981).

69. Ibid.

70. Ibid.

71. *Oregon v. Mitchell.*, 400 U.S. 112, 91 S.Ct. 260 (1970).

72. Ibid., 400 U.S. 112 at 126, 91 S.Ct. 260 at 266.

73. Ibid., 400 U.S. 112 at 129, 91 S.Ct. 260 at 267.

74. *National League of Cities v. Usery*, 426 U.S. 833, 96 S.Ct. 2465 (1976).

75. *Washington v. Davis*, 426 U.S. 229, 96 S.Ct. 2040 (1976).

76. *Village of Arlington Heights v. Metropolitan Housing Development Corporation*, 429 U.S. 252, 97 S.Ct. 555 (1977).

77. *Maine v. Thiboutot*, 448 U.S. 1, 100 S.Ct. 2502 (1980); *Owen v. City of Independence*, 445 U.S. 622, 100 S.C. 1398 (1980); and *Civil Rights Act of 1971*, 42 U.S.C. §1983.

78. *Maine v. Thiboutot*, 448 U.S. 1 at 22, 100 S.Ct. 2502 at 2513.

79. Ibid., 448 U.S. 1 at 34–37, 100 S.Ct. 2502 at 2520–21.

80. *Owen v. City of Independence*, 445 U.S. 622 at 655, 100 S.Ct. 1398 at 1422–23.

81. *Public Utility Regulatory Policies Act of 1978*, 92 Stat. 3121, 16 U.S.C. §2621, and *Federal Energy Regulatory Commission v. Mississippi*, 456 U.S. 742, 102 S.Ct. 2126 (1982).

82. The court decision is unreported.

83. *Federal Energy Regulatory Commission v. Mississippi*, 456 U.S. 742 at 766, 102 S.Ct. 2126 at 2141 (1982).

84. *Garcia v. San Antonio Metropolitan Transit Authority*, 469 U.S. 528 at 531, 105 S.Ct. 1005 at 1007 (1985).

85. The Florida's Supreme Court's lead in striking down the distinction has been followed by many other state supreme courts (*Hargrove v. Cocoa Beach*,

96 So.2d 139 [Fla. 1957]). The New York State Legislature in 1929 took the unusual action of waiving sovereign immunity and in 1936 waived the immunity of local governments (*New York Laws of 1929*, chap. 467 and *New York Laws of 1936*, chap. 323, *New York General Municipal Law*, §50-b). Also consult Joseph F. Zimmerman, *The Government and Politics of New York State* (New York: New York University Press, 1981).

86. "Statement of William Bradford Reynolds, Assistant Attorney General, Civil Rights Division before the Committee on Labor and Human Resources, Subcommittee on Labor, U.S. Senate Concerning the Impact of *Garcia v. San Antonio Metropolitan Transit Authority* on September 10, 1985," p. 2.

87. Robert B. Hawkins, Jr., "The Chairman's View," *Intergovernmental Perspective* 11, Spring/Summer 1985, p. 22.

88. R. Perry Sentell, Jr., "Gesticulations of Garcia," *Urban Georgia* 35, October 1985, pp. 34–35.

89. *Hodel v. Virginia Surface Mining and Reclamation Association*, 452 U.S. 264 at 312, 101 S.Ct. 2389 at 2392 (1981).

90. *Hillsborough County v. Automated Medical Laboratories*, 471 U.S. 707, 105 S.Ct. 2371 (1985).

91. *Fisher v. City of Berkeley, California*, 475 U.S. 260 at 273, 106 S.Ct. 1045 at 1053 (1986). See also the *Sherman Antitrust Act* 26 Stat. 209, 15 U.S.C. §1.

92. *California Coastal Commission v. Granite Rock Company*, 480 U.S. 572, 107 S.Ct. 1419 (1987). See also the *Coastal Zone Management Act of 1972*, 86 Stat. 1280, 16 U.S.C. §1451.

93. *California Federal Savings and Loan Association v. Guerra*, 479 U.S. 272 at 291, 107 S.Ct. 683 at 695 (1987). See *California Laws of 1978*, chap. 1321, §1; *California Fair Employment and Housing Act*; *California Government Code Annotated*, §12945(b)(2); and *Pregnancy Discrimination Act of 1978*, 92 Stat. 1076, 41 U.S.C. §2000e.

94. *Fort Halifax Packing Company v. Coyne*, 482 U.S. 1 at 22, 107 S.Ct. 2211 at 2223. See also the *National Labor Relations Act of 1935*, 49 Stat. 449, 15 U.S.C. §151, and the *Employee Retirement Income Security Act of 1974*, 88 Stat. 829, 29 U.S.C. §1001.

95. *CTS Corporation v. Dynamics Corporation of America*, 481 U.S. 69 at 93, 107 S.Ct. 1637 at 1652 (1987). Consult also the *Williams Act of 1968*, 82 Stat. 454, 15 U.S.C. §§78m(d-e), 78n(d-f).

96. *Tax Equity and Fiscal Responsibility Act of 1982*, 96 Stat. 596, 26 U.S.C. §103(j)(1).

97. *South Carolina v. Baker*, 485 U.S. 505 at 511, 108 S.Ct. 1355 at 1361 (1988).

98. *City of New York v. Federal Communications Commission*, 486 U.S. 57, 108 S.Ct. 1637 (1988).

99. *Mississippi Power & Light Company v. Mississippi*, 387 U.S. 354, 108 S.Ct. 2428 (1988).

100. *Employment Division, Department of Human Resources of Oregon v. Smith*, 294 U.S. 872, 1120 S.Ct. 1595, and *North Dakota v. United States*, 495 U.S. 423, 110 S.Ct. 1986 (1990).

101. *Tax Equity and Fiscal Responsibility Act of 1982*, 96 Stat. 1063, 26 U.S.C. §§623(a), 631(a). See also the *Age Discrimination in Employment Act of 1967*, 81 Stat. 602, 29 U.S.C. §621, and *Constitution of Missouri*, Art. V, §26.

102. *Gregory v. Ashcroft*, 501 U.S. at 457, 473, 111 S.Ct. 2395 at 2399, 2408.

103. *Low-Level Radioactive Waste Policy Amendments of 1985*, 99 Stat. 1842, 42 U.S.C. §2021b.

104. Consult Joseph F. Zimmerman, *Interstate Cooperation: Compacts and Administrative Agreements* (Westport, CT: Praeger Publishers, 2002), pp. 106–09.

105. *New York v. United States*, 505 U.S. 144 at 188, 112 S.Ct. 2408 at 2435 (1992).

106. *Gun-Free School Zones Act of 1990*, 104 Stat. 4844, 18 U.S.C. §922(q)(2)(A).

107. *United States v. Lopez*, 540 U.S. 549 at 567, 115 S.Ct. 1624 at 1634 (1995).

108. *Prinz v. United States*, 521 U.S. 898, 117 S.Ct. 2365 (1997), and *Brady Handgun Violence Prevention Act of 1993*, 107 Stat. 1536, 18 U.S.C. §921.

109. *Brady Handgun Violence Prevention Act of 1993*, 107 Stat. 1536, 18 U.S.C. §922(s)(2).

110. *Prinz v. United States*, 521 U.S. 898 at 935, 117 S.Ct. 2365 at 2384 (1997).

111. *Seminole Tribe of Florida v. Florida*, 517 U.S. 44, 116 S.Ct. 1114 (1996).

112. *Pennsylvania v. Union Gas Company*, 491 U.S. 1 at 13, 109 S.Ct. 2273 at 2281 (1989). Consult also *Comprehensive Environmental Response, Compensation, and Liability Act of 1980*, 94 Stat. 2767, 26 U.S.C. §4611, and *Superfund Amendments and Reauthorization Act of 1986*, 100 Stat. 1613, 42 U.S.C. §9601 note.

113. *Indian Gaming Regulatory Act of 1988*, 108 Stat. 2472, 25 U.S.C. §2710(d)(3).

114. *Seminole Tribe of Florida v. Florida*, 517 U.S. 44 at 76, 116 S.Ct. 1114 at 1133 (1996). See *Ex Parte Young*, 209 U.S. 123, 28 S.Ct. 441 (1908).

115. *Rhode Island Department of Environmental Management v. United States*, 304 F.3d 31 (C.A. 1 [RI] 2002).

116. *Federal Maritime Commission v. South Carolina State Ports Authority*, 535 U.S. 743, 122 S.Ct. 1864 (2002).

117. *Lapides v. Board of Regents of the University System of Georgia*, 535 U.S. 613, 122 S.Ct. 1640 (2002). See also the *Removal of Causes Act of 1920*, 41 Stat. 554, 28 U.S.C. §1441.

118. *Civil Rights Remedies for Gender-Motivated Violence Act of 1994*, 108 Stat. 1941, 42 U.S.C. §12981.

119. *United States v. Morrison*, 529 U.S. 598 at 618, 120 S.Ct.1740 at 1753 (2000).

120. Ibid., 529 U.S. 598 at 627, 120 S.Ct. 1740 at 1759.

121. *Sierra Club v. Ruckelshaus*, 344 F. Supp. 253 (1972), and *Fri v. Sierra Club*, 412 U.S. 541, 93 S.Ct. 2770 (1973).

122. Primary ambient air quality standards are national ones designed to protect the health of susceptible citizens. Secondary air quality standards generally are more stringent and are designed to prevent adverse environmental effects such as damage to animals, climate, vegetation, and water quality.

123. Challenges to administrative rules and regulations promulgated by federal departments and agencies must be brought in the U.S. court of appeals.

124. *Sierra Club v. Environmental Protection Agency*, 540 F.2d 114 (D.C. Cir. 1976). For an excellent analysis of this controversy, consult Albert C. Hyde, "The Politics of Environmental Decision-Making: The Non-Decision Issue" (unpublished Ph.D. dissertation, State University of New York at Albany, 1980).

125. *Clean Air Act Amendments of 1977*, 91 Stat. 731, 42 U.S.C. §7470.

126. Ibid., 91 Stat. 739, 42 U.S.C. §7476.

127. *An Act to Amend PL 108-35, Title 28, United States Code, to Provide for the Selection of Court of Appeals to Decide Multiple Appeals Filed with Respect to the Same Agency Order*, 101 Stat. 1731, 28 U.S.C. §2112(a). Consult also Marcia Coyle, "Ban OK'd on Agency-Review Forum Shopping," *National Law Review* 10, January 25, 1988, p. 9.

128. *An Act to Amend PL 109-35, Title 28, United States Code, to Provide for the Selection of Court of Appeals to Decide Multiple Appeals Filed with Respect to the Same Agency Order*, 101 Stat. 1731, 28 U.S.C. §2112(a).

129. 44 *Federal Register*, June 4 1979, p. 32008.

130. Ibid., pp. 32009–2010.

131. *Smithfield v. Chesapeake Bay Foundation*, 484 U.S. 49, 108 S.Ct. 376 (1987).

7. Metamorphic Federalism

1. *Voting Rights Act of 1965*, 79 Stat. 437, 42 U.S.C. §1973. For an analysis of the act, consult Joseph F. Zimmerman, "The Federal Voting Rights Act and Alternative Election Systems," *William and Mary Law Review* 19, Summer 1978, pp. 621–60. See also the dissent by Justice Hugo L. Black in *Perkins v. Matthew*, 400 U.S. 379 at 404, 91 S.Ct. 431 at 445 (1971).

2. *Transportation Safety Act of 1974*, 88 Stat. 2156, 49 U.S.C. Appendix §1801.

3. Herbert Wechsler, "The Political Safeguards of Federalism: The Role of the States in the Composition and Selection of the National Government," *Columbia Law Review* 54, 1953, pp. 543–60.

4. *Garcia v. San Antonio Metropolitan Transit Authority*, 469 U.S. 528 at 556, 105 S.Ct. 1005 at 1020 (1985).

5. *Unfunded Mandates Reform Act of 1995*, 109 Stat. 48, 2 U.S.C. §1501.

6. *Poultry Products Inspection Act of 1968*, 82 Stat. 791, 21 U.S.C. §451.

7. *Atomic Energy Act of 1959*, 73 Stat. 688, 42 U.S.C. §2021.

8. *National Traffic and Motor Vehicle Safety Act of 1966*, 80 Stat. 719, 15 U.S.C. §1392(d).

9. *United States Grain Standards Act of 1968*, 82 Stat. 906, 7 U.S.C. §71; *Resource Conservation and Recovery Act of 1976*, 90 Stat. 1795, 42 U.S.C. §6901; and *Federal Railroad Safety Act of 1970*, 84 Stat. 971, 45 U.S.C. §431.

10. *Atomic Energy Act of 1959*, 73 Stat 688, 42 U.S.C. §2021.

11. *Equal Employment Opportunity Act of 1972*, 86 Stat. 103, 42 U.S.C. §2000(e)(5).

12. For additional details, consult Zimmerman, "The Federal Voting Rights Act and Alternative Election Systems." See also Joseph F. Zimmerman, *The Government and Politics of New York* (New York: New York University Press, 1981).

13. *United Jewish Organizations of Williamsburg v. Carey*, 430 U.S. 144, 97 S.Ct. 996 (1977).

14. For a description and analysis of alternative electoral systems, consult Joseph F. Zimmerman, "Eliminating Disproportionate Representation in the House," in *The U.S. House of Representatives: Reform or Rebuild?*, ed. Joseph F. Zimmerman and Wilma Rule (Westport, CT: Praeger Publishers, 2000), pp. 163–86.

15. Joseph F. Zimmerman, "Election Systems and Representative Democracy: Reflections on the Voting Rights Act of 1965," *National Civic Review* 84, Fall 1995, pp. 287–309.

16. *Abandoned Shipwreck Act of 1987*, 102 Stat. 432, 43 U.S.C. §2101, and *Commercial Motor Vehicle Safety Act of 1986*, 100 Stat. 3207, 49 U.S.C. §2701.

17. *Johnson Act of 1951*, 64 Stat. 1134, 15 U.S.C. §1172(a).

18. *Coastal Zone Management Act of 1972*, 86 Stat. 1280, 16 U.S.C. §1451, and *Nuclear Waste Policy Act of 1982*, 96 Stat. 2217, 42 U.S.C. §10135.

19. *Toxic Substances Control Act of 1976*, 90 Stat. 2003, 15 U.S.C. §2601.

20. *Port and Tanker Safety Act of 1978*, 92 Stat. 1471, 33 U.S.C. §214 (1979 Supp.). This act has been replaced by 46 U.S.C. §§7101, 7106, 7109.

21. *Nuclear Waste Policy Act of 1982*, 96 Stat. 2217, 42 U.S.C. §10125.

22. "Approving the Site at Yucca Mountain, Nevada," 116 Stat. 735.

23. *Coast Guard Authorization Act of 1984*, 98 Stat. 2862, 46 U.S.C. §2302.

24. *Atlantic Striped Bass Conservation Act Amendments of 1986*, 100 Stat. 989, 16 U.S.C. §1851.

25. *Abandoned Shipwreck Act of 1987*, 102 Stat. 432, 43 U.S.C. §2101.

26. *Riegle-Neal Interstate Banking and Branching Efficiency Act of 1994*, 108 Stat. 2343, 12 U.S.C. §1831u.

27. Ibid., 108 Stat. 2352, 12 U.S.C. §36g.

28. *An Act to Revise and Codify Title 49, United States Code*, 108 Stat. 272, 49 U.S.C. §31705 (1994).

29. Consult, Joseph F. Zimmerman, *Interstate Cooperation: Compacts and Administrative Agreements* (Westport, CT: Praeger Publishers, 2002), pp. 165, 190–92.

30. *Gramm-Leach-Bliley Financial Modernization Act of 1999*, 113 Stat. 1338, 12 U.S.C. §1811.

31. Consult Joseph F. Zimmerman, "How Perfect Is the Economic Union? Interstate Trade Barriers," a paper presented at the annual meeting of the American Political Science Association, Philadelphia, Pennsylvania, August 28, 2003.

32. *Electronic Signatures in Global and National Commerce Act of 2000*, 114 Stat. 464, 15 U.S.C. §7001.

33. *Hotel and Motel Fire Safety Act of 1990*, 104 Stat. 747, 5 U.S.C. §5701. See also the *Federal Fire Prevention and Control Act of 1974*, 88 Stat. 1535, 15 U.S.C. §2224.

34. *Muhammad Ali Boxing Reform Act of 2000*, 114 Stat. 322, 15 U.S.C. §6301.

35. Ibid., 114 Stat. 323, 15 U.S.C. §6307c.

36. Ibid.

37. *Hearings Before the Subcommittee on Air and Water Pollution of the Committee on Public Works, United States Senate on "Problems and Progress Associated with Control of Automobile Exhaust Emissions"* (Washington, DC: U.S. Government Printing Office, 1967), p. 116.

38. 49 C.F.R. §177, App. A.

39. Ibid.

40. *Buckley v. Valeo*, 424 U.S. 1 at 52, 96 S.Ct. 612 at 651 (1976), and *First National Bank v. Bellotti*, 435 U.S. 765, 98 S.Ct. 1407 (1978).

41. "An Ordinance for Ascertaining the Mode of Disposing of Lands in the Western Territory," *Journals of the American Congress, from 1774 to 1788* (Washington, DC: 1823), pp. 395–400. See p. 398 in particular.

42. *Morrill Act of 1862*, 12 Stat. 503, 7 U.S.C. §301.

43. *McGee v. Mathias*, 71 U.S. 314, 4 Wall. 143 (1866).

44. *Hatch Act of 1887*, 24 Stat. 440, 7 U.S.C. §362.

45. *Carey Act of 1894*, 28 Stat. 422, 43 U.S.C. §641.

46. *Atomic Energy Act of 1946*, 60 Stat. 755, 42 U.S.C. §2011.

47. *Atomic Energy Act of 1954*, 69 Stat. 919, 42 U.S.C. §2011.

48. *Surface Transportation Assistance Act of 1982*, 96 Stat. 2097, 23 U.S.C. §101.

49. *Regulatory Federalism: Policy, Process, Impact, and Reform* (Washington, DC: U.S. Advisory Commission on Intergovernmental Relations, 1984).

50. Ibid., p. 139.

51. Ibid., pp. 139–44.

52. *Air Quality Act of 1967*, 81 Stat. 485, 42 U.S.C. §1857.

53. *Hearing Before the Subcommittee on Air and Water Pollution of the Committee on Public Works, United States Senate on* "Problems and Progress Associated with Control of Automobile Exhaust Emissions" (Washington, D.C.: U.S. Government Printing Office, 1967), p. 2514.

54. *Clean Air Amendments of 1970*, 84 Stat. 1676, 42 U.S.C. §1857.

55. R. Shep Melnick, *Regulation and the Courts: The Case of the Clean Air Act* (Washington, D.C.: Brookings Institution, 1983), p. 254.

56. *Clean Air Act Amendments of 1977*, 91 Stat. 722, 42 U.S.C. §7424.

57. Barry Goldwater, Jr., "Smog in the Clean Air Act," *Congressional Record*, April 5, 1979, p. H2054.

58. "Ohio Told to Meet Clean Air Deadline," *New York Times*, October 18, 1979, p. A16.

59. 100 Stat. 1329-199, 42 U.S.C. §7503. Consult also Matthew L. Wald, "Clean Air Deadline Is History," *New York Times*, January 3, 1988, p. E9.

60. *Clean Air Act Amendments of 1990*, 104 Stat. 2399, 42 U.S.C. §7407(d).

61. Ibid., 104 Stat. 2412, 42 U.S.C. §7502.

62. Ibid., 104 Stat. 2423, 42 U.S.C. §7511, and 104 Stat. 2463, 42 U.S.C. §7514.

63. Ibid., 104 Stat. 1591, 42 U.S.C. §7651b(f).

64. *EPA's Acid Rain Program: Results of Phase I, Outlook for Phase II* (Washington, DC: U.S. Environmental Protection Agency, 2001), p. 2.

65. Thomas J. Butler, Gene E. Likens, and Barbara J. Stunder, "Regional-Scale Impacts of Phase I of the Clean Air Act Amendments in the USA: The Relation Between Emissions and Concentrations, Both Wet and Dry," *Atmospheric Environment* 35, 2001, p. 1028.

66. *EPA's Acid Rain Program*, p. 39 .

67. Ibid., p. 2.

68. Erin Duggan, "Panel Calls for Better Pollution Controls," *Times Union (Albany, NY)*, April 23, 2003, p. B2.

69. *Water Quality Act of 1965*, 79 Stat. 903, 33 U.S.C. §1151.

70. *Environmental Quality: The Ninth Annual Report of the Council on Environmental Quality* (Washington DC: U.S. Government Printing Office, 1978), pp. 110, 113.

71. Gladwin Hill, "E.P.A. Head, Conceding Errors, Reports Gain on Water Pollution," *New York Times*, October 10, 1979, p. A24. See also Douglas M. Costle, "Toward a Quiet Victory: A Report Card on the Clean Water

Program," a paper presented at the fifty-second Annual Conference of the Water Pollution Control Federation, Houston, Texas, October 9, 1979 (mimeographed).

72. *Clean Water Act of 1977*, 91 Stat. 1567, 33 U.S.C. §1251, and *Federal Register*, August 29, 1979, pp. 5073–76. See also *National Municipal Policy and Strategy for Construction Grants, NPDES Permits, and Enforcement under the Clean Water Act* (Washington, DC: U.S. Environmental Protection Agency, 1979).

73. *Clean Water Act of 1977*, 91 Stat. 1552–583, 33 U.S.C. §1311, and *Water Quality Act of 1987*, 101 Stat. 29–30, 33 U.S.C. §§1311, 1314.

74. Rob Gurwitt, "The Tap Has Run Dry on EPA Extensions to the Clean Water Act," *Governing* 1, January 1988, p. 16. See also Philip Shabecoff, "Most Sewage Plants Meeting Latest Goal of Clean Water Act," *New York Times*, July 28, 1988, pp. 1, A18.

75. "U.S. Is Faulted for Role in Water Quality," *New York Times*, October 8, 1990, p. A9.

76. Katharine Q. Seelye, "U.S. Report Faults Efforts to Track Water Pollution," *New York Times*, May 27, 2003, pp. 1, A19.

77. Guy Gugliotta and Eric Pianin, "EPA: Few Fined for Polluting Water," *Washington Post*, June 6, 2003, p. 1.

78. John B. Stephenson, *Water Quality: EPA Should Improve Guidance and Support to Help States Develop Standards That Better Target Cleanup Efforts* (Washington, DC: U.S. General Accounting Office, 2003), pp. 5, 9.

79. "An Environmental Report Card," *New York Times*, June 26, 2003, p. A32.

80. Guy Gugliotta, "IG investigates Whether EPA Misled Public on Water Quality: Agency Audits Suggest Reports Overstated Utilities' Record," *Washington Post*, August 6, 2003, p. A15.

81. Melnick, *Regulation and the Courts*, p. 385.

82. The term apparently was first used by Justice Joseph McKenna of the U.S. Supreme Court, who wrote in 1917 state securities laws were aimed at "speculative schemes which have no more basis than so many feet of 'blue sky,'" *Hall v. Geiger-Jones Company*, 242 U.S. 539 at 550, 37 S.Ct. 217 at 220–21 (1917).

83. Manning G. Warren, III, "Reflections on Dual Regulation of Securities: A Case Against Preemption," *Boston College Law Review* 25, 1984, p. 495.

84. *Securities Act of 1933*, 48 Stat. 74, 15 U.S.C. §§77a-77aa; *Securities Exchange Act of 1934*, 48 Stat. 881; *Public Utility Holding Company Act of 1935*,

49 Stat. 803, 15 U.S.C. §§79–79z-6; *Trust Indenture Act of 1939*, 53 Stat. 1149, 15 U.S.C. §§77aaa to 77 bbbb; *Investment Advisers Act of 1940*, 54 Stat. 847, 15 U.S.C. §§80b-1 to 80b-21; *Investment Company Act of 1940*, 54 Stat. 789, 11 U.S.C. §§ 72, 107, 15 U.S.C. §§80a-1 to 80a-52; *Private Securities Litigation Reform Act of 1995*, 109 Stat. 743, 15 U.S.C. §78u-4; *National Securities Markets Improvement Act of 1996*, 110 Stat. 3416, 15 U.S.C. §§77a-77mm; *Securities Litigation Uniform Standards Act of 1998*, 112 Stat. 3227, 15 U.S.C. §78a; and *Sabanes-Oxley Act of 2002*, 116 Stat. 745, 15 U.S.C. §7201.

85. *National Securities Markets Improvement Act of 1996*, 110 Stat. 3416, 15 U.S.C. §§771-77mm, and *Sabanes-Oxley Act of 2002*, 116 Stat. 752, 15 U.S.C. §7211. For an analysis of the preemptive effect of the first act, consult Manning G. Warren, "Reflections on Dual Regulation of Securities: A Case for Reallocation of Regulatory Responsibilities," *Washington University Law Quarterly* 78, Summer 2000, 497–512.

86. *New York Laws of 1921*, chap. 649, *New York General Business Law*, §352.

87. Patrick McGeehan, "SEC Joining Spitzer's Probe of Stock Analysts," *Times Union (Albany, NY)*, April 26, 2002, pp. 1, A5.

88. Stephen Labaton, "10 Wall St. Firms Settle with U.S. in Analyst Inquiry," *New York Times*, April 29, 2003, pp. 1, C4.

89. Jeffrey Krasner, "Investors Get Little in States' Settlement with Wall St.," *Boston Globe*, April 28, 2003, p. 1.

90. Langdon, Thomas, Jr., "States, Intent on Regulating, Look at Morgan," *New York Times*, July 15, 2003, pp. C1, C4.

91. H.R. 2179 (*Securities Fraud Deterrence and Investor Restitution Act of 2003*).

92. Gretchen Morgenson, "Bill to Limit Oversight of Wall St. Gains," *New York Times*, July 11, 2003, p. C2.

93. For congressional responses to several Burger Court decisions, consult Carol F. Lee, "The Political Safeguards of Federalism? Congressional Responses to Supreme Court Decisions on State and Local Liability," *Urban Lawyer* 20, Spring 1998, pp. 301–340.

94. *Clean Air Act Amendments of 1970*, 84 Stat. 1676, 42 U.S.C. §1857.

95. *Friends of the Earth v. Environmental Protection Agency*, 499 F.2d 1118 (2d Cir. 1974).

96. *Clean Air Act Amendments of 1977*, 91 Stat. 695, 42 U.S.C. §7410.

97. *Federal Register*, December 5, 1977, p. 61453.

98. *Surface Transportation Assistance Act of 1982*, 96 Stat. 2097, 23 U.S.C. §101, and *National Interstate and Defense Highway Act of 1956*, 70 Stat. 374, 23 U.S.C. §101.

99. *Tandem Truck Safety Act of 1984*, 98 Stat. 2829, 42 U.S.C. §2301.

100. Ibid., 98 Stat. 2830, 42 U.S.C. §§2301-302.

101. *Motor Carrier Safety Act of 1984*, 98 Stat. 2834, 2837, 42 U.S.C. §§2502, 2508.

102. *National Highway System Designation Act of 1995*, 109 Stat. 577.

103. Ibid., 109 Stat. 591, 23 U.S.C. §410(d)(7).

104. *Age Discrimination in Employment Act of 1967*, 81 Stat. 381, 29 U.S.C. §623, and *Tax Equity and Fiscal Responsibility Act of 1982*, 96 Stat. 324, 26 U.S.C. §1.

105. *Age Discrimination in Employment Amendments of 1986*, 100 Stat. 3342, 29 U.S.C. §623.

106. *Unfunded Mandates Reform Act of 1995*, 109 Stat. 48, 2 U.S.C. §1501.

107. Ibid., 109 Stat. 49, 2 U.S.C. §1503.

108. Ibid., 109 Stat. 53, 2 U.S.C. §658b(b-e).

109. Ibid., 109 Stat. 54, 2 U.S.C. §658b(e).

110. Ibid., 109 Stat. 55, 2 U.S.C. §658c(a).

111. Ibid., 109 Stat. 57, 2 U.S.C. §658(a)(2)(B).

112. Ibid., 109 Stat. 67, 2 U.S.C. §1552.

113. *The Role of Federal Mandates in Intergovernmental Relations* (Washington, DC: U.S. Advisory Commission on Intergovernmental Relations, 1996).

114. 110 Stat. 4004 and *National Gambling Impact Study Commission Act of 1996*, 110 Stat. 1487.

115. "States Feel Relief from Unfunded Mandates," *Governors' Bulletin*, June 17, 1996, p. 1.

116. Daniel H. Cole and Carol S. Comer, "Rhetoric, Reality, and the Law of Unfunded Federal Mandates," *Stanford Law and Policy Review* 8, Summer 1997, p. 118.

117. Elizabeth Garrett, "States in a Federal System: Enhancing the Political Safeguards of Federalism? The Unfunded Mandates Reform Act of 1995," *Kansas Law Review* 45, July 1997, p.183.

118. John C. Eastman, "Re-entering the Arena: Restoring a Judicial Role for Enforcing Limits on Federal Mandates," *Harvard Journal of Law & Public Policy* 25, Summer, 2002, p. 952.

119. Joseph F. Zimmerman, *State-Local Relations: A Partnership Approach*, 2nd ed. (Westport, CT: Praeger Publishers, 1995), pp. 88–100.

120. *Paul v. Virginia*, 75 U.S. 168, 8 Wall. 168 (1868).

121. *United States v. South-Eastern Underwriters Association*, 322 U.S. 533, 64 S.Ct. 1162 (1944).

122. *McCarran-Ferguson Act of 1945*, 59 Stat. 33, 15 U.S.C. §1011.

123. *Gramm-Leach-Bliley Financial Modernization Act of 1999*, 113 Stat. 1353, 15 U.S.C. §6751.

124. *Parker v. Brown*, 317 U.S. 341, 63 S.Ct. 307 (1945).

125. *Lafayette v. Louisiana Power and Light Company*, 434 U.S. 389, 98 S.Ct. 1123 (1978).

126. *Community Communications Corporation v. City of Boulder*, 455 U.S. 389, 102 S.Ct. 835 (1982).

127. Ibid., 455 U.S. 40 at 56–57, 102 S.Ct. 835 at 841.

128. *Local Government Antitrust Act of 1984*, 98 Stat. 2750, 15 U.S.C. §§34-36. Consult also *The Act of October 15, 1914* (Clayton Antitrust Act), 38 Stat. 730, 15 U.S.C. §12.

129. "Localities Get Antitrust Relief," *Intergovernmental Perspective* 10, Fall 1984, p. 4.

130. *National League of Cities v. Usery*, 426 U.S. 833, 96 S.Ct. 2465 (1976) and *Garcia v. San Antonio Metropolitan Transit Authority*, 469 U.S. 528, 105 S.Ct. 1005 (1985).

131. *Report to Accompany H.R. 3530* (Washington, DC: Committee on Education and Labor, U.S. House of Representatives, 1985), p. 30.

132. *Fair Labor Standards Amendments of 1985*, 99 Stat. 787, 29 U.S.C. §201.

133. M. J. C. Vile, *The Structure of American Federalism* (Oxford: Oxford University Press, 1961), p. 35.

134. Daniel J. Elazar, *American Federalism: A View from the States*, 3rd ed. (New York: Harper & Row, 1984), pp. 109–49.

135. Paul L. Posner, *Regulatory Programs; Balancing Federal and State Responsibilities for Standard Setting and Implementation* (Washington, DC: U.S. General Accounting Office, 2002).

136. Ibid., p. 11.

137. Ibid., pp. 20–22.

138. Ibid., p. 35.

139. Examples include S. 275 (*Professional Boxing Amendments Act of 2003*), S. 3107 (*Driver's License Fraud Prevention Act of 2003*), H.R. 4633 (*Driver's License Modernization Act of 2003*), and H.R. 2179 (*Securities Fraud Deterrence and Investor Restitution Act of 2003*).

140. Joseph F. Zimmerman, "National-State Relations: Cooperative Federalism in the Twentieth Century," *Publius* 31, Spring 2001, pp. 15–30.

141. *Chisholm v. Georgia*, 2 U.S. 419 at 435, 2 Dall. 419 at 435 (1793).

142. Daniel J. Elazar, *The American Partnership: Intergovernmental Cooperation in the Nineteenth Century United States* (Chicago: University of Chicago Press, 1962).

143. Letter to author from Director Daniel J. Elazar of Temple University's Center for the Study of Federalism, December 7, 1992. See also, John Kincaid, "From Cooperative to Coercive Federalism," in "American Federalism: The Third Century," ed. John Kincaid, *Annals of the American Academy of Political and Social Science* 509, May 1990, pp. 139–52.

144. *Do-Not-Call Implementation Act of 2003*, 117 Stat. 557, 15 U.S.C. §6101.

145. *New York Laws of* 2003, chap. 124, *New York General Business Law*, §399Z(2)(b). Elizabeth Benjamin, "State Do-Not-Call List Goes Federal," *Times Union (Albany, NY)*, July 8, 2003, p. B2.

146. Joseph F. Zimmerman, *The Initiative: Citizen Law-Making* (Westport, CT: Praeger Publishers, 1999); *The Referendum: The People Decide Public Policy* (Westport, CT: Praeger Publishers, 2001); and *The Recall: Tribunal of the People* (Westport, CT: Praeger Publishers, 1997).

147. Henry M. Hart, Jr., "The Relations Between State and Federal Law," *Columbia Law Review* 54, April 1954, p. 541.

148. Edward I. Koch, "The Mandate Millstone," *Public Interest* 61, Fall 1980, p. 44.

149. Congress in 1998 recognized the need for a federal-state compact by granting its consent to states to enter into *The National Crime Prevention and Privacy Compact*, 112 Stat. 1874, 42 U.S.C. §14601. See also Joseph F. Zimmerman, *Interstate Relations: The Neglected Dimension of Federalism* (Westport, CT: Praeger Publishers, 1996).

Bibliography

Books and Reports

Anderson, William. *Intergovernmental Relations in Review.* Minneapolis: University of Minnesota Press, 1960.

Antieu, Chester J. *States Rights Under Federal Constitutions.* Dobbs Ferry, NY: Oceana, 1984.

Bailey, Thomas A. *The American Pageant: A History of the Republic.* 3rd ed. Boston: D. C. Heath, 1967.

Barnes, Jeb. *Overruled? Legislative Overrides, Pluralism and Contemporary Court-Congress Relations.* Stanford: Stanford University Press, 2004.

Beard, Charles A. *An Economic Interpretation of the Constitution of the United States.* New York: Macmillan, 1913.

Bittermann, Henry J. *State and Federal Grants-in-Aid.* New York: Mentzer, Bush, 1938.

Brogan, Dennis W. *Politics in America.* Garden City, NY: Anchor Books, 1960.

Bryce, James. *The American Commonwealth.* 3rd ed. 2 vols. New York: Macmillan, 1900.

Calhoun, John C. *Disquisition on Government.* New York: Political Science Classics, 1947.

Clark, Jane P. *The Rise of a New Federalism: Federal-State Cooperation in the United States.* New York: Columbia University Press, 1938.

Commager, Henry S., ed. *Documents of American History to 1898.* 8th ed. New York: Appleton-Century-Crofts, 1968.

Committee on Energy and Environment. *The Agreement State Program: A State Perspective.* Washington, DC: National Governors' Association, 1983.

Conlan, Timothy. *From New Federalism to Devolution: Twenty-Five Years of Intergovernmental Reform.* Washington, DC: Brookings Institution Press, 1998.

Corwin, Edward S. *The Commerce Power Versus States' Rights.* Princeton: Princeton University Press, 1936.

————. *National Supremacy: Treaty Power vs. State Power.* New York: Henry Holt, 1913.

Dahl, Robert A. *Dilemmas of Pluralist Democracy: Autonomy vs. Control.* New Haven: Yale University Press, 1982.

Derthick, Martha, and Paul J. Quirk. *The Politics of Deregulation.* Washington, DC: Brookings Institution, 1985.

Elazar, Daniel J. *American Federalism: A View from the States.* 3rd ed. New York: Harper & Row, 1984.

————. *The American Partnership: Intergovernmental Cooperation in the Nineteenth Century United States.* Chicago: University of Chicago Press, 1962.

————. *Exploring Federalism.* Tuscaloosa: University of Alabama Press, 1987.

Epstein, David F. *The Political Theory of the Federalist.* Chicago: University of Chicago Press, 1984.

Farrand, Max. *The Fathers of the Constitution.* New Haven: Yale University Press, 1921.

————. *The Records of the Federal Convention of 1787.* New Haven: Yale University Press, 1966.

Fife, Emerson D. *Government by Cooperation.* New York: Macmillan, 1932.

Ford, Paul L., ed. *The Writings of Thomas Jefferson*, vol. 9. New York: G. P. Putnam, 1898.

Frankfurter, Felix. *The Commerce Clause Under Marshall, Taney, and Waite.* Chapel Hill: University of North Carolina Press, 1937.

Friedrich, Carl J. *Trends of Federalism in Theory and Practice.* New York: Praeger Publishers 1968.

Friendly, Henry J. *Federal Jurisdiction: A General View.* New York: Columbia University Press, 1973.

Goals for State-Federal Action: 1984–1986. Washington, DC: National Conference of State Legislatures, n.d.

Goldwin, Robert A., ed. *A Nation of States: Essays on the American Federal System.* 2nd ed. Chicago: Rand McNally College Publishing, 1974.

Graves, W. Brooke. *American Intergovernmental Relations: Their Origins, Historical Development, and Current Status.* New York: Charles Scribner's Sons, 1964.

————, ed. "Intergovernmental Relations in the United States." *Annals of the American Academy of Political and Social Science* 207, January 1940, pp. 1–218.

————. *Uniform State Action: A Possible Substitute for Centralization.* Chapel Hill: University of North Carolina Press, 1934.

Grodzins, Morton. *The American System: A New View of Government in the United States*. Chicago: Rand McNally & Company, 1966.

"Guarding Your Credit Record." *Consumer Reports* 69, November 2004, p. 55.

Haider, Donald. *When Governments Come to Washington: Governors, Mayors, and Intergovernmental Lobbying*. Riverside, NJ: Free Press, 1974.

Haines, Charles G. *The Role of the Supreme Court in American Government and Politics*. New York: Russell & Russell, 1966.

Hand, Learned. *The Bill of Rights*. New York: Atheneum, 1964.

Hofstadter, Richard, William Miller, and Daniel Aaron. *The American Republic*. Englewood Cliffs, NJ: Prentice-Hall, 1959.

Hunt, Gaillard, ed. *The Writings of James Madison*. New York: G. P. Putnam's Sons, 1901.

To Improve Cooperation Among the States. Chicago: Council of State Governments, 1962.

Interstate River Basin Development. Chicago: Council of State Governments, 1947.

Jacobs, Clyde E. *The Eleventh Amendment and Sovereign Immunity*. Westport, CT: Greenwood Press, 1972.

Jackson, Robert H. *Full Faith and Credit: The Lawyer's Clause of the Constitution*. New York: Columbia University Press, 1945.

Jensen, Merrill. *The Making of the American Constitution*. Princeton, NJ: Van Nostrand, 1964.

Jones, Charles O. *Clean Air: The Policies and Politics of Pollution Control*. Pittsburgh: University of Pittsburgh Press, 1975.

Kaminski, John P., and Gaspare J. Saladino. *The Documentary History of the Ratification of the Constitution*. Madison: State Historical Society of Wisconsin, 1981.

Ketcham, Ralph, ed. *The Anti-Federalist Papers and the Constitutional Convention Debates*. New York: New American Library, 1986.

Kettl, Donald F. *The Regulation of American Federalism*. Baton Rouge: Louisiana State University Press, 1983.

Key, V.O., Jr. *The Administration of Federal Grants to States*. Chicago: Public Administration Service, 1937.

Kincaid, John, ed. "American Federalism: The Third Century." *Annals of the American Academy of Political and Social Science* 509, May 1990, pp. 11–152.

Knapp, Michael M. and Craig H. Blakely. *The Education Bock Grant at the Local Level: The Implementation of Chapter 2 of the*

Education Consolidation and Improvement Act in Districts and Schools. Menlo Park, CA: SRI International, 1986.

Laski, Harold J. *The American Democracy: A Commentary and an Interpretation.* New York: Viking Press, 1948.

Leach, Richard H. *American Federalism.* New York: W.W. Norton Company, 1970.

———, ed. *Intergovernmental Relations in the 1980s.* New York: Marcel Dekker, 1983.

———, ed. "Intergovernmental Relations in America Today." *Annals of the American Academy of Political and Social Science* 416, November 1974, pp. 1–169.

Lindblom, Charles E. *The Intelligence of Democracy: Decision Making Through Mutual Adjustment.* New York: Free Press, 1965.

Lowi, Theodore J. *The End of Liberalism: The Second Republic of the United States,* 2nd ed. New York: W. W. Norton, 1979.

MacMahon, Arthur W. *Administering Federalism in a Democracy.* New York: Oxford University Press, 1972.

———, ed. *Federalism: Mature and Emergent.* Garden City, NY: Doubleday and Company, 1955.

Madison, James. *Journal of the Federal Convention.* Chicago: Albert, Scott & Company, 1893.

Main, Jackson T. *The Antifederalists: Critics of the Constitution 1781–1788.* Chapel Hill: University of North Carolina Press, 1961.

Martin, Roscoe C. et al. *River Basin Administration and the Delaware.* Syracuse: Syracuse University Press, 1960.

Maxwell, James A. *Tax Credits and Intergovernmental Fiscal Relations.* Washington, DC: Brookings Institution, 1962.

McCurley, Robert L., Jr. *Federally Mandated State Legislation.* Washington, DC: National Conference of State Legislatures, 1986.

McMaster, John B., and Frederick D. Stone. *Pennsylvania and the Federal Constitution: 1787–1788.* New York: Da Capo Press, 1970.

Meier, Kenneth J. *The Political Economy of Regulation: The Case of Insurance.* Albany: State University of New York Press, 1988.

Melnick, R. Shep. *Regulation and the Courts: The Case of the Clean Air Act.* Washington, DC: Brookings Institution, 1983.

Morley, Felix. *Freedom and Federalism.* Chicago: Henry Regnery Company, 1959.

Nagle, Robert F. *The Implosion of American Federalism.* New York: Oxford University Press, 2002.

Noonan, John T. *Narrowing the Nation's Power: The Supreme Court Sides with the States.* Berkeley: University of California Press, 2002.

Ostrom, Vincent. *The Intellectual Crisis in American Public Administration.* University: University of Alabama Press, 1973. *Policy Positions: 1980–81.* Washington, DC: National Governors' Association, 1980.

Preemption: Drawing the Line: A State and Local Government Report on Federal Preemption and Mandates. Washington, DC: Academy for State and Local Government, 1986.

Reagan, Michael D., and John G. Sanzone. *The New Federalism.* 2nd ed. New York: Oxford University Press, 1981.

Restrictions on the Stringency of State and Local Air Quality Programs. Washington, DC: State and Territorial Air Pollution Program Administrators and the Association of Local Air Pollution Control Officials, 2002.

Roberts, Owen J. *The Court and the Constitution.* Cambridge: Harvard University Press, 1951.

Rossiter, Clinton, ed. *The Federalist Papers.* New York: New American Library, 1961.

Sandler, Ross, and David Scoenbrod. *Democracy by Decree: What Happens When Courts Run Government.* New Haven: Yale University Press, 2003.

Shavior, Daniel. *Federalism in Taxation.* Washington, DC: AEI Press, 1993.

Sherk, George W. *Dividing the Waters: The Resolution of Interstate Water Conflicts in the United States.* Boston: Kluwer Law International, 2000.

Singewald, Karl. *The Doctrine of Non-Suability of the State in the United States.* Baltimore: Johns Hopkins Press, 1916.

Stewart, William H. *Concepts of Federalism.* Lanham, MD: University Press of America, 1984.

Storing, Herbert J. *What the Anti-Federalists Were For.* Chicago: University of Chicago Press, 1981.

Story, Joseph. *Commentaries on the Constitution of the United States.* Boston: Hilliard, Gray, 1833.

Sundquist, James L. *Constitutional Reform and Effective Government.* Washington, DC: Brookings Institution, 1986.

Sundquist, James L., and David W. Davis. *Making Federalism Work.* Washington, DC: Brookings Institution, 1969.

Thompson, Kenneth E., Jr. *Deceive to Win: The Maine–New Hampshire Border Controversy.* Portland, ME: Thompson Group, 2003.

Tietenberg, T. H. *Emissions Trading: An Exercise in Reforming Pollution Policy.* Baltimore: Johns Hopkins University Press, 1985.

Tipton, Diane. *Nullification and Interposition in American Political Thought.* Albuquerque: Division of Research, Institute for Social Research and Development, University of New Mexico, 1969.

Tocqueville, Alexis de. *Democracy in America.* New York: Vintage Books, 1954.

Van Doren, Carl. *The Great Rehearsal.* New York: Viking Press, 1948.

Vile, M. J. C. *The Structure of American Federalism.* Oxford: Oxford University Press, 1961.

Walker, David B. *The Rebirth of Federalism.* New York: Chatham House Publishers, 2000.

———. *Toward a Functioning Federal System.* Cambridge, MA: Winthrop Publishers, 1981.

Walker, Robert H., ed. *The Reform Spirit in America: A Documentation of Reform in the American Republic.* New York: G. P. Putnam, 1976.

Warren, Charles. *The Supreme Court in United States History.* Rev. ed. Boston: Little, Brown, 1926.

Wasby, Stephen L. *The Supreme Court in the Federal Judicial System.* 3rd ed. Chicago: Nelson-Hall, 1988.

Wheare, Kenneth C. *Federal Government.* 4th ed. New York: Oxford University Press, 1964.

White, Leonard D. *The States and the Nation.* Baton Rouge: Louisiana State University Press, 1953.

White, Morton. *"The Federalist" and the Constitution.* New York: Oxford University Press, 1987.

Wilson, Woodrow. *Congressional Government.* Boston: Houghton Mifflin, 1925.

Wolfe, Christopher. *Judicial Activism: Bulwark of Freedom or Precarious Security?* Pacific Grove, CA: Brooks/Cole Publishing, 1991.

Wright, Deil S. *Understanding Intergovernmental Relations*, 3rd ed. Pacific Grove, CA: Brooks/Cole Publishing, 1988.

Yarbrough, Tinsley E. *Race and Redistricting: The Shaw-Cromartie Cases.* Lawrence: University of Kansas Press, 2002.

Zimmerman, Joseph F. *Contemporary American Federalism: The Growth of National Power.* Leicester: Leicester University Press, 1992.

———. *Federal Preemption: The Silent Revolution.* Ames: Iowa State University Press, 1991.

———. *The Government and Politics of New York State*. New York: New York University Press, 1981.

———. *Interstate Cooperation: Compacts and Administrative Agreements*. Westport, CT: Praeger Publishers, 2002.

———. *Interstate Economic Relations*. Albany: State University of New York Press, 2004.

———. *Interstate Relations: The Neglected Dimension of Federalism*. Westport, CT: Praeger Publishers, 1996.

———. The *Referendum: The People Decide Public Policy*. Westport, CT: Praeger Publishers, 2001.

———. *State-Local Relations: A Partnership Approach*. 2nd ed. Westport, CT: Praeger Publishers, 1995.

Zimmerman, Joseph F., and Wilma Rule, eds. *The U.S. House of Representatives: Reform or Rebuild?* Westport, CT: Praeger Publishers, 2000.

Public Documents

American Federalism: Toward a More Effective Partnership. Washington, DC: U.S. Advisory Commission on Intergovernmental Relations, 1975.

Awakening the Slumbering Giant: Intergovernmental Relations and Federal Grant Law. Washington, DC: U.S. Advisory Commission on Intergovernmental Relations, 1980.

Boyd, Eugene. *American Federalism, 1776 to 1995*. Washington, DC: Congressional Research Service, 1995.

A Catalog of Federal Grant-in-Aid Programs to State and Local Governments: Grants Funded FY 1978. Washington, DC: U.S. Advisory Commission on Intergovernmental Relations, 1979.

Categorical Grants: Their Role and Design. Washington, DC: U.S. Advisory Commission on Intergovernmental Relations, 1978.

Citizen Participation in the American Federal System. Washington, DC: U.S. Advisory Commission on Intergovernmental Relations, 1979.

Commission on Intergovernmental Relations. *A Report to the President for Transmittal to the Congress*. Washington, DC: U.S. Government Printing Office, 1955.

Commission on the Organization of the Executive Branch of the Federal Government. *Overseas Administration, Federal-State Relations, Federal Research*. Washington, DC: U.S. Government Printing Office, 1949.

Criteria for Preparation and Evaluation of Radiological Emergency Response Plans and Preparedness in Support of Nuclear Power Plants. Washington, DC: U.S. Nuclear Regulatory Commission and Federal Emergency Management Agency, 1987.

Cuciti, Peggy L. *Federal Constraints on State and Local Governments.* Washington, DC: Congressional Budget Office, 1979.

Danger on Our Highways: The Critical Problem of Unsafe Large and Heavy Trucks. Albany: New York State Legislative Commission on Critical Transportation Choices, 1988.

Devolving Federal Program Responsibilities and Revenue Sources to State and Local Governments. Washington, DC: U.S. Advisory Commission on Intergovernmental Relations, 1986.

Education Block Grant Alters State Role and Provides Greater Local Discretion. Washington, DC: U.S. General Accounting Office, 1984.

Emergency Planning: Federal Involvement in Preparedness Exercise at Shoreham Nuclear Plant. Washington, DC: U.S. General Accounting Office, 1986.

Emerging Issues in American Federalism. Washington, DC: U.S. Advisory Commission on Intergovernmental Relations, 1985.

Environmental Protection: Overcoming Obstacles to Innovative State Regulatory Programs. Washington, DC: U.S. General Accounting Office, 2002.

Environmental Quality: The Ninth Annual Report of the Council on Environmental Quality. Washington, DC: U.S. Government Printing Office, 1978.

EPA's Acid Rain Program: Results of Phase I, Outlook for Phase II. Washington, DC: U.S. Environmental Protection Agency, 2001.

Federal Aid to States Fiscal Year 1980. Washington, DC: U.S. Department of the Treasury, 1981.

The Federal Influence on State and Local Roles in the Federal System. Washington, DC: U.S. Advisory Commission on Intergovernmental Relations, 1981.

Federal-Interstate Compact Commissions: Useful Mechanisms for Planning and Managing River Basin Operations. Washington, DC: U.S. General Accounting Office, 1981.

Federal Mandate Relief for State, Local, and Tribal Governments. Washington, DC: U.S. Advisory Commission on Intergovernmental Relations, 1996.

The Federal Role in the Federal System: The Dynamics of Growth. Washington, DC: U.S. Advisory Commission on Intergovernmental Relations, 1981.

Final Task Force Report on the Agreement State Program. Washington, DC: U.S. Nuclear Regulatory Commission, 1977.

Financial Privacy: Status of State Actions on Gramm-Leach-Bliley Act's Privacy Provisions. Washington, DC: U.S. General Accounting Office, 2002.

"First Principles" of American Federalism: A Working Paper. Washington, DC: U.S. Advisory Commission on Intergovernmental Relations, 1982.

Fiscal Balance in the American Federal System. Washington, DC: U.S. Advisory Commission on Intergovernmental Relations, 1967.

Formula Grants: 2000 Census Redistributes Federal Funding Among States. Washington, DC: U.S. General Accounting Office, 2003.

Freshwater Supply: States' Views of How Federal Agencies Could Help Them Meet the Challenges of Expected Shortages. Washington, DC: U.S. General Accounting Office, 2003.

General Revenue Sharing: An ACIR Re-evaluation. Washington, DC: U.S. Advisory Commission on Intergovernmental Relations, 1974.

Grant Formulas: A Catalog of Federal Aid to States and Localities. Washington, DC: U.S. Advisory Commission on Intergovernmental Relations, 1987.

Hearings Before the Subcommittee on Air and Water Pollution of the Committee on Public Works, United States Senate on "Problems and Progress Associated with Control of Automobile Exhaust Emissions." Washington, DC: U.S. Government Printing Office, 1967.

Hillman, Richard J. *SEC Operations: Oversight of Mutual Fund Industry Presents Management Challenges.* Washington, DC: U.S. General Accounting Office, 2004.

How Much Power Do New York State and Local Governments Have to Abate Airport Noise? Albany, NY: New York State Legislative Commission on Critical Transportation Choices, 1984.

Hunter, Lawrence A., and Ronald J. Oakerson. *Reflections on Garcia and Its Implications for Federalism.* Washington, DC: U.S. Advisory Commission on Intergovernmental Relations, 1986.

Implementing Nationally Uniform Truck Laws. Albany: New York State Legislative Commission on Critical Transportation Choices, August 1983.

Intellectual Property: State Immunity in Infringement Actions. Washington, DC: U.S. General Accounting Office, 2001.

Intergovernmental Regulatory Relief Act of 1985: Hearings Before the Subcommittee on Intergovernmental Relations, United States

Senate on S.483. Washington, DC: U.S. Government Printing Office, 1986.

Interstate Compacts and Agencies. Lexington, KY: Council of State Governments, 2003.

Is Constitutional Reform Necessary to Reinvigorate Federalism: A Roundtable Discussion. Washington, DC: U.S. Advisory Commission on Intergovernmental Relations, 1987.

Lead in Drinking Water Regulation: Public Education Guidance. Washington, DC: U.S. Environmental Protection Agency, 2002.

Letter from Governor Mario M. Cuomo of New York to U.S. Secretary of Energy John S. Herrington dated March 28, 1985. *Public Papers of Governor Mario M. Cuomo 1985*. Albany: Executive Chamber, 1989. pp. 928–29.

"Licensing of Nuclear Power Plants Where State and/or Local Governments Decline to Cooperate in Offsite Emergency Planning." *United States Nuclear Regulatory Commission News Releases*, March 10, 1987, p. 2.

Low-Level Radioactive Wastes: States Are Not Developing Disposal Facilities. Washington, DC: U.S. General Accounting Office, 1999.

A Market Approach to Air Pollution Control Could Reduce Compliance Costs Without Jeopardizing Clean Air Goals. Washington, DC: U.S. General Accounting Office, 1982.

Maternal and Child Health Block Grant: Program Changes Emerging under State Administration. Washington, DC: U.S. General Accounting Office, 1984.

Means for Improving State Participation in the Siting, Licensing, and Development of Federal Nuclear Waste Facilities. Washington, DC: Office of State Programs, U.S. Nuclear Regulatory Commission, 1979.

Medicare: Information Systems Modernization Needs Stronger Management and Support. Washington, DC: U.S. General Accounting Office, 2001.

Memorandum Regarding Final Orders: Civil Action No. 72-911-G. Boston: U.S. District Court, November 1, 1985.

Nemer, Kirk D. *Waiver of Eleventh Amendment Immunity from Suit: State Survey Relating to Copyright Infringement Claims*. Washington, DC: Congressional Research Service, Library of Congress, 1988.

New York State Air Quality Implementation Plan: The Moynihan/Holtzman Amendment Submission: Transit Improvements in the New York City Metropolitan Area. Albany: New York

State Department of Environmental Conservation and State Department of Transportation, 1979.

North American Free Trade Agreement: Coordinated Operational Plan Needed to Ensure Mexican Trucks' Compliance with U.S. Standards. Washington, DC: U.S. General Accounting Office, 2002.

NRC Coziness with Industry: An Investigation Report. Washington, DC: Subcommittee on General Oversight and Investigations, U.S. House of Representatives, 1987.

Nuclear Regulation: Unique Features of Shoreham Nuclear Plant Emergency Planning. Washington, DC: U.S. General Accounting Office, 1986.

Nuclear Regulatory Commission: Oversight of Security at Commercial Nuclear Power Plants Needs to be Strengthened. Washington, DC: U.S. General Accounting Office, 2003.

"Nuclear Regulatory Commissioners Vote to Seek Public Comment on Proposed Rule Change in Emergency Planning Rule." *United States Nuclear Regulatory Commission News Releases,* March 3, 1987.

Nuclear Waste: Yucca Mountain Project Behind Schedule and Facing Major Scientific Uncertainties. Washington, DC: U.S. General Accounting Office, 1993.

Official Agency Directory. Washington, DC: Grain Inspection, Packers and Stockyards Administration, Federal Grain Inspection Service, U.S. Department of Agriculture, 2003.

"An Ordinance for Ascertaining the Mode of Disposing of Lands in the Western Territory." *Journals of the American Congress, from 1774 to 1788.* Washington, DC, 1823, pp. 395–400.

The Partnership For Health Act: Lessons from a Pioneering Block Grant. Washington, DC: U.S. Advisory Commission on Intergovernmental Relations, 1977.

Posner, Paul L. *Federal Assistance: Grant System Continues to Be Highly Fragmented.* Washington, DC: U.S. General Accounting Office, 2003.

———. *Regulatory Programs: Balancing Federal and State Responsibilities for Standard Setting and Implementation.* Washington, DC: U.S. General Accounting Office, 2002.

Professional Boxing: Issues Related to the Protection of Boxers' Health, Safety, and Economic Interests. Washington, DC: U.S. General Accounting Office, 2003.

Proposed Changes in Federal Matching and Maintenance of Effort Requirements for State and Local Governments. Washington, DC: U.S. General Accounting Office, 1980.

Rail Safety: States' Reaction to Proposed Elimination of Inspection Funding. Washington, DC: U.S. General Accounting Office, 1987.

Reagan Administration Regulatory Achievements. Washington, DC: Presidential Task Force on Regulatory Relief, 1983.

Reagan, Ronald. "Federalism: Executive Order 12612, October 26, 1987." *Weekly Compilation of Presidential Documents,* November 2, 1987, p. 1231.

———. "Regulatory Program of the U.S. Government—Message from the President Received During the Adjournment—PM 73." *Congressional Record,* August 14, 1985, pp. S11023–24.

Reauthorization of the State and Local Cost Estimate Act: Statement of J. William Gadsby Before the Subcommittee on Government Efficiency, Federalism, and the District of Columbia, United States Senate. Washington, DC: U.S. General Accounting Office, 1987.

The Register of Copyrights. *Copyright Liability of States and the Eleventh Amendment.* Washington, DC: Library of Congress, 1988.

Regulatory Federalism: Policy, Process, Impact, and Reform. Washington, DC: U.S. Advisory Commission on Intergovernmental Relations, 1984.

Report to Accompany H.R. 3530. Washington, DC: Committee on Education and Labor, U.S. House of Representatives, 1985.

The Role of Equalization in Federal Grants. Washington, DC: U.S. Advisory Commission on Intergovernmental Relations, 1964.

The Role of Federal Mandates in Intergovernmental Relations. Washington, DC: U.S. Advisory Commission on Intergovernmental Relations, 1995.

The Role of OSHA—Approved State Plans in the National OSHA Program. Washington, DC: Occupational Safety and Health Administration, 2001.

The Safe Drinking Water Act: A Case Study of an Unfunded Federal Mandate. Washington, DC: Congressional Budget Office, 1995.

State and Local Roles in the Federal System. Washington, DC: U.S. Advisory Commission on Intergovernmental Relations, 1982.

State Implementation Guidance for the Lead and Copper Rule Minor Revisions. Washington, DC: U.S. Environmental Protection Agency, 2001.

"State of New York Executive Order No. 75, April 3, 1973." *Public Papers of Nelson A. Rockefeller: Fifty-Third Governor of the State of New York, 1973.* Albany: State of New York, n.d.: 811–12.

State Programs: Background. Washington, DC: Occupational Safety and Health Administration, 1985.

A State Response to Urban Problems: Recent Experience Under the "Buying In" Approach. Washington, DC: U.S. Advisory Commission on Intergovernmental Relations, 1970.

State Taxation of Interstate Mail Order Sales. Washington, DC: U.S. Advisory Commission on Intergovernmental Relations, 1992.

States Use Added Flexibility Offered by the Preventive Health and Health Services Block Grant. Washington, DC: U.S. General Accounting Office, 1984.

Stenberg, Carl W. *State Involvement in Federal-Local Grant Programs: A Case Study of the "Buying In" Approach.* Washington, DC: U.S. Advisory Commission on Intergovernmental Relations, 1970.

Stephenson, John. *Environmental Protection: Recommendations for Improving the Underground Storage Tank Program.* Washington, DC: U.S. General Accounting Office, 2003.

———. *Water Quality: EPA Should Improve Guidance and Support to Help States Develop Standards That Better Target Cleanup Efforts.* Washington, DC: U.S. General Accounting Office, 2003.

Telecommunications: Characteristics and Competitiveness of the Internet Backbone Market. Washington, DC: U.S. General Accounting Office, 2002.

Thomas, Kenneth R. *Federalism and the Constitution: Limits on Congressional Power.* Washington, DC: Congressional Research Service, 2001.

Title I Funding: Poor Children Benefit Though Funding Per Poor Child Differs. Washington, DC: U.S. General Accounting Office, 2002.

Trends in Federal and State Capital Investment in Highways. Washington, DC: U.S. General Accounting Office, 2003.

"Unfunded Federal Mandates." *Congressional Digest* 74, March 1995, pp. 68–95.

U.S. Commission on the Organization of the Executive Branch of Government. *Overseas Administration, Federal-State Relations, Federal Research.* Washington, DC: U.S. Government Printing Office, 1949.

USDA's Oversight of State Meat and Poultry Inspection Programs Could Be Strengthened. Washington, DC: U.S. General Accounting Office, 1983.

U.S. Environmental Protection Agency. *Safe Drinking Water Act Cost Impacts on Selected Water Systems.* Springfield, VA: National Technical Information Service, 1987.

Viewpoints and Guidelines on Court Appointed Citizens Monitoring Commissions in School Desegregation. Washington, DC: U.S. Department of Justice, 1978.

Water Infrastructure: Information on Federal and State Financial Assistance. Washington, DC: U.S. General Accounting Office, 2002.

Welfare Reform: With TANF Flexibility, States Vary in How They Implement Work Requirements and Time Limits. Washington, DC: U.S. General Accounting Office, 2002.

Workforce Investment Act: States and Localities Increasingly Coordinate Services for TANF Clients, but Better Information Needed on Effective Approaches. Washington, DC: U.S. General Accounting Office, 2002.

Zimmerman, Joseph F. *Federal Preemption of State and Local Authority.* Washington, DC: U.S. Advisory Commission on Intergovernmental Relations, 1990.

———. *Federally Induced Costs Affecting State and Local Governments.* Washington, DC: U.S. Advisory Commission on Intergovernmental Relations, 1994.

———. *Measuring Local Discretionary Authority.* Washington, DC: U.S. Advisory Commission on Intergovernmental Relations, 1981.

———. *Pragmatic Federalism: The Reassignment of Functional Responsibility.* Washington, DC: U.S. Advisory Commission on Intergovernmental Relations, 1976.

———. *State Mandating of Local Expenditures.* Washington, DC: U.S. Advisory Commission on Intergovernmental Relations, 1978.

Zimmerman, Joseph F., and Sharon Lawrence. *Federal Statutory Preemption of State and Local Authority: History, Inventory, and Issues.* Washington, DC: U.S. Advisory Commission on Intergovernmental Relations, 1992.

Articles

Adler, Matthew D. "State Sovereignty and the Anti-Commandeering Cases." *Annals of the American Academy of Political and Social Science* 574, March 2001, pp. 158-72.

Abel, David. "3 States Will Sue EPA Over Emissions." *Boston Globe*, January 31, 2003, p. B1.

Agranoff, Robert. "Managing Within the Matrix: Do Collaborative Intergovernmental Relations Exist? *Publius: The Journal of Federalism* 31, Spring 2001, pp. 31–56.

Alexander, James R. "State Sovereignty in the Federal System: Constitutional Protections Under the Tenth and Eleventh Amendments? *Publius: The Journal of Federalism* 16, Spring 1986, pp. 1–15.

Allotta, John. "Alden v. Maine: Infusing Tenth Amendment and General Federalism Principles into Eleventh Amendment Jurisprudence." *Case Western Reserve Law Review* 51, Spring 2001, pp. 505–38.

Althoff, Megan M. "The National Bank Act's Federal Preemption of State Electronic Funds Transfer Acts." *The Journal of Corporation Law* 25, Summer 2000, pp. 843–65.

Althouse, Ann. "Inside the Federalism Cases: Concern About the Federal Courts." *Annals of the American Academy of Political and Social Science* 574, March 2001, pp. 132–44.

Apple, R. W., Jr. "Senate Rejects Reagan Plan and Votes 67–33 to Override his Veto of Highway Funds." *New York Times*, April 3, 1987, pp. 1, A25.

Archibold, Randal C. "Albany Says It Can't Certify Indian Pt. Plan." *New York Times* January 31, 2003, pp. B1, B5.

———. "Closed or Not, Indian Point and Its Perils Won't Vanish." *New York Times*, January 28, 2003, pp. B1, B8.

———. "Disaster Plan for Indian Point Is Called Inadequate." *New York Times*, January 11, 2003, pp. 1, B4.

———. "FEMA Says It Can't Approve Emergency Plan for Indian Pt." *New York Times*, February 22, 2003, pp. B1, B8.

———. "Officials Quarrel over Plan for Indian Point Emergency." *New York Times*, February 4, 2003, p. B5.

———. "State Consultant Reiterates: Indian Point Plan Is Weak." *New York Times*, March 7, 2003, p. B5.

———. "3 Counties Maneuver in Bid to Close Down Indian Point." *New York Times*, January 16, 2003, p. B5.

———. "U.S. Faults Safety Study on Indian Pt." *New York Times*, February 13, 2002, pp. B1, B4.

Archibold, Randal C., and Matthew L. Wald. "U.S. Approves Evacuation Plan for Indian Point Nuclear Plant." *New York Times*, July 26, 2003, pp. 1, B4.

Arenson, Karen W. "Impact on Universities Will Range from None to a Lot." *New York Times*, June 25, 2003, p. A22.

Arneson, Ben A. "Federal Aid to the States." *American Political Science Review* 16, August 1922, pp. 443–54.

Atlas, Riva D., and Diana B. Henriques. "U.S. Closes Mutual Fund Intermediary." *New York Times*, November 26, 2003, pp. C1, C4.

"The Attack on Women's Sports." *New York Times*, February 17, 2003, p. A20.

Baker, Al. "Albany Facing New U.S. Rule on Potential Cuts in Medicaid." *New York Times* January 20, 2003, p. B3.

———. "Telecommuter Loses Case for Benefits." *New York Times*, July 3, 2003, pp. B1, B6.

Baker, William C. "30 Years After the Clean Water Act: Chesapeake's Still Waiting." *Bay Journal* 13, September 2003, pp. 20–21.

Barnett, James D. "Cooperation Between the Federal and State Governments." *National Municipal Review* 17, May 1928, pp. 283–91.

———. "The Delegation of Legislative Power by Congress to the States." *American Political Science Review* 2, 1908, pp. 347–77.

Barnett, Randy E. "Necessary and Proper." *UCLA Law Review* 44, February 1997, pp. 745–93.

Barrett, Devlin. "Indian Point Disaster Plan Gets Federal Agency's OK." *Times Union*, (Albany, NY), July 26, 2003, pp. 1, A6.

Barron, Gerald, et al. "New Approaches to Safe Drinking Water." *Journal of Law, Medicine and Ethics* 30, Fall 2002, pp. S105–09.

Bartfeld, Esther. "Point-Nonpoint Source Trading: Looking Beyond Potential Cost Savings." *Environmental Law* 23, January 1993, pp. 43–106.

Baybeck, Brady, and William Lowry. "Federalism Outcomes and Ideological Preferences: The U.S. Supreme Court and Preemption Cases." *Publius: The Journal of Federalism* 30, Summer 2000, pp. 73–97.

Bayot, Jennifer. "Card Companies May Be Forced to Return Fees." *New York Times*, February 11, 2003, pp. C1, C9.

Becker, Elizabeth. "U.S. Ready to End Tariffs on Textiles in Hemisphere." *New York Times*, February 11, 2003, pp. C1, C10.

Befort, Stephen F. "Demystifying Federal Labor and Employment Law Preemption." *Labor Lawyer* 13, Winter/Spring 1998, pp. 429–43.

Benjamin, Elizabeth. "Indian Point Study Faults Evacuation Plan." *Times Union (Albany, NY)*, January 11, 2003, pp. 1, A8.

———. "State Do-Not-Call List Goes Federal." *Times Union (Albany, NY)*, July 8, 2003, p. B2.

———. "Tougher DWI Limit Finally Sails Through." *Times Union (Albany, NY)*, December 18, 2002, pp. 1, A8.

Bennett, Neyah K. "Banking Law—Federal Monetary Control Act Looses Preemptive Struggle Over State Ban on Compound Interest—*Grunbeck v. Dime Savings Bank of New York* FSB, 74 F.3d 331 (1st Cir. 1996)." *Suffolk University Law Review* 30, Fall 1997, pp. 917–25.

Bloom, Lackland H., Jr. "Interpretive Issues in Seminole and Alden." *Southern Methodist University Law Review* 55, Spring 2002, pp. 377–92.

Bork, Robert H., and Daniel E. Troy. "Locating the Boundaries: The Scope of Congress's Power to Regulate Commerce." *Harvard Journal of Law and Public Policy* 25, Summer 2002, pp. 849–93.

Boroff, Philip, and Monique Wise. "Reforms Sought for Stock Analysts." *Times Union (Albany, NY)*, October 23, 2002, pp. E1, E5.

Bowsher, Charles A. "Federal Cutbacks Strengthen State Role." *State Government News* 29, February 1986, pp. 18–21.

Braden, George B. "Umpire to the Federal System." *University of Chicago Law Review* 10, October 1942, pp. 27–48.

"Brattleboro Board Questions Evacuation Plan." *Keene (NH) Sentinel*, June 25, 2003, p. 3.

Briceland, Alan V. "Virginia's Ratification of the U.S. Constitution." *Newsletter* (Institute of Government, University of Virginia) 61, October 1984, pp. 1–14.

Bridis, Ted. "Ruling Aids Music Piracy Fight." *Times Union (Albany, NY)*, January 22, 2003, pp. E1, E5.

Brown, Ernest J. "The Open Economy: Justice Frankfurter and the Position of the Judiciary." *Yale Law Review* 67, December 1957, pp. 219–39.

Buckley, James L. "The Trouble with Federalism: It Isn't Being Tried." *Commonsense* 1, Summer 1978, pp. 1–17.

"Busing in Boston." *New Perspectives* 17, Fall 1985, pp. 36–37.

Butler, Thomas J., Gene E. Likens, and Barbara J. Stunder. "Regional-Scale Impacts of Phase I of the Clean Air Act Amendments in the USA: The Relation Between Emissions and Concentrations, Both Wet and Dry." *Atmospheric Environment* 35, 2001, pp. 1015–28.

Butterfield. "As Expiration Looms, Gun Ban's Effect Is Debated." *New York Times*, September 10, 2004, p. 14.

Bycznski, Lynn. "Judge Raises Taxes to Pay for School Bias Remedy." *National Law Journal* 10, October 5, 1987, p. 25.

"California Curbed." *New York Times*, January 8, 2003, p. A22.

Cambanis, Thanassis. "Appeals Court Bars Tobacco Disclosure." *Boston Globe*, December 4, 2002, p. 1

Caminker, Evan H. "Judicial Solicitude for State Dignity." *Annals of the American Academy of Political and Social Science* 574, March 2001, pp. 81–91.

Cardwell, Diane. "Pataki Says He Remains Undecided on Indian Pt." *New York Times*, August 2, 2003, pp. B1, B4.

Carnahan, Ira. "Removing the Scarlet A: Age-Discrimination Laws Can Backfire on Older Job Seekers." *Forbes* 170, August 12, 2002, p. 78.

Carrow, Milton M. "Sovereign Immunity in Administrative Law." *Journal of Public Law* 9, 1960, pp. 1–22.

Carstens, Anne-Marie. "Lurking in the Shadows of Judicial Process: Special Masters in the Supreme Court's Original Jurisdiction Cases." *Minnesota Law Review* 86, February 2002, pp. 625–704.

Carvajal, Alejandr. "State and Local 'Free Burma' Laws: The Case for Sub-National Trade Barriers." *Law and Policy in International Business* 29, Winter 1998, pp. 257–74.

Chamberlain, Natasha. "Remedial Provision of Lead Contamination Control Act Violates Tenth Amendment." *Journal of Land, Resources, and Environmental Law* 17, 1997, pp. 95–107.

Chemers, Robert M., and Robert J. Franco. "The Preemption of State Claims Under ERISA." *Illinois Bar Journal* 78, November 1990, pp. 550–54.

Chen, David W. "State Remains Liable for Half of Yonker's Integration Costs." *New York Times*, May 23, 2002, p. B8.

Cho, Chung-Lae, and Deil S. Wright. "Managing Carrots and Sticks: Changes in State Administrators' Perceptions of Cooperative and Coercive Federalism During the 1990s." *Publius: The Journal of Federalism* 31, Spring 2001, pp. 57–80.

"The City's Precious Watershed." *New York Times*, July 15, 2002, p. A16.

Clark, Charles E. "New Hampshire's First Look at Anti-ratification Arguments." *Keene (NH) Sentinel*, November 18, 1987, p. 5.

"Clean Air, Courtesy of California." *New York Times*, August 14, 2003, p. A24.

Cohen, William. "Congressional Power to Validate Unconstitutional State Laws: A Forgotten Solution to an Old Enigma." *Stanford Law Review* 35, February 1983, pp. 387–422.

Cole, Daniel H., and Carol S. Comer. "Rhetoric, Reality, and the Law of Unfunded Federal Mandates." *Stanford Law and Policy Review* 8, Summer 1997, pp. 103–25.

"The Coming of Copyright Perpetuity." *New York Times*, January 16, 2003, p. A28.

Conlan, Timothy J., and Francois Vergniolle de Chantel. "The Rehnquist Court and Contemporary American Federalism." *Political Science Quarterly* 116, 2001, pp. 253–75.

Corwin, Edward S. "National-State Cooperation—Its Present Possibilities." *Yale Law Journal* 46, February 1937, pp. 599–623.

Cosgrove, Richard T. "*Reno v. Condon*: The Supreme Court Takes a Right Turn in Its Tenth Amendment Jurisprudence by Upholding the Constitutionality of the Driver's Privacy Protection Act." *Fordham Law Review* 68, May 2000, pp. 1543–93.

Cox, Gail D. "Change of Course: Status Quo Is Threatened on America's Most-Litigated River." *National Law Journal* 16, September 1993, pp. 1, 36.

Coyle, Marcia. "Ban OK'd on Agency-Review Forum Shopping." *National Law Review* 10, January 25, 1988, p. 9.

———. "Is Rehnquist Tinkering with Revolution?" *National Law Journal* 21, August 16, 1999, pp. B7-B8.

———. "States Get New Shield from Suits." *National Law Journal* 24, June 3, 2002, pp. 1, A8.

———. "States' Immunity Redux." *National Law Journal* 21, March 29, 1999, pp. 1, A9.

Coyle, Marcia, and Harvey Berkman. "Justices Weigh in on Side of States." *National Law Journal* 21, July 5, 1999, pp. 1, A11.

Crihfield, Brevard and H. Clyde Reeves. "Intergovernmental Relations: A View from the States." *The Annals of the American Academy of Political and Social Science*, 416, November 1974, pp. 99–107.

Crotty, Michael G. "*Bragg v. West Virginia Mining Association*: The Eleventh Amendment Challenge to Mountaintop Coal Mining." *Villanova Environmental Law Journal* 13, 2002, pp. 387–413.

"Danger to Wetlands." *New York Times*, January 11, 2003, p. A14.

Department of Transportation, "Hazardous Materials: Inconsistent Rulings IR-7 Through IR–15." *Federal Register*, November 27, 1984, p. 46633.

"Desegregation Ends." *New York Times,* http://nytimes.com/2003/ 09/25/politics/25MCCA.html (accessed December 28, 2003).

Dinan, John. "Congressional Responses to the Rehnquist Court's Federalism Decisions." *Publius: The Journal of Federalism* 32, Summer 2002, pp. 1–24.

Distaso, John. "NRC Adopts New Nuke Evac Rule." *Union Leader (Manchester, NH),* October 30, 1987, pp. 1, 9.

Dixon, Terence A. "Security Interests: Unregistered Copyrights." *National Law Journal* 25, November 18, 2002, p. B17.

Donohue, Laura K., and Juliette N. Kayyem. "Federalism and the Battle Over Counterterrorist Law: State Sovereignty, Criminal Law Enforcement, and National Security." *Studies in Conflict and Terrorism* 25, January-February 2002, pp. 1–18.

Douglas, Paul H. "The Development of a System of Federal Grants-in-Aid I." *Political Science Quarterly* 35, June 1920, pp. 255–71.

———. "The Development of a System of Federal Grants-in-Aid II." *Political Science Quarterly* 35, December 1920, pp. 522–44.

Dudley, Susan. "The Future of Clean Air Futures." *Public Utilities Fortnightly* 30, August 1, 1992, pp. 11–13.

Duggan, Erin. "Mixed Reviews for Regional Emissions Plan." *Times Union (Albany, NY),* July 25, 2003, p. B2.

———. "Panel Calls for Better Pollution Controls." *Times Union (Albany, NY),* April 23, 2003, p. B2.

Durham, G. Homer. "Politics and Administration in Intergovernmental Relations." *Annals of the American Academy of Political and Social Science* 207, January 1940, pp. 1–6.

Dwyer, "The Role of State Law in an Era of Federal Preemption: Lessons from Environmental Regulation." *Law and Contemporary Problems* 60, Summer 1997, pp. 203–29.

Eastman, John C. "Re-entering the Arena: Restoring a Judicial Role for Enforcing Limits on Federal Mandates." *Harvard Journal of Law and Public Policy* 25, Summer 2002, pp. 931–52.

Eaton, Leslie. "State Unemployment Fund Is Operating in the Red." *New York Times,* January 29, 2003, p. B3.

Ehrenhalt, Alan. "Devolution's Double Standard." *Governing* 16, April 2003, pp. 6, 8.

Eichenwald, Kurt. "2 Banks Settle Accusations They Aided in Enron Fraud." *New York Times,* July 29, 2003, pp. 1, C7.

Eichhorn, Cory. "Eleventh Amendment Immunity Jurisprudence in an Era of Globalization: The Tension Between State Sovereign Rights and Federal Treaty Obligations." *University of Miami Inter-American Law Review* 32, Fall 2001, pp. 523–40.

Eichorn, L. Mark. "*Cuyler v. Adams* and the Characterization of Compact Law." *Virginia Law Review* 77, October 1991, pp. 1387–410.

"Energy Secretary Rethinking Cross-Sound Cable Decision." *New York Times*, September 27, 2003, p. B7.

"Environmental Report Card." *New York Times*, June 26, 2003, p. A32.

"E.P.A. Begins Cleanup at 10 Toxic Waste Sites and Says 10 Others Will Wait." *New York Times*, July 17, 2003, p. A24.

"Federal Judge Orders a Panel to Monitor State Schools for Retarded." *Boston Globe*, March 16, 1986, p. 16.

Fellows, Lawrence. "Connecticut Scores Sound's Pilot Fee." *New York Times*, September 30, 1973, p. 25.

Feron, James. "Judge Tells Yonkers Crowd 'Chapter Is Closed' in Case." *New York Times*, June 17, 1988, p. B2.

———. "Yonkers Council, in a 4 to 3 Vote, Defies Judge on Integration Plan." *New York Times*, August 2, 1988, p. 1.

———. "Yonkers Seeks to End Pact on Housing Ruling." *New York Times*, March 3, 1988, p. B2.

Fetter, Henry D. "Copyright Revision and the Preemption of State Misappropriation Law: A Study in Judicial and Congressional Interaction." *Copyright Law Symposium* 27, 1982, pp. 1–10.

"Fighting School Resegregation." *New York Times*, January 27, 2003, p. A24.

Finnegan, Michael C. "New York City's Watershed Agreement: A Lesson in Sharing Responsibility." *Pace Environmental Law Review* 14, Summer 1997, pp. 577–644.

Fisk, Alan. "Disabled Are Suing States on Voting: Blind Voter Triggers Suit for 20,000 in Maryland." *National Law Journal* 23, April 14, 2001 (Internet edition).

Fitzgerald, Jim. "Report Lengthens Escape Route Plan." *Times Union (Albany, NY)*, July 4, 2003, p. B2.

———. "State Puts Fate of Nuclear Plants in Federal Hands." *Times Union (Albany, NY)*, January 31, 2003, p. B2.

Foderaro, Lisa W. "Problems Are Compounded at Indian Point Plants." *New York Times*, May 1, 2003, p. B5.

———. "Study Sees a Longer Time for Evacuating Indian Pt." *New York Times*, July 3, 2003, p. B5.

———. "Two Counties to Withhold Documents on Indian Point Plant." *New York Times*, May 2, 2003, p. B2.

"Forward on Filtration." *New York Times*, July 11, 2003, p. A16.

Frahm, Robert A. "SETTLEMENT: A Four-Year Effort Begins to Help Undo Hartford's School Segregation." *Hartford Courant,* January 24, 2003 pp. 1, 8.

Franklin, Ben A. "Nuclear Panel Denies Waiver on New Hampshire Reactor." *New York Times,* April 23, 1987, p. A24.

Franklin, James L. "Court Denies License Delay at Seabrook." *Boston Globe,* March 15, 1990, pp. 1, 22.

Fried, Charles. "Supreme Court Folly." *New York Times,* July 6, 1999, p. A17.

Friedman, Barry. "The Law and Economics of Federalism: Valuing Federalism." *Minnesota Law Review* 82, December 1997, pp. 317–412.

Fuhr, Cecily. "Sovereign Impunity: The 'Uniform Laws' Theory Tries (and Fails) to Take a Bankruptcy-Sized Bite Out of the Eleventh Amendment." *Washington Law Review* 77, April 2002, pp. 511–44.

"Full Participation in Seabrook Drill Is Critical to Plan, Critics Assert." *Keene (NH) Sentinel,* March 3, 1986, p. 6.

Furchgott, Roy. "For an Ailing Retina: Instant Diagnosis from Afar." *New York Times,* July 3, 2003, p. G5.

Garnett, Stanley. "Why Taxes Do Distort Emissions Trading." *Public Utilities Fortnightly* 33, February 15, 1995, pp. 42–49.

Garrett, Elizabeth. "States in a Federal System: Enhancing the Political Safeguards of Federalism? The Unfunded Mandates Reform Act of 1995." *Kansas Law Review* 45, July 1997, pp. 113–183.

Gausman, Carlton J. "The Interstate Compact as a Solution to Regional Problems: The Kansas City Metropolitan Culture District." *Kansas Law Review* 45, May 1997, pp. 897–920.

Goldfarb, William. "Watershed Management: Slogan or Solution?" *Boston College Environmental Affairs Law Review* 21, Spring 1994, pp. 483–503.

Goldwater, Barry, Jr. "Smog in the Clean Air Act." *Congressional Record,* April 5, 1979, p. H2054.

Goodman, Frank, ed. "The Supreme Court's Federalism: Real or Imagined?" *Annals of the American Academy of Political and Social Science* 574, March 2001.

Gordon, Marcy. "Senator Eyes Insurance Rules." *Times Union (Albany, NY),* October 23, 2003, p. E4.

Gormley, Michael. "Martin Act Gives Spitzer Weapon for Disclosure." *Times Union (Albany, NY),* April 20, 2002, p. B9.

Graf, Michael W. "Regulating Pesticide Pollution in California under the 1986 Safe Drinking Water and Toxic Exposure Act

(Proposition 65)." *Ecology Law Quarterly* 28, September-October 2001, pp. 663–759.

Graves, W. Brooke. "Federal Leadership in State Legislation." *Temple Law Quarterly* 10, July 1936, pp. 385–405.

———. "The Future of the American States." *American Political Science Review* 30, February 1936, pp. 24–50.

———. ed. "Intergovernmental Relations in the United States." *Annals of the American Academy of Political and Social Science* 207, January 1940, pp. 1–218.

———. "State Constitutional Provision for Federal-State Cooperation." *Annals of the American Academy of Political and Social Science* 18, September 1935, pp. 142–48.

Green, Tristin K. "Complete Preemption: Removing the Mystery from Removal." *California Law Review* 86, March 1998, pp. 363–95.

Greenblatt, Alan. "The Avengers General." *Governing* 16, May 2003, pp. 52, 54, 56.

———. "Super-Activist: Expanding the Scope of Consumer Protection." *Governing* 16, November 2002, p. 22.

Greene, Susan. "Norton Threatens Calif. Water Cut." *Denver Post*, December 17, 2002, pp. 1, B6.

Greenhouse, Linda. "Context and the Court." *New York Times*, June 25, 2003, pp. 1, A22.

———. "Justices Back Affirmative Action by 5 to 4, But Wider Vote Bans a Racial Point System." *New York Times*, June 24, 2003, pp. 1, A23.

———. "The Justices Decide Who's in Charge." *New York Times*, June 27, 1999, sec. 4, pp. 1, 4.

———. "Justices, 6-3, Rule Workers Can Sue States Over Leave." *New York Times*, May 28, 2003, pp. 1, A18.

———. "Justices Uphold Ban on States' Sales of Drivers' License Information." *New York Times*, January 12, 2000, p. A29.

———. "Local Lawmakers Immune from Suits Too, Court Says." *New York Times*, March 4, 1998, p. A14.

———. "Supreme Court Shields States from Lawsuits on Age Bias." *New York Times*, January 12, 2000, pp. 1, A18.

———. "Supreme Court Takes Case of Black Voting Districts." *New York Times*, January 18, 2003, p. A12.

———. "20-Year Extension of Existing Copyrights Is Upheld." *New York Times*, January 16, 2003, p. A24.

———. "U.S. Court Bars Mexican Trucks Pending an Environmental Study." *New York Times*, January 17, 2003, pp. 1, A17.

———. "Whistleblower Act Is in Peril After Court Widens an Issue." *New York Times*, November 30, 1999, p. A20.

Grogan, Colleen M. "The Influence of Federal Mandates on State Medicaid and AFDC Decision-Making." *Publius: The Journal of Federalism* 29, Summer 1999, pp. 1–30.

Gudridge, Patrick O. "*United States v. Locke*, 120 S.Ct. 1135." *American Journal of International Law* 94, October 2000, pp. 745–50.

Gugliotta, Guy. "IG Investigates Whether EPA Misled Public on Water Quality: Agency Audits Suggest Reports Overstated Utilities' Record." *Washington Post*, August 6, 2003, p. A15.

Gugliotta, Guy, and Eric Pianin. "EPA: Few Fined for Polluting Water." *Washington Post*, June 6, 2003, p. 1.

Gulick, Luther. "Reorganization of the State." *Civil Engineering* 3, August 1933, pp. 419–26.

Guthrie, William D. "The Eleventh Article of Amendment to the Constitution of the United States." *Columbia Law Review* 8, 1908, pp. 183–207.

Hakim, Danny. "Automakers Drop Suits on Air Rules." *New York Times*, August 12, 2003, pp. C1, C5.

———. "States Plan Suit to Prod U.S. on Global Warming." *New York Times* October 4, 2003, pp. C1–2.

———. "Trash from Toronto Upsets Michigan Town." *New York Times*, January 19, 2003, pp. C1, C5.

———. "U.S. Court Rejects Tire Safety Rule, Saying Margin for Error Is Too Great." *New York Times*, August 7, 2003, pp. C1, C10.

Harberson, Albert. "Licensed by the States." *State Government News* 45, August 2002, pp. 20–25.

Harlin, Kevin. "Verizon Wants Higher Access Fees for Competitors." *Times Union (Albany, NY)*, March 28, 2003, pp. E1, E5.

Harris, Andrew. "Boston Overcorrected for Past Biases." *National Law Journal* 25, April 7, 2003 (Internet edition).

Hausman, Jerry A., and J. Gregory Sidak. "A Consumer-Welfare Approach to the Mandatory Unbundling of Telecommunications Networks." *Yale Law Journal* 109, December 1999, pp. 417–505.

Hawkins, Robert B., Jr. "The Chairman's View." *Intergovernmental Perspective* 11, Spring/Summer 1985, pp. 22–23.

Healy, Patrick. "U.S. Orders Use of Cable Under Sound." *New York Times*, August 29, 2003, pp. B1–B2.

Heilprin, John. "New Rules Cast Doubt on Wetlands Protection." *Times Union (Albany, NY)*, January 11, 2003, p. 3.

Henriques, Diana B., and Jonathan Fuerbringer. "Bankers Opposing New State Curbs on Unfair Loans." *New York Times*, February 14, 2002, pp. C1, C5.

Hernandez, Peggy. "Garrity Expected to Yield Control of Schools Today." *Boston Globe*, September 3, 1985, p. 15.

Hernandez, Raymond. "N.A.A.C.P. Suspends Yonkers Head." *New York Times*, November 1, 1995, pp. B1, B4.

———. "Neither Separate Nor Equal." *New York Times*, December 20, 1996, pp. B1, B8.

Herszenhorn, David M. "Indian Bureau Rejects Bid for Group's Status as Tribe." *New York Times*, January 22, 2003, p. B5.

Heuer, Max. "Supreme Court Hears Debate over Copyright Change." *Union Leader (Manchester, NH)*, October 10, 2002, pp. 1, A18.

Hill, Michael. "Ruling Targets Telecommuting." *Times Union (Albany, NY)*, July 3, 2003, p. E1.

Hill, Rebecca L. "California v. F.E.R.C.: Federal Preemption of State Water Laws." *Journal of Energy, Natural Resources and Environmental Law* 12, No. 1, 1992, pp. 261–83.

Hilts, Philip J. "Congress Votes Bill on Labeling of Foods and Health Claims." *New York Times*, October 25, 1990, pp. 1, B11.

"Hinsdale Not Satisfied with Disaster Plan." *Union Leader (Manchester, NH)*, June 11, 2003, p. B1.

Holsendolph, Ernest. "Double-Trailer Plan Stirs Outcry in Some Unexpected Quarters." *New York Times*, April 11, 1983, p. A15.

———. "State Officials Gather to Plan Resistance to Big Truck Rules." *New York Times*, April 15, 1983, p. B10.

Hu, Winnie. "Accord Is Reached in School Bias Suit Involving Yonkers." *New York Times*, January 9, 2002, pp. 1, B4.

———. "Indian Point Battle Lines Are Redrawn." *New York Times*, February 1, 2003, p. B5.

———. "Judge Approves Settlement in Yonkers Desegregation Suit." *New York Times*, March 27, 2002, p. B6.

Hughes, David W. "When NIMBYs Attack: The Heights to Which Communities Will Climb to Prevent the Siting of Wireless Towers." *Journal of Corporation Law* 23, Spring 1998, pp. 469–500.

Hulse, Carl. "Provision in Energy Bill Brings Unease in G.O.P." *New York Times*, September 16, 2003, p. A12.

Hummer, Paul M., and Michael F. Consedine. "Insurance Catches Up to Internet Revolution." *National Law Journal* 22, March 20, 2000, pp. B9, B15.

Jackson, Vicki C. "Federalism and the Court: Congress as the Audience." *Annals of the American Academy of Political and Social Science* 574, March 2001, pp. 145–57.

———. "Federalism and the Uses and Limits of Law: Printz and Principle?" *Harvard Law Review* 111, June 1998, pp. 2180–2259.

Jaffe, Louis L. "Suits Against Governments and Officers: Sovereign Immunity." *Harvard Law Review* 77, November 1963, pp. 1–39.

Jehl, Douglas. "U.S. Plan Could Ease Limits on Wetlands Development." *New York Times*, January 11, 2003, p. A10.

Johnson, Kirk. "For First Time, Conservation Groups Endorse Filtering Plant for City Water Supply." *New York Times*, May 23, 2003, p. B3.

———. "Pataki Seeks Changes in Decision on City Water Filtration Plant." *New York Times*, July 17, 2003, p. B2.

———. "Rules Approved to Reduce Pollutants at Power Plants." *New York Times*, March 27, 2003, p. D5.

———. "10 States to Discuss Curbs on Power-Plant Emissions." *New York Times*, July 25, 2003, p. B5.

Joyce, Kate M. "Who'll Stop the Rain?" *Albany Law Environmental Outlook* 7, 2002, pp. 94–128.

Kaleem, Jaweed. "Telemarketers Not Ready to Hang It Up." *Times Union (Albany, NY)*, August 13, 2003, pp. 1, A8.

Kearney, Richard C., and John J. Stucker. "Interstate Compacts and the Management of Low Level Radioactive Wastes." *Public Administration Review* 45, January/February 1985, pp. 210–20.

Kelly, Janet M. "The States on Unfunded Mandates: Where There's a Will, There's a Way." *South Carolina Policy Forum* 8, Winter 1997, pp. 29–34.

Kelly, Matthew J. "Federal Preemption by the Airline Deregulation Act of 1978: How Do State Tort Claims Fare?" *Catholic University Law Review* 49, Spring 2000, pp. 873–902.

Kelly, Tina. "Watershed Deal Calls for City to Act, But Saves It Billions." *New York Times*, November 26, 2002 (Internet edition).

Kelso, Charles D. and R. Randall Kelso. "Standing to Sue: Transformations in Supreme Court Methodology, Doctrine, and Results." *Toledo Law Review* 28, Fall, 1996, pp. 93–150.

Kennedy, Robert F., Jr. "A Culture of Mismanagement: Environmental Protection and Enforcement at the New York City Department of Environmental Protection." *Pace Environmental Law Review* 15, Winter 1997, pp. 233–92.

Key, V. O., Jr. "State Legislation Facilitative of Federal Action." *Annals of the American Academy of Political and Social Science* 207, January 1940, pp. 7–13.

Kincaid, John, ed. "American Federalism: The Third Century." *Annals of the American Academy of Political and Social Science* 509, May 1990, pp. 1–152.

———. "From Cooperative to Coercive Federalism." In "American Federalism: The Third Century," edited by John Kincaid. *Annals of the American Academy of Political and Social Science* 509, May 1990, pp. 139–52.

Kirkham, Christopher W. "Busting the Administrative Trust: An Experimentalist Approach to Universal Service Administration in Telecommunications Policy." *Columbia Law Review* 98, April 1998, pp. 620–64.

Klein, Robert W. "Insurance Regulation in Transition." *Journal of Risk and Insurance* 62, September 1995, pp. 363–405.

Koch, Edward I. "The Mandate Millstone." *The Public Interest* 61, Fall 1980, pp. 42–57.

Kocieniewski, David. "States to Fight Easing of Rules on Pollution by Power Plants." *New York Times*, August 29, 2003, pp. B1, B8.

Koenig, Louis W. "Federal and State Cooperation Under the Constitution." *Michigan Law Review* 36, March 1938, pp. 752–85.

Kolker, Michael S. "National League of Cities: The Tenth Amendment, and the Conditional Spending Power." *Urban Law Annual* 21, 1981, pp. 217–37.

Krasner, Jeffrey. "Investors Get Little in States' Settlement with Wall Street." *Boston Globe*, April 28, 1003, p. 1.

Kravitz, Mark R. "Removal Remands." *National Law Journal* 23, June 25, 2001, p. A10.

Kruger, Joseph, and Melanie Dean. "Looking Back on SO₂ Trading: What's Good for the Environment Is Good for the Market." *Public Utilities Fortnightly* 135, August 1997, pp. 30–38.

Labaton, Stephen. "10 Wall St. Firms Settle with U.S. in Analyst Inquiry." *New York Times*, April 29, 2003, pp. 1, C4.

———. "U.S. Moves to Allow Trading of Radio Spectrum Licenses." *New York Times*, May 16, 2003, pp. 1, C2.

Lambert, Bruce. "Congress Puts Authorization of L.I. Cable in Energy Bill." *New York Times*, November 18, 2003, p. B5.

Langdon, Thomas, Jr. "States, Intent on Regulating, Look at Morgan. *New York Times*, July 15, 2003, pp. C1, C4.

Laski, Harold J. "The Obsolescence of Federalism." *New Republic* 98, May 3, 1939, pp. 362–69.

"Last California District Approves Pact on Colorado River Water." *New York Times*, October 4, 2003, p. A8.

Lawson, Gary, and Patricia B. Granger. "The 'Proper' Scope of Federal Power: A Jurisdictional Interpretation of the Sweeping Clause." *Duke Law Journal* 43, November 1993, pp. 267–336.

Leach, Richard H., ed., "Intergovernmental Relations in the United States." *Annals of the American Academy of Political and Social Science* 416, November 1974, pp. 1–193.

Lebenguth, M. Scott. "Ending Federal Preemption of State Water Regulation." *Williamette Law Review* 29, Winter 1991, pp. 95–112.

Lee, Carol F. "The Political Safeguards of Federalism? Congressional Responses to Supreme Court Decisions on State and Local Liability." *Urban Lawyer* 20, Spring 1988, pp. 301–340.

Lee, Jennifer 8. "E.P.A. Reintroduces Standards to Control Ozone and Smog and Encounters Criticism." *New York Times*, May 16, 2003, p. A18.

———. "2 Companies Aid to Agree to Settle Suits on Emissions." *New York Times*, April 9, 2003, p. A14.

———. "U.S. and States Joint to Fight Internet-Auction Fraud." *New York Times*, May 1, 2003, p. C4.

———. "Vowing to Enforce the Clean Air Act, While Also Trying to Change it." *New York Times*, April 22, 2003, p. A21.

Leighton, Wayne A. "Prescriptive Regulations and Telecommunications: Old Lessons Not Learned." *Cato Journal* 20, Winter 2001, pp. 379–400.

Lemov, Penelope. "Blocking ERISA." *Governing* 16, May 2003, p. 74.

Lichtblau, Erik. "Detroit Agrees on Monitor for Police." *New York Times*, June 12, 2003, A24.

———. "Republicans Want Terrorism Law Made Permanent." *New York Times*, April 9, 2003, pp. B1, B13.

Livingstone, John D. "Uniformity of Patent Law Following Florida Prepaid: Should the Eleventh Amendment Put Patent Owners Back in the Middle Again?" *Emory Law Journal* 20, Winter 2001, pp. 323–62.

Lobsenz, George. "Lawmakers Pick Nevada to Host Nuke Waste Dump." *Union Leader (Manchester, NH)*, December 18, 1987, p. 16.

"Localities Get Antitrust Relief." *Intergovernmental Perspective* 10, Fall 1984, p. 4.

Luken, Susan M. "Irreconcilable Differences: The Spending Clause and the Eleventh Amendment: Limiting Congress's Use of Conditional Spending to Circumvent Eleventh Amendment Immunity." *University of Cincinnati Law Review* 70, Winter 2002, pp. 693–714.

Macey, Jonathan R. "Federal Deference to Local Regulators and the Economic Theory of Regulation: Toward a Public-Choice Explanation of Federalism." *Virginia Law Review* 76, March 1990, pp. 165–91.

Macey, Jonathan R., and Geoffrey P. Miller. "The McCarran-Ferguson Act of 1945: Reconceiving the Federal Role in Insurance Regulation." *New York University Law Review* 68, April 1993, pp. 13–87.

———. "Origin of the Blue Sky Laws." *Texas Law Review* 70, December 1991, pp. 347–96.

Madigan, Nick. "In a City of Few Limits, One Just Got Lower." *New York Times*, September 24, 2003, p. A18.

Magagnini, Stephen. "Some Learn Indian Justice the Hard Way." *Sacramento Bee*, April 7, 2003 (Internet edition).

March, Richard. "Seabrook Drill Called a Failure." *Keene (NH) Sentinel*, March 1, 1986, pp. 1–2.

Marek, Elizabeth A. "Education by Decree." *New Perspectives* 17, Summer 1985, pp. 36–41.

"Massachusetts Governor Seeks to Stop Nuclear Plant Opening." *New York Times*, September 21, 1986, p. 24.

May, Clifford D. "Shoreham Dispute Centers on Policy." *New York Times*, April 16, 1986, p. B2.

McCoy, Charles S. "Federalism: The Lost Tradition? *Publius: The Journal of Federalism* 31, Spring 2001, pp. 1–14.

McGeehan, Patrick. "First Boston Rejects Demand by State for Civil Settlement." *New York Times*, October 21, 2002, p. A15.

———. "How Settlement Is Worded Could be Costly to Merrill." *New York Times*, May 10, 2002, p. C4

———. "SEC Joining Spitzer's Probe of Stock Analysts." *Times Union (Albany, NY)*, April 26, 2002, pp. 1, A5.

———. "Wall St. Deal Says Little on Individuals." *New York Times*, December 21, 2002, pp. C1 and C14.

McGeehan, Patrick, and Norm Alster. "Massachusetts Charges Fraud in Complaint on First Boston." *New York Times*, October 22, 2002, pp. C1, C13.

McKay, Jim. "Driver's License Debate." *Government Technology* 16, April 2003, pp. 31–32, 34.

McKinley, James C., Jr. "Deadlock Ends on Tightening D.W.I. Laws." *New York Times*, December 3, 2002, pp. B1, B6.

———. "Lawmakers Step Lightly Along a Nuclear Tightrope." *New York Times*, August 7, 2003, pp. B1, B6.

"Meat Safety at Risk." *New York Times*, February 1, 2003, p. A18.

Meese, Edwin, III. "The Attorney General's View of the Supreme Court: Toward a Jurisprudence of Original Intention." *Public Administration Review* 45, November 1985, pp. 701–704.

Meltzer, Daniel J. "State Sovereign Immunity: Five Authors in Search of a Theory." *Notre Dame Law Review* 75, March 2000, pp. 1011–66.

Meyland, Sarah J. "Land Use & the Protection of Drinking Water Supplies." *Pace Environmental Law Review* 10, Spring 1993, pp. 563–602.

Miller, Anne. "Colonie Battles AT&T on Rights." *Times Union (Albany, NY)*, July 14, 2003, pp. B1, B5.

"Misguided Marijuana War." *New York Times*, February 4, 2003, p. A28.

Morenson, Gretchen. "Bill to Limit Oversight of Wall St. Gains." *New York Times*, July 11, 2003, p. C2.

———. "In Hierarchy on Wall St., Short Shrift to Little Guy." *New York Times*, April 29, 2003, pp. C1, C5.

Morgenson, Gretchen, and Patrick McGeehan. "Wall St. and the Nursery School: A New York Story." *New York Times*, November 14, 2002, pp. 1, C10.

———. "Wall Street Firms Are Ready to Pay $1 Billion in Fines." *New York Times*, December 20, 2002, pp. 1, C5.

"Mr. Spitzer and the SEC." *Times Union (Albany, NY)*, November 18, 2003, p. A18.

Murphy, Dean E. "A California Cultivator of Medical Marijuana Is Convicted on Federal Charges." *New York Times*, February 1, 2003, p. A14.

———. "California Water Users Miss Deadline on Pact for Sharing." *New York Times*, January 1, 2003, p. A11.

———. "Failed Deal in California Cuts Water for Nevada." *New York Times*, January 2, 2003, p. A10.

———. "Government Adds to Threat of Denying Farmers Water." *New York Times*, January 17, 2003, p. A14.

———. "U.S. Moves to Cut California Water Supply." *New York Times*, December 17, 2002, p. A33.

Murphy, Kathleen. "Federal Oversight Urged for State Boxing Commissions." *Stateline.org*, February 26, 2003, p. 1.

Mustokoff, Matthew. "Sovereign Immunity and the Crisis of Constitutional Absolutism: Interpreting the Eleventh Amendment After *Alden v. Maine*." *Maine Law Review* 53, 2001, pp. 81–109.

Nathan, Richard P. "The New Federalism Versus the Emerging New Structuralism." *Publius: The Journal of Federalism* 5, Summer 1975, pp. 111–29.

Nathan, Richard P., and Paul R. Dommel. "Federal-Local Relations Under Block Grants." *Political Science Quarterly* 93, Fall 1978, pp. 421–42.

Nathan, Richard P., and John R. Lago. "Intergovernmental Fiscal Roles and Relations." *Annals of the American Academy of Political and Social Science* 509, May 1990, pp. 36–47.

Neumeier, Matthew M. "Recent Trends in Federal Preemption of Law Claims Under the Federal Home Owners' Loan Act of 1933." *Banking Law Journal* 119, July 2002, pp. 621–34.

"Nevada's Radioactive Jackpot." *New York Times*, January 5, 1988, A18.

Northrop, Patricia T. "The Constitutional Insignificance of Funding for Federal Mandates." *Duke Law Journal* 46, February 1997, pp. 903–30.

O'Brien, David M. "The Rehnquist Court and Federal Preemption: In Search of a Theory." *Publius: The Journal of Federalism* 23, Fall 1993, pp. 15–31.

———. "The Supreme Court and Intergovernmental Relations: What Happened to 'Our New Federalism'?" *Journal of Law and Politics* 9, Summer 1993, pp. 609–37.

Odato, James M. "Stalled DWI Bill Costing Millions." *Times Union (Albany, NY)*, November 26, 2002, pp. 1, A10.

"Ohio Told to Meet Clean Air Deadline." *New York Times*, October 18, 1979, p. A16.

"$1.4B Settles Stocks Inquiry." *Times Union (Albany, NY)*, April 29, 2003, pp. E1, E5.

Oppel, Richard A., Jr. "Congress Is Close to Eliminating a Privacy Law." *New York Times*, October 25, 2003, pp. C1, C15.

Otero-Phillips, Camille V. "What's in the Forecast? A Look at the EPA's Use of Computer Models in Emissions Trading." *Rutgers Computer 7 Technology Law Journal* 24, Spring 1998, pp. 187–222.

Patchel, Kathleen. "Interest Group Politics, Federalism, and the Uniform Laws Process: Some Lessons from the Uniform Commercial Code." *Minnesota Law Review* 78, November 1993, pp. 83–164.

Pear, Robert. "Bush Signs Legislation Intended to End Voting Disputes." *New York Times* October 30, 2002, p. A22.

———. "Justices Voice Skepticism on Taking Drug-Cost Case." *New York Times*, January 23, 2003, p. A18.

Pemberton, Jackson. "A New Message: On Amendment XVII." *The Freeman* 26, November 1976, pp. 654–60.

Penney, Michael. "Application of the Primary Jurisdiction Doctrine to Clean Air Act Citizen Suits." *Boston College Environmental Affairs Law Review* 29, 2002, pp. 399–426.

Percy, Stephen L. "ADA, Disability Rights, and Evolving Regulatory Federalism." *Publius: The Journal of Federalism* 23, Fall 1993, pp. 87–105.

Perlex, Jane. "U.S. Aide Quits, Charging Pressure on LILCO Drill." *New York Times*, April 15, 1986, p. B1.

Perlman, Ellen. "The Gorrilla That Swallows State Laws: Federal Preemption Sounds Like a Technical Term." *Governing* 7, August 1994, pp. 46–48.

Perry, Tony. "Inland Water Sale Rejected: Coastal Cutback Threatened." *Los Angeles Times*, December 10, 2002 (Internet edition).

Perz-Pena, Richard and Patrick McGeehan. "Assault on Wall St. Misdeeds Raises Spitzer"s Profile." *New York Times*, November 4, 2002, pp. 1, B6.

Petragnani, Amy M. "The Dormant Commerce Clause: On Its Last Leg." *Albany Law Review* 57, Fall 1994, pp. 1215–253.

Pianin, Eric. "EPA to Allow Polluters to Buy Clean Water Credits." *Washington Post*, January 14, 2003, p. A3.

Plitt, Steven, Valerie J. Fasolo, and Daniel Maldonado. "The Changing Landscape of Eleventh Immunity in the Context of the Americans with Disabilities Act and the Rehabilitation Act after Garrett: Are Arizona School Districts Beyond Suit?" *Arizona State Law Journal* 34, Fall 2002, pp. 871–919.

Pokorny, Brad, and Ray Richard. "Seabrook Tests Evacuation Plans." *Boston Globe*, February 27, 1986, p. 23.

Polgreen, Lydia. "Indian Point Is Said to Pass U.S. Test in Mock Attack." *New York Times*, August 12, 2003, p. B5.

"A Pollutant By Any Other Name." *New York Times*, February 22, 2003, p. A16.

Postrel, Virginia. "A Look at Wine Sales over the Internet Shows the Price of Some Regulations in the Name of Consumer Protection." *New York Times*, July 17, 2003, p. C2.

Powell, H. Jefferson. "The Original Understanding of Original Intent." *Harvard Law Review* 98, March 1985, pp. 885–948.

"The Power of Congress to Subject Interstate Commerce to State Regulation." *University of Chicago Law Review* 3, 1935, pp. 636–40.

"Pre-Emption as a Preferential Ground: A New Canon of Construction." *Stanford Law Review* 12, December 1959, pp. 208–25.

Pristin, Terry. "Appeals Court Upholds Ban on Online Sale of Cigarettes." *New York Times*, February 14, 2003, p. B7.

"Public Service Argues for 2-Mile Safety Zone." *Keene (NH) Sentinel*, September 27, 1986, p. 3.

Reid, T. R. "Troubled Waters: Fight Brews over Mighty Colorado River." *Washington Post*, January 19, 2003, p. A11.

Reiman, Pamela S., and Stephen C. Yohay. "Compliance with Clean Air Act Employer Trip Reduction Requirements." *Employee Relations Law Journal* 19, Spring 1994, pp. 621–38.

Reitze, Arnold W., Jr., and Michael K. Stagg. "Air Emissions Standards and Guidelines under the Clean Air Act for the Incineration of Hospital, Medical, and Infectious Waste." *Environmental Law* 28, Winter 1998, pp. 791–844.

Revesz, Richard L. "Rehabilitating Interstate Competition: Rethinking the 'Race-to-the-Bottom' Rationale for Federal Environmental Regulation." *New York University Law Review* 67, December 1992, pp. 1210–1254.

Ribstein, Larry E., and Bruce H. Kobayashi. "An Economic Analysis of Uniform State Laws." *Journal of Legal Studies* 25, January 1996, pp. 131–87.

Rich, Michael J. "Targeting Federal Grants: The Community Development Experience, 1950–86." *Publius: The Journal of Federalism* 21, Winter 1991, pp. 29–49.

Rimer, Sara. "Boston School Plan Isn't Biased Against Whites, Judge Rules." *New York Times*, April 25, 2003, p. A24.

Robinson, Nicholas A. "Sustainable Science for a Sustainable Environment: Legal Systems, Decisionmaking, and the Science of Earth's Systems: Procedural Missing Links." *Ecology Law Quarterly* 27, 2001, pp. 1077–1161.

Robinson, Richard S. "Preemption, the Right of Publicity, and a New Federal Statute." *Cardozo Arts and Entertainment Journal* 16, 1998, pp. 183–206.

Ross, Nathan E. "Federalism Versus the Greater Good." *Journal of Dispute Resolution*, no. 1, 2000, pp. 199–214.

Rossmann, Antonio. "The Law and the River." *New York Times*, January 18, 2003, p. A17.

Rubin, Edward L., and Malcolm Feeley. "Federalism: Some Notes on a National Neurosis." *University of California Los Angeles Law Review* 41, April 1994, pp. 903–52.

Sacher, Steven J., and Judy C. Bauserman. "The ERISA Preemption Amendments of 1991: Punitive Damages in the Offing?" *Benefits Law Journal* 4, Autumn 1991, pp. 335–44.

Santora, Marc. "Gambling Foes Try to Curb Growth of Connecticut's 2 Casino Giants." *New York Times*, September 4, 2003, pp. B1, B5.

———. "Rowland Vows to Shut Down Cross-Sound Cable That Helps Power Long Island." *New York Times*, September 6, 2003, p. B6.

Savage, David G. "High Court Gives States Protection in Age-Bias Suits." *Washington Times*, January 12, 2000, pp. A1, A14.

Schneeweiss, Jonathan. "Watershed Protection Strategies: A Case Study of the New York City Watershed in Light of the 1996 Amendments to the Safe Drinking Water Act." *Villanova Environmental Law Journal* 8, 1997, pp. 77–119.

Schuck, Peter H. "Some Reflections on the Federalism Debate." *Yale Law and Policy Review* 14, 1996, pp. 1–22.

Schultze, Charles L. "Federal Spending: Past, Present, and Future." In *Setting National Priorities: The Next Ten Years*, edited by Henry Owen and Charles L. Schultze, Washington, DC: Brookings Institution, 1976, 323–69.

Schwarcz, Steven L. "A Fundamental Inquiry into the Statutory Rulemaking Process of Private Legislatures." *Georgia Law Review* 29, Summer 1995, pp. 909–989.

Scicchitano, Michael J., and David M. Hedge. "From Coercion to Partnership in Federal Partial Preemption; SMCRA, RCRA, and OSHA Act." *Publius: The Journal of Federalism* 23, Fall 1993, pp. 107–121.

Seelye, Katharine Q. "Administration Adopts Rule on Antipollution Exemption." *New York Times*, August 28, 2003, p. A20.

———. "9 Northeastern States Challenge Administration on Pollution Rule." *New York Times*, January 1, 2003, pp. 1, A12.

———. "U.S. Report Faults Efforts to Track Water Pollution." *New York Times*, May 27, 2003, pp. 1, A19.

Sentell, R. Perry, Jr. "Gesticulations of Garcia." *Urban Georgia* 35, October 1985, pp. 33–35.

Sevastopulo, Demetri. "US Class-Action Lawsuits Face Reform." *Financial Times*, June 13, 2003, p. 11.

Shabecoff, Philip. "Most Sewage Plants Meeting Latest Goal of Clean Water Act." *New York Times*, July 28, 1988, pp. 1, A18.

Sherer, Christopher E. "The Resurgence of Federalism: State Employees and the Eleventh Amendment." *Hamline Journal of Public Law and Policy* 23, Fall 2001, pp. 1–34.

"Shoreham Drill Gets Positive Initial Appraisal." *New York Times*, February 16, 1986, p. 48.

Siegel, Norman E. "FIFRA and Preemption: Can State Common Law and Federal Regulations Coexist? *Papas v. Upjohn Co.*, 926 F.2d 1019." *Washington University Journal of Urban and Contemporary Law* 41, Spring 1992, pp. 257–70.

Sinozich, Paula A., ed. "The Role of Preemption in Administrative Law." *Administrative Law Review* 45, Spring 1993, pp. 107–224.

Smith, Deann, and Donna McGuire. "Judge Halts KC School District Desegregation Case." *Kansas City Star*, August 14, 2003, p. 1.

Sostek, Anya. "Slow to Toe the DJI Line." *Governing* 16, May 2003, pp. 42, 44.

Squire, Ryan C. "Effectuating Principles of Federalism: Reevaluating the Federal Spending Power as the Great Tenth Amendment Loophole." *Pepperdine Law Review* 25, 1998, pp. 869–937.

"States Feel Relief from Unfunded Mandates." *Governors' Bulletin*, June 17, 1996, p. 1.

Stein, George. "Spitzer: End Allotting Hot Stocks to CEOs." *Times Union (Albany, NY)*, December 6, 2002, pp. E1, E4.

Stevens, Ted. "The Internet and the Telecommunications Act of 1996." *Harvard Journal on Legislation* 35, Winter 1998, pp. 5–31.

Strahan, Philip E. "The Real Effects of U.S. Banking Deregulation." *Federal Reserve Bank of St. Louis Review* 85, July/August 2003, pp. 111–28.

"Suit Challenges School Policy over Race." *New York Times*, February 11, 2003, p. A26.

"The Supreme Court Docket: States' Rights vs. Civil Rights." *New York Times*, January 16, 2003, p. A28.

"Supreme Court Okays Seabrook." *Keene (NH) Sentinel*, April 27, 1990, p. 1.

"Supreme Mischief." *New York Times*, June 24, 1999, p. A26.

Swindler, William F. "Our First Constitution: The Articles of Confederation." *American Bar Association Journal* 69, February 1981, pp. 166–69.

Syles, Richard T. "Nuclear Power Plants and Emergency Planning: An Intergovernmental Nightmare." *Public Administration Review* 44, September-October 1984, pp. 393–401.

Teske, Paul, and Andrey Kuljiev. "Federalism, Preemption, and Implementation of the Telecommunications Act." *Publius: The Journal of Federalism* 30, Winter/Spring 2000, pp. 53–67.

Teske, Paul, Michael Mintrom, and Samuel Best. "Federal Preemption and State Regulation of Transportation and Telecommunications." *Publius: The Journal of Federalism* 23, Fall 1993, pp. 71–85.

"Text of Reagan's Speech Accepting the Republican Nomination." *New York Times*, July 18, 1980, p. A8.

Thomas, Landon, Jr. "New York Sets Conflict Rules with Banks." *New York Times*, August 26, 2003, p. C4.

———. "States, Intent on Regulating, Look at Morgan." *New York Times*, July 15, 2003, pp. C1, C4.

Thomas, Landon, Jr., and Gretchen Morgenson. "2 Analysts Likely to Pay $20 Million in Fraud Case." *New York Times*, April 28, 2003, pp. C1, C8.

Thompson, Walter. "The Trend Toward Federal Centralization." *Annals of the American Academy of Political and Social Science* 113, May 1924, pp. 172–82.

Thrash, Thomas W. "Federal Automotive Safety Standards and Georgia Products Liability Law: Conflict or Coexistence?" *Georgia State Bar Journal* 26, February 1990, pp. 107–112.

"Too Lax About DWI." *Times Union (Albany, NY)*, December 1, 2002, p. B4.

Trinchero, Mark P., and Holly R. Smith. "Federal Preemption of State Universal Service Regulations under the Telecommunications Act of 1996." *Federal Communications Law Journal* 51, March 1999, pp. 303–47.

Tubbesing, Carl. "The Dual Personality of Federalism." *State Legislatures* 24, April 1998, pp. 14–18.

Tucker, Cynthia. "All-Black Districts No Longer Useful." *Times Union (Albany, NY)*, May 6, 2003, p. A11.

"Two Sates Seeking Tougher Sanctions Against Microsoft." *New York Times*, May 6, 2003, C3.

Tye, Larry. "NRC Approves Licensing of Seabrook." *Boston Globe*, March 2, 1990, pp. 1, 12.

"Utility to Spend $1.2 Billion to Cut Emissions." *New York Times*, April 19, 2003, A9.

Vairo, Georgene M. "A Federal Question?" *National Law Journal* 24, December 17, 2001, p. B11.

———. "Forum Selection: Judge Shopping." *National Law Journal* 23, November 27, 2000, p. A16.

———. "Forum Selection: Removal Traps." *National Law Journal* 23, July 9, 2001, p. A14.

———. "An Update on Removal." *National Law Journal* 26, October 14, 2002, p. B8.

Vaishnav, Anand. "City Defends Assignment Plan: US Court Hears School Lawsuit." *Boston Globe*, February 11, 2003, p. B2.

Van Hernel, Peter J. "A Way Out of the Maze: Federal Agency Preemption of State Licensing and Regulation of Complementary and Alternative Medicine Practitioners." *American Journal of Law and Medicine* 27, no. 2–3, 2001, pp. 329–44.

Vazqiez, Carlos M. "Treaties and the Eleventh Amendment." *Virginia Journal of International Law* 42, Winter 2002, pp. 713–42.

Von Zielbauer, Paul. "Hartford Moves to Curb Gambling and Stop a Casino." *New York Times*, January 7, 2003, pp. B1–B2.

Wade, Betsy. "New Federal Law Encourages Fire Safety in Hotels." *New York Times*, September 30, 1990, sec. 5, p. xx3.

Wald, Matthew L. "Clean Air Deadline Is History." *New York Times*, January 3, 1988, p. E9.

———. "Flaw Is Found in Plan to Bury Nuclear Waste." *New York Times*, October 21, 2003, p. A21.

———. "Indian Point Report Contradicts Experts on Effect of Attack." *New York Times*, January 21, 2003, p. B5.

———. "Indian Point Security Test Is Called Too Easy." *New York Times*, September 16, 2003, p. B5.

———. "Nevada States Case Against Waste Dump in Mountain." *New York Times*, December 3, 2002, p. A24.

———. "Northeast to Fight New Pollution Policy." *Times Union (Albany, NY)*, December 1, 2002, p. A6.

———. "Safety Problem at Nuclear Plants Is Cited." *New York Times*, September 8, 2003, p. A14.

———. "Study Warns Attack on Fuel Could Pose Serious Hazards." *New York Times*, January 30, 2003, p. A13.

Wallick, Ruth. "GATT and Preemption of State and Local Laws." *Government Finance Review* 10, October 1994, pp. 46–47.

Wang, Alexander K. "Southern California's Quest for Clean Air: Is EPA's Dilemma Nearing an End?" *Environmental Law* 24, July 1994, pp. 1137–1158.

Warren, Charles. "New Light on the Federal Judiciary Act of 1789." *Harvard Law Review* 37, 1923–24, pp. 93–132.

Warren, Manning G., III. "Reflections on Dual Regulation of Securities: A Case Against Preemption." *Boston College Law Review* 25, 1984, pp. 495–538.

———. "Reflections on Dual Regulation of Securities: A Case for Reallocation of Regulatory Responsibilities." *Washington University Law Quarterly* 78, Summer 2000, pp. 497–512.

Warren, William T. "Free Trade and Federalism." *State Legislatures* 22, May 1996, pp. 12–16.

"The Way We Were & Are." *Governing* 16, October 2002, pp. 37–39.

Walters, Jonathan. "Preemption Washington." Governing 17, September 2004, p. 12.

Wechsler, Herbert. "The Political Safeguards of Federalism: The Role of the States in the Composition and Selection of the National Government." *Columbia Law Review* 54, 1953, pp. 543–60.

Weiland, Paul S. "Federal and State Preemption of Environmental Law: A Critical Analysis." *Harvard Environmental Law Review* 24, 2000, pp. 237–86.

Weiss, Kenneth R. "New Coastal Drilling Blocked." *Los Angeles Times*, December 3, 2002 (Internet edition).

"West Virginia to Join Appeal in Microsoft Case." *New York Times*, December 3, 2002, p. C6.

Williamson, Richard S. "Block Grants—A Federalist Tool." *State Government* 54, no. 4, 1981, pp. 114–17.

———. "The Self-Government Balancing Act: A View from the White House." *National Civic Review* 71, January 1982, pp. 19–22.

Willing, Richard. "Attitudes Ease Toward Medical Marijuana." *USA Today*, May 29, 2003, p. A4.

Wilson, James G. "The Eleventh Amendment Cases: Going 'Too Far' with Judicial Neofederalism." *Loyola of Los Angeles Law Review* 33, June 2000, pp. 1687–1717.

Winter, Greg. "Schools Resegregate, Study Finds." *New York Times*, January 21, 2003, p. A14.

Wright, Deil S. "Intergovernmental Relations: An Analytical Overview." *Annals of the American Academy of Political and Social Science* 416, November 1974, pp. 1–16.

"Yonkers Residents Fight Low Income Housing." *Times Union*, *(Albany, NY)*, June 6, 1988, p. 1.

Young, Ernest A. "Dual Federalism, Concurrent Jurisdiction, and the Foreign Affairs Exception." *George Washington Law Review* 69, February 2001, pp. 139–88.

Zimmerman, James. "Restrictions on Forum-Selection Clauses in Franchise Agreements and the Federal Arbitration Act: Is State

Law Preempted?" *Vanderbilt Law Review* 51, April 1998, pp. 759–86.

Zimmerman, Joseph F. "Congressional Regulation of Subnational Governments." *PS: Political Science and Politics* 26, June 1993, pp. 177–81.

———. "Election Systems and Representative Democracy: Reflections on the Voting Rights Act of 1965." *National Civic Review* 84, Fall 1995, pp. 287–309.

———. "Eliminating Disproportionate Representation in the House." In *The U.S. House of Representatives: Reform or Rebuild?* edited by Joseph F. Zimmerman and Wilma Rule, 163–86. Westport, CT: Praeger Publishers, 2000.

———. "Federal Judicial Remedial Power: The Yonkers Case." *Publius: The Journal of Federalism* 20, Summer 1990, pp. 45–61.

———. ed. "Federal Preemption." *Publius: The Journal of Federalism* 23, Fall 1993, pp. 1–121.

———. "Federal Preemption Under Reagan's New Federalism." *Publius: The Journal of Federalism* 21, Winter 1991, pp. 7–28.

———. "The Federal Voting Rights Act and Alternative Election Systems." *William and Mary Law Review* 19, Summer 1978, pp. 621–60.

———. "Financing National Policy Through Mandates." *National Civic Review* 81, Summer-Fall 1992, pp. 367–73.

———. "Local Representation: Designing a Fair System." *National Civic Review* 60, June 1980, pp. 307–12.

———. "Mandating in New York State." In *State Mandating of Local Expenditures*. Washington, DC: U.S. Advisory Commission on Intergovernmental Relations, 1978, pp. 69–85.

———. "The Metropolitan Area Problem." *Annals of the American Academy of Political and Social Science* 416, November 1974, pp. 133–47.

———. "National-State Relations: Cooperative Federalism in the Twentieth Century." *Publius: The Journal of Federalism* 31, Spring 2001, pp. 15–30.

———. "The 104th Congress and Federalism." *Current Municipal Problems* 23, no. 4, 1997, pp. 494–514.

———. "Overview of Voting Rights Laws" in *Communities & The Voting Rights Act*." Denver: National Civic League, 1996, pp. 8–16.

———. "Preemption in the U.S. Federal System." *Publius: The Journal of Federalism* 23, Fall 1993, pp. 1–13.

———. "Regulating Intergovernmental Relations in the 1990s." *Annals of the American Academy of Political and Social Science* 509, May 1990, pp. 48–72.

———. "Relieving the Fiscal Burdens of State and Federal Mandates and Restraints." *Current Municipal Problems* 19, no. 2, 1992, pp. 216–24.

———. "The Role of the State Legislature in Air Pollution Abatement." *Suffolk University Law Review* 5, Spring 1971, pp. 850–77.

———. "The State Mandate Problem." *State and Local Government Review* 19, Spring 1987, pp. 78–84.

———. "Trends in Congressional Preemption." *The Book of the States 2003*. Lexington, KY: The Council of State Governments, 2003, pp. 32–37.

Unpublished Materials

"Address of William Bradford Reynolds, Assistant Attorney General, Civil Rights Division, Counselor to the Attorney General, United States Department of Justice before the Conservative Law Students—A Federalist Society Chapter, Washington University, St. Louis, Missouri, October 28, 1987."

Bork, Robert H. "The Constitution, Original Intent, and Economic Rights." An address presented at the University of San Diego Law School, November 18, 1985.

Bowman, Ann O'M. "Interstate Equilibrium: Competition and Cooperation in the U.S. Federal System." A paper presented at the annual meeting of the American Political Science Association, Philadelphia, Pennsylvania, August 28, 2003.

Brennan, William Jr. "The Constitution of the United States: Contemporary Ratification." A paper presented at a text and teaching symposium, Georgetown University, Washington, D.C., October 12, 1985.

Costle, Douglas M. "Toward a Quiet Victory: A Report Card on the Clean Water Program." A paper presented at the fifty-second Annual Conference of the Water Pollution Control Federation, Houston, Texas, October 9, 1979 (mimeographed).

Crotty, Patricia M. "The New Federalism Game: Options for the States." A paper presented at the annual meeting of the Northeastern Political Science Association, Philadelphia, Pennsylvania, November 14–16, 1985.

Hyde, Albert C. "The Politics of Environmental Decision Making: The Non-Decision Issue" Unpublished Ph.D. dissertation, State University of New York at Albany, 1980.

"Members Certify GLBA Reciprocity Requirement Met." News release issued by the National Association of Insurance Commissioners, Kansas City, Missouri, September 10, 2002.

Nickerson, Brian J. "Interest Group Involvement in New York State Public School Aid: Litigation and Lobbying." Unpublished Ph.D. dissertation, State University of New York at Albany, 2002.

Reynolds, William Bradford. "The Bicentennial: A Constitutional Restoration." A paper presented at the University of Texas, Austin, February 19, 1987.

"Statement of William Bradford Reynolds, Assistant Attorney General, Civil Rights Division before the Committee on Labor and Human Resources, Subcommittee on Labor, U.S. Senate Concerning Impact of *Garcia v. San Antonio Metropolitan Transit Authority* on September 10, 1985."

Stenberg, Carl W. "Federal-Local Relations in a Cutback Environment: Issues and Future Directions." A paper presented at the Annual Conference of the American Politics Group of the United Kingdom Political Studies Association, Manchester, England, January 4, 1980.

Zimmerman, Joseph F. "Congressional Preemption: Regulatory Federalism." A paper presented at the annual meeting of the American Political Science Association, Chicago, September 4, 2004.

———. "How Perfect Is the Economic Union? Interstate Trade Barriers." A paper presented at the annual meeting of the American Political Science Association, Philadelphia, Pennsylvania, August 28, 2003.

———. "Interstate Disputes: The Supreme Court's Original Jurisdiction." A paper presented at the annual conference of the American Politics Group, Canterbury Christ Church University College, Canterbury, England, January 7, 2005.

———. "The Interstate Insurance Product Regulation Compact." A paper presented at a meeting of the National Conference of State Legislatures Executive Committee's Task Force to Streamline and Simplify Insurance Regulation, New York, New York, March 22, 2003.

———. "Interstate Trade Barriers: Their Erection and Removal." A paper presented at the annual conference of the American Politics Group of the United Kingdom Political Studies

Association, University of Reading, Reading, England, January 4, 2003.

———. "Regulatory Federalism: Congressional Preemption." A paper presented at the annual conference of the American Politics Group of the United Kingdom Political Studies Association, Oxford University, Oxford, England, January 3, 2004.

———. "The United States Federal System: A Kaleidoscipic View." A paper presented at a research seminar, Rothermere American Institute, Oxford University, Oxford, England, November 23, 2004.

Index

DATE DUE
